STAR WARS®
INVASION

THE NEW JEDI ORDER
(25–40 years after the Battle of Yavin)

As this era began, Luke Skywalker had unified the Jedi Order into a cohesive group of powerful Jedi Knights. It was a time of relative peace, yet darkness approached on the horizon. Now, Skywalker's descendants face new and resurgent threats to the galaxy, and to the balance of the Force.

The events in this story take place approximately twenty-five years after the Battle of Yavin.

STAR WARS®
INVASION

2 RESCUES

Script
TOM TAYLOR

Art
COLIN WILSON

Colors
WES DZIOBA

Letters
MICHAEL HEISLER

Cover Art
JO CHEN

DARK HORSE BOOKS®

president and publisher
MIKE RICHARDSON

collection designer
STEPHEN REICHERT

editor
RANDY STRADLEY

assistant editor
FREDDYE LINS

NEIL HANKERSON executive vice president TOM WEDDLE chief financial officer RANDY STRADLEY vice president of publishing MICHAEL MARTENS vice president of business development ANITA NELSON vice president of business affairs MICHA HERSHMAN vice president of marketing DAVID SCROGGY vice president of product development DALE LAFOUNTAIN vice president of information technology DARLENE VOGEL director of purchasing KEN LIZZI general counsel DAVEY ESTRADA editorial director SCOTT ALLIE senior managing editor CHRIS WARNER senior books editor DIANA SCHUTZ executive editor CARY GRAZZINI director of design and production LIA RIBACCHI art director CARA NIECE director of scheduling

special thanks to Jann Moorhead, David Anderman, Troy Alders, Leland Chee, Sue Rostoni, and Carol Roeder at Lucas Licensing

STAR WARS: INVASION VOLUME 2—RESCUES

This volume collects issues #1–#6 of the Dark Horse comic-book series *Star Wars: Invasion—Rescues*.

Published by
Dark Horse Books
A division of Dark Horse Comics, Inc.
10956 SE Main Street
Milwaukie, OR 97222

darkhorse.com
starwars.com

To find a comics shop in your area, call the Comic Shop Locator Service toll-free at 1-888-266-4226

Library of Congress Cataloging-in-Publication Data

Taylor, Tom, 1978-
Rescues / script, Tom Taylor ; art, Colin Wilson ; colors, Wes Dzioba ; letters, Michael Heisler ; cover art, Jo Chen.
-- 1st ed.
p. cm. -- (Star Wars--Invasion ; v. 2)
Summary: Twenty years after the defeat of the Empire and the establishment of the New Republic, a new threat has come and, despite the misgivings of Jedi Master Luke Skywalker, a daring rescue mission is undertaken.
ISBN 978-1-59582-630-5
1. Graphic novels. [1. Graphic novels. 2. Science fiction.] I. Wilson, Colin, 1949 Oct. 31- ill. II. Heisler, Michael.
III. Title.
PZ7.7.T393Res 2011
741.5'973--dc22
2010045851

First edition: April 2011
ISBN 978-1-59582-630-5

1 3 5 7 9 10 8 6 4 2
Printed by Midas Printing International, Ltd., Huizhou, China.

In the wake of the Yuuzhan Vong invasion, Luke Skywalker leads the New Jedi Order to aid planets under attack, while also trying to discover the secrets behind this strange new enemy.

Artorias, the homeworld of the royal Galfridian family, has been overrun by the enemy. Now, though separated, each member of the family fights the invaders with the hope that one day they can be reunited and free their planet.

Finn trains to become a Jedi on Yavin 4. His father, Caled, secretly leads survivors against the Yuuzhan Vong on Artorias. Kaye and Nina, Finn's sister and mother, have commandeered the ship on which they and many others were captives. But other refugees are not so lucky . . .

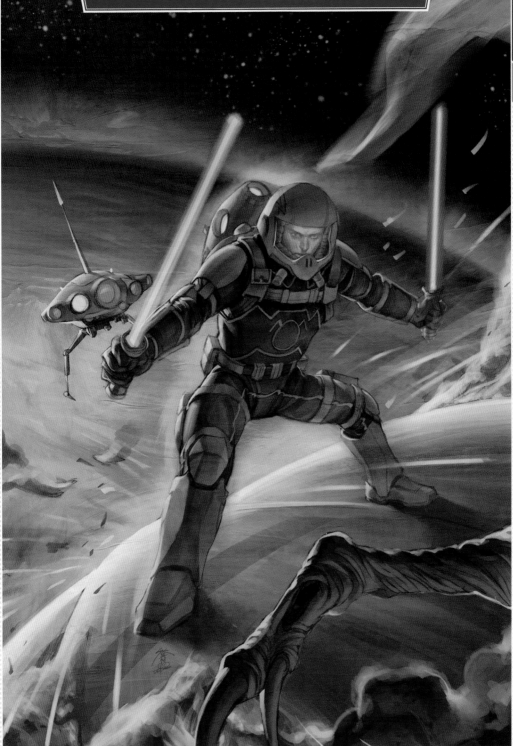

ILLUSTRATION BY JO CHEN

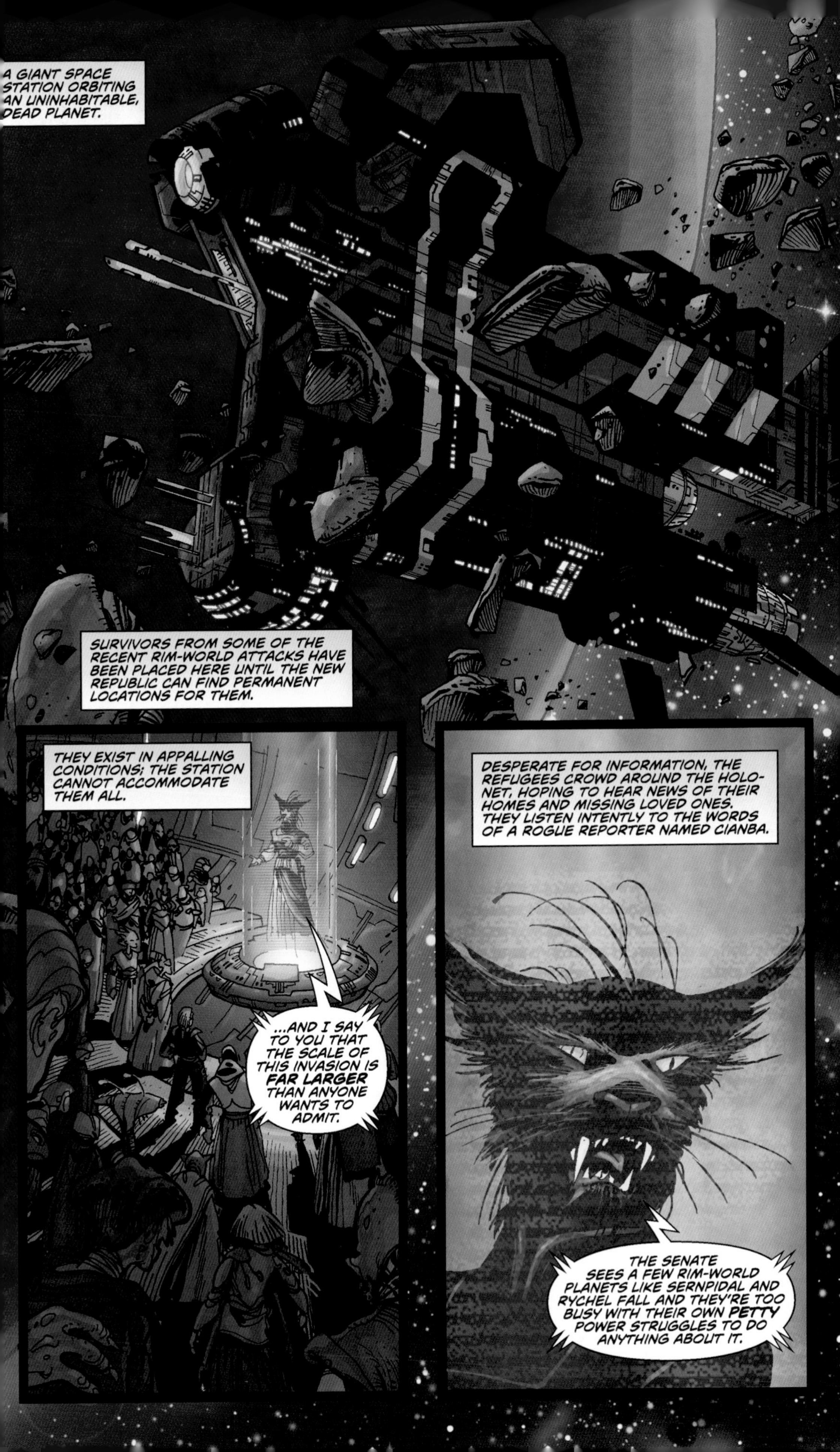
A GIANT SPACE STATION ORBITING AN UNINHABITABLE, DEAD PLANET.
SURVIVORS FROM SOME OF THE RECENT RIM-WORLD ATTACKS HAVE BEEN PLACED HERE UNTIL THE NEW REPUBLIC CAN FIND PERMANENT LOCATIONS FOR THEM.
THEY EXIST IN APPALLING CONDITIONS; THE STATION CANNOT ACCOMMODATE THEM ALL.
...AND I SAY TO YOU THAT THE SCALE OF THIS INVASION IS **FAR LARGER** THAN ANYONE WANTS TO ADMIT.
DESPERATE FOR INFORMATION, THE REFUGEES CROWD AROUND THE HOLONET, HOPING TO HEAR NEWS OF THEIR HOMES AND MISSING LOVED ONES. THEY LISTEN INTENTLY TO THE WORDS OF A ROGUE REPORTER NAMED CIANBA.
THE SENATE SEES A FEW RIM-WORLD PLANETS LIKE SERNPIDAL AND RYCHEL FALL AND THEY'RE TOO BUSY WITH THEIR OWN **PETTY** POWER STRUGGLES TO DO ANYTHING ABOUT IT.

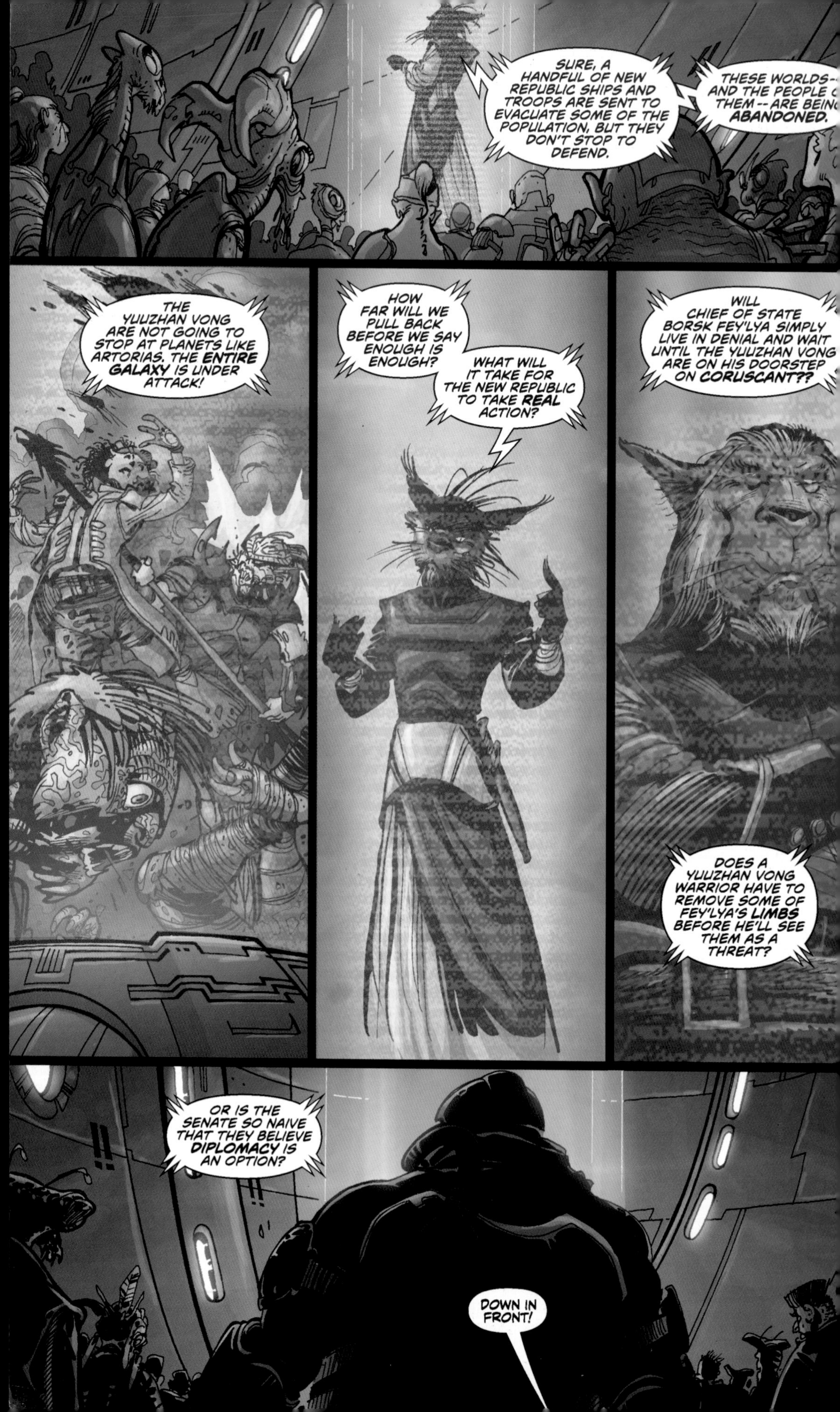
SURE, A HANDFUL OF NEW REPUBLIC SHIPS AND TROOPS ARE SENT TO EVACUATE SOME OF THE POPULATION, BUT THEY DON'T STOP TO DEFEND.
THESE WORLDS-- AND THE PEOPLE O THEM -- ARE BEIN ABANDONED.
THE YUUZHAN VONG ARE NOT GOING TO STOP AT PLANETS LIKE ARTORIAS. THE ENTIRE GALAXY IS UNDER ATTACK!
HOW FAR WILL WE PULL BACK BEFORE WE SAY ENOUGH IS ENOUGH?
WHAT WILL IT TAKE FOR THE NEW REPUBLIC TO TAKE REAL ACTION?
WILL CHIEF OF STATE BORSK FEY'LYA SIMPLY LIVE IN DENIAL AND WAIT UNTIL THE YUUZHAN VONG ARE ON HIS DOORSTEP ON CORUSCANT??
DOES A YUUZHAN VONG WARRIOR HAVE TO REMOVE SOME OF FEY'LYA'S LIMBS BEFORE HE'LL SEE THEM AS A THREAT?
OR IS THE SENATE SO NAIVE THAT THEY BELIEVE DIPLOMACY IS AN OPTION?
DOWN IN FRONT!

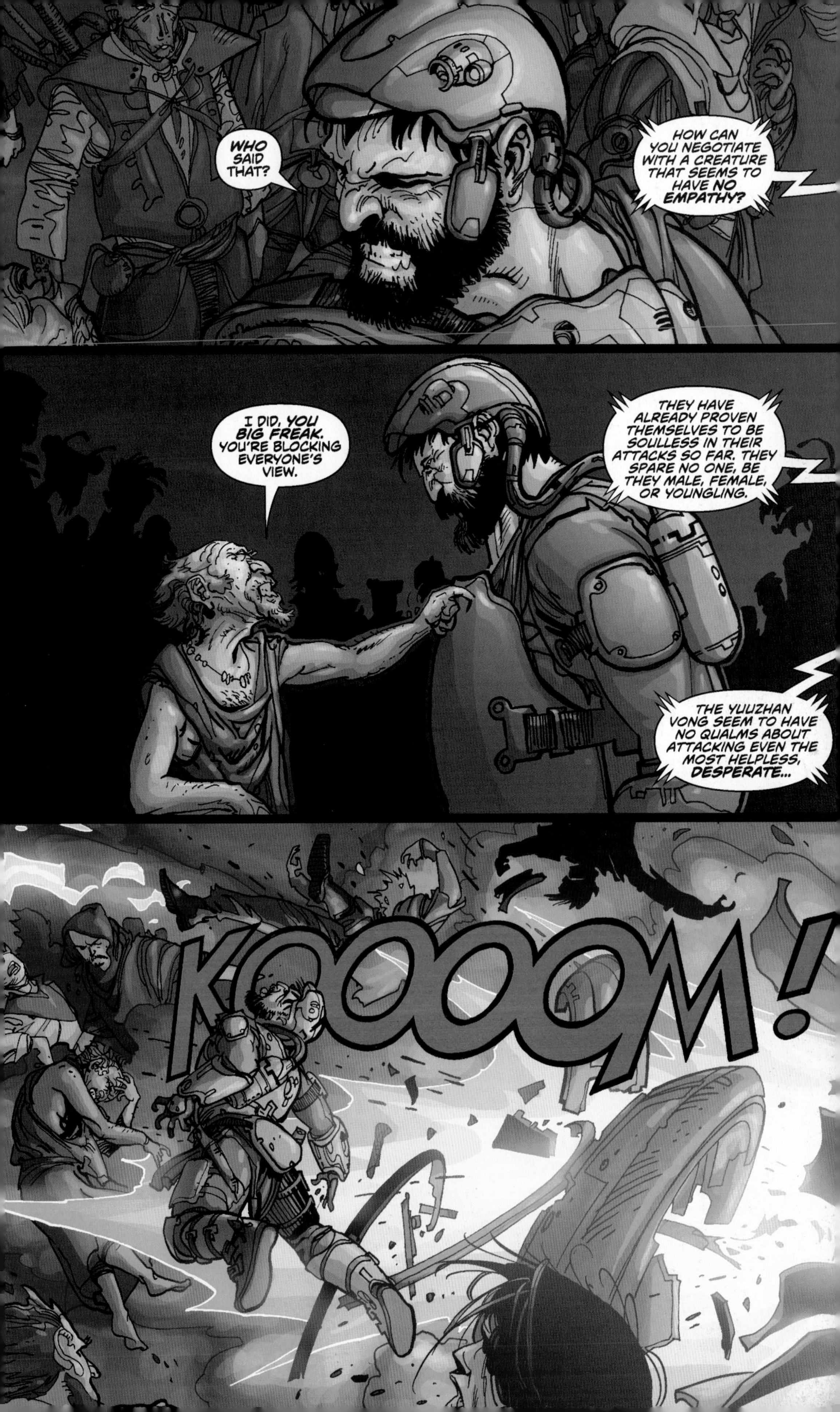
WHO SAID THAT?
HOW CAN YOU NEGOTIATE WITH A CREATURE THAT SEEMS TO HAVE NO EMPATHY?
I DID, YOU BIG FREAK. YOU'RE BLOCKING EVERYONE'S VIEW.
THEY HAVE ALREADY PROVEN THEMSELVES TO BE SOULLESS IN THEIR ATTACKS SO FAR. THEY SPARE NO ONE, BE THEY MALE, FEMALE, OR YOUNGLING.
THE YUUZHAN VONG SEEM TO HAVE NO QUALMS ABOUT ATTACKING EVEN THE MOST HELPLESS, DESPERATE...
KOOOOM!

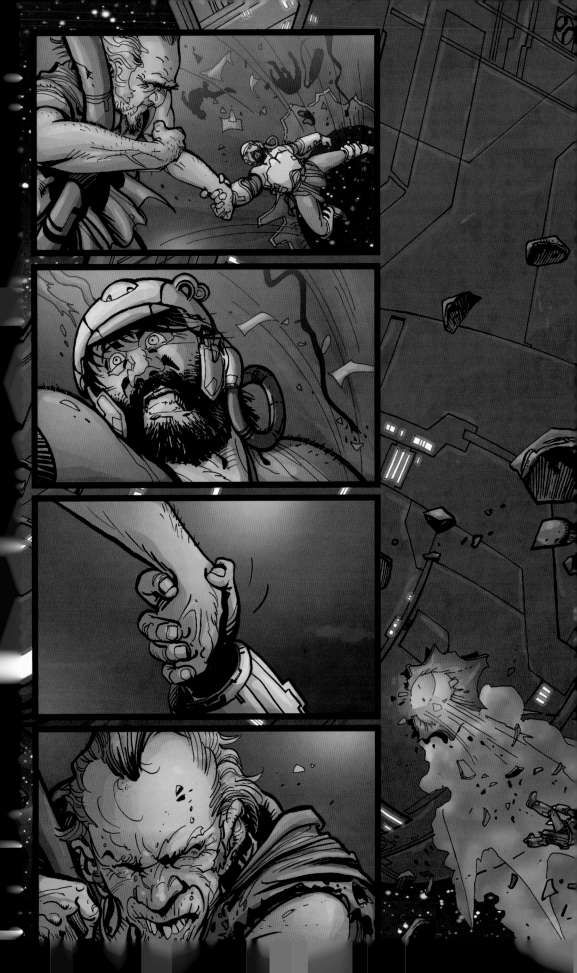

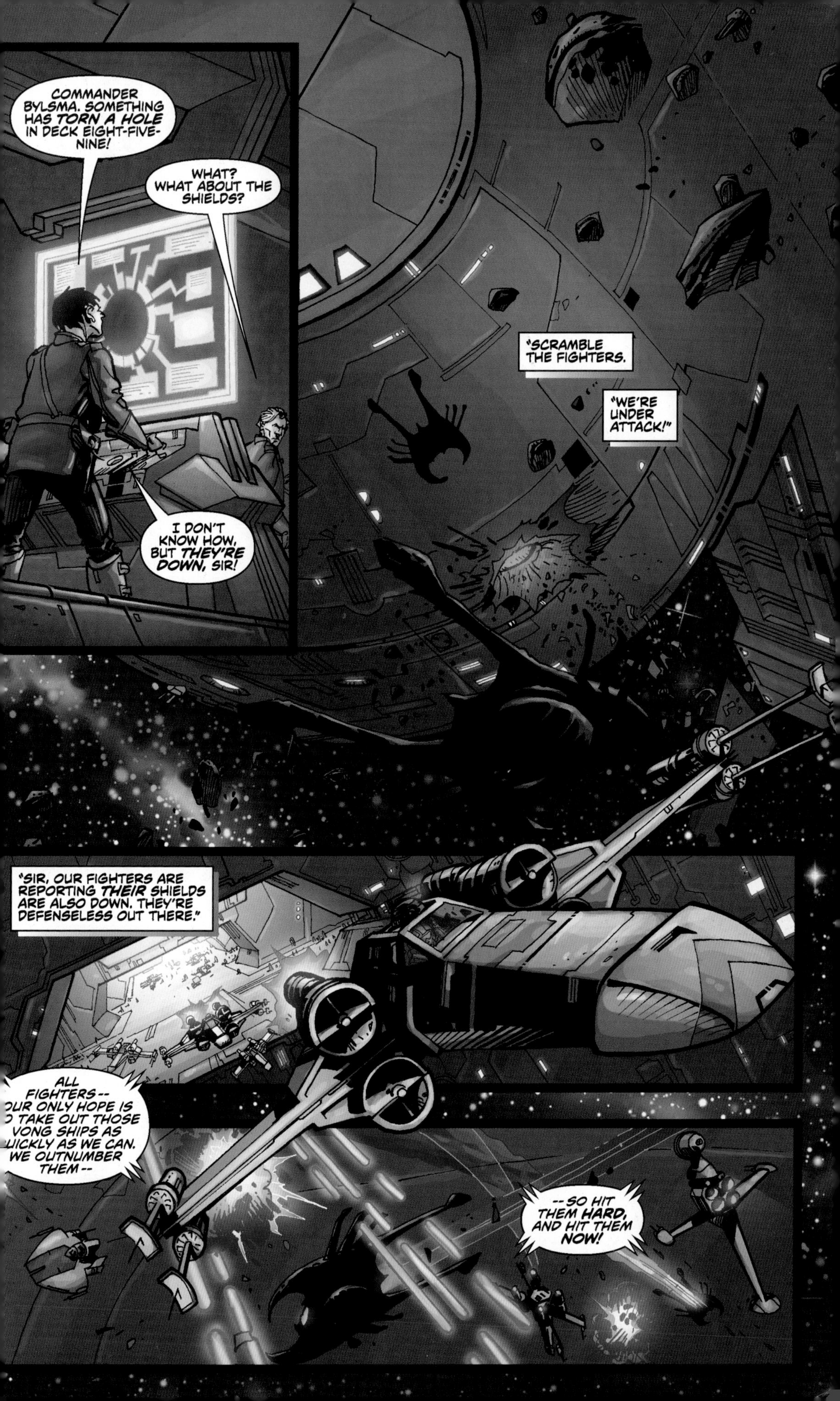
COMMANDER BYLSMA. SOMETHING HAS TORN A HOLE IN DECK EIGHT-FIVE-NINE!
WHAT? WHAT ABOUT THE SHIELDS?
I DON'T KNOW HOW, BUT THEY'RE DOWN, SIR!
"SCRAMBLE THE FIGHTERS.
"WE'RE UNDER ATTACK!"
"SIR, OUR FIGHTERS ARE REPORTING THEIR SHIELDS ARE ALSO DOWN. THEY'RE DEFENSELESS OUT THERE."
ALL FIGHTERS -- OUR ONLY HOPE IS TO TAKE OUT THOSE VONG SHIPS AS QUICKLY AS WE CAN. WE OUTNUMBER THEM --
-- SO HIT THEM HARD, AND HIT THEM NOW!

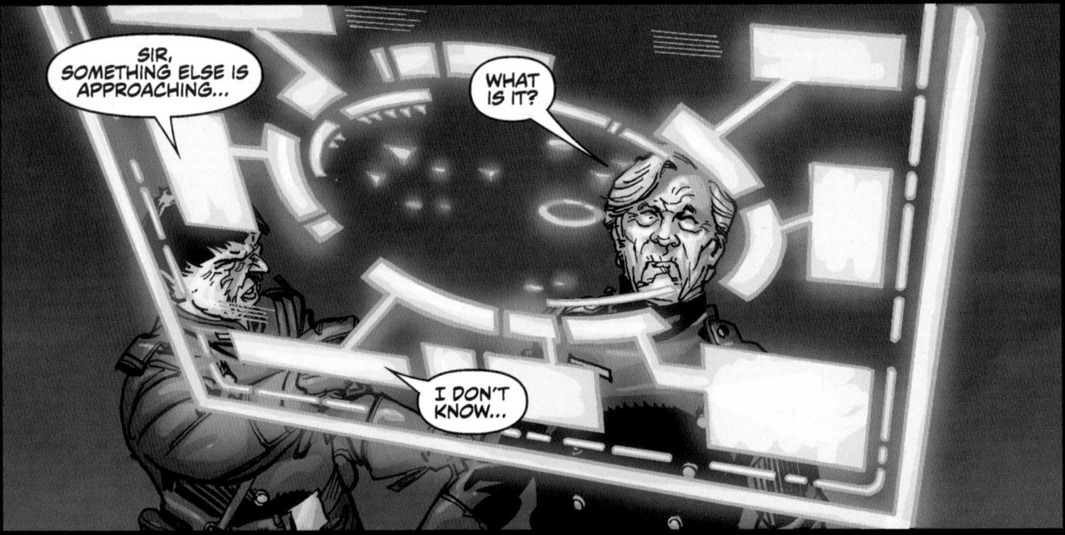
SIR, SOMETHING ELSE IS APPROACHING...
WHAT IS IT?
I DON'T KNOW...

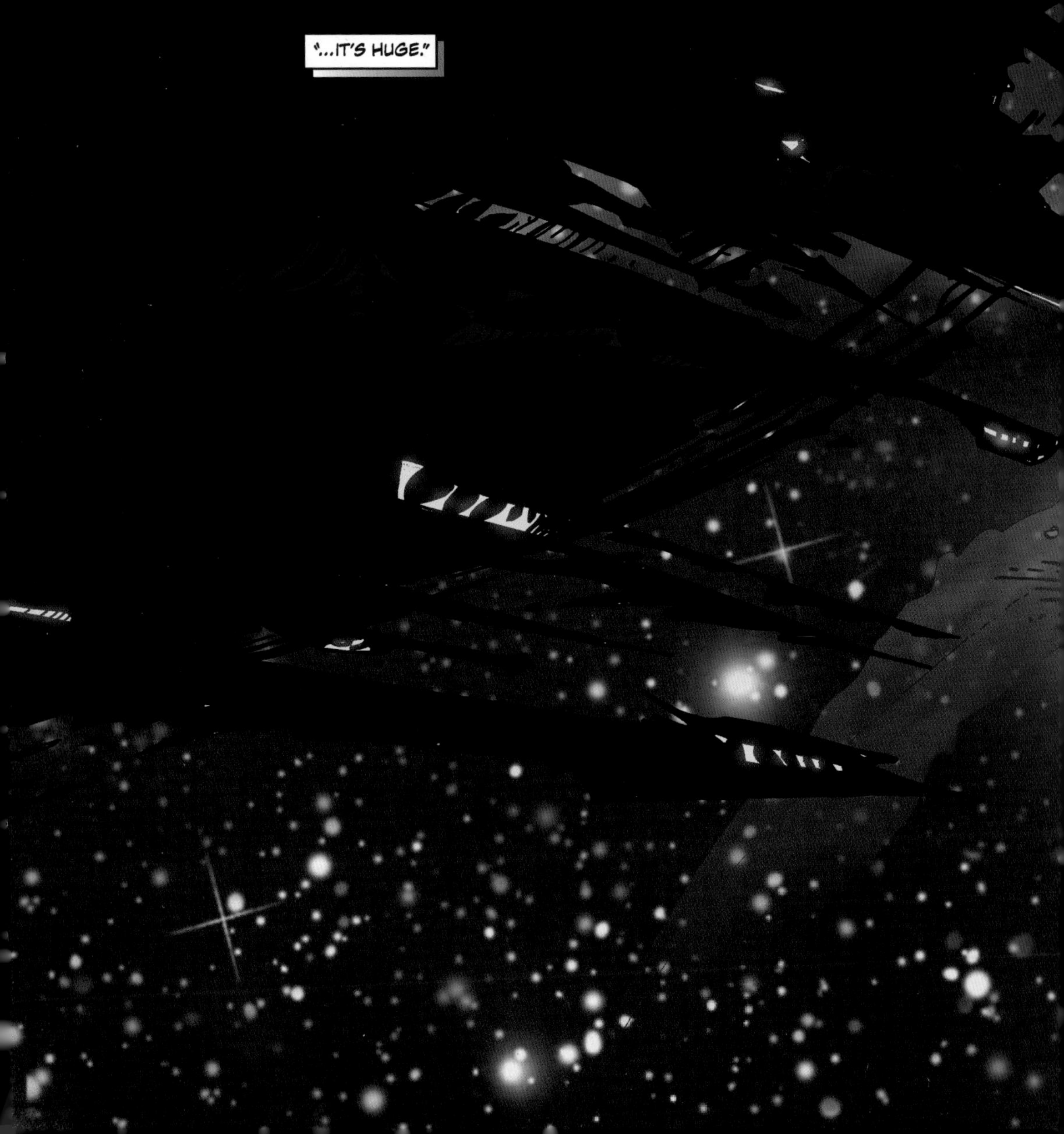
"...IT'S HUGE."

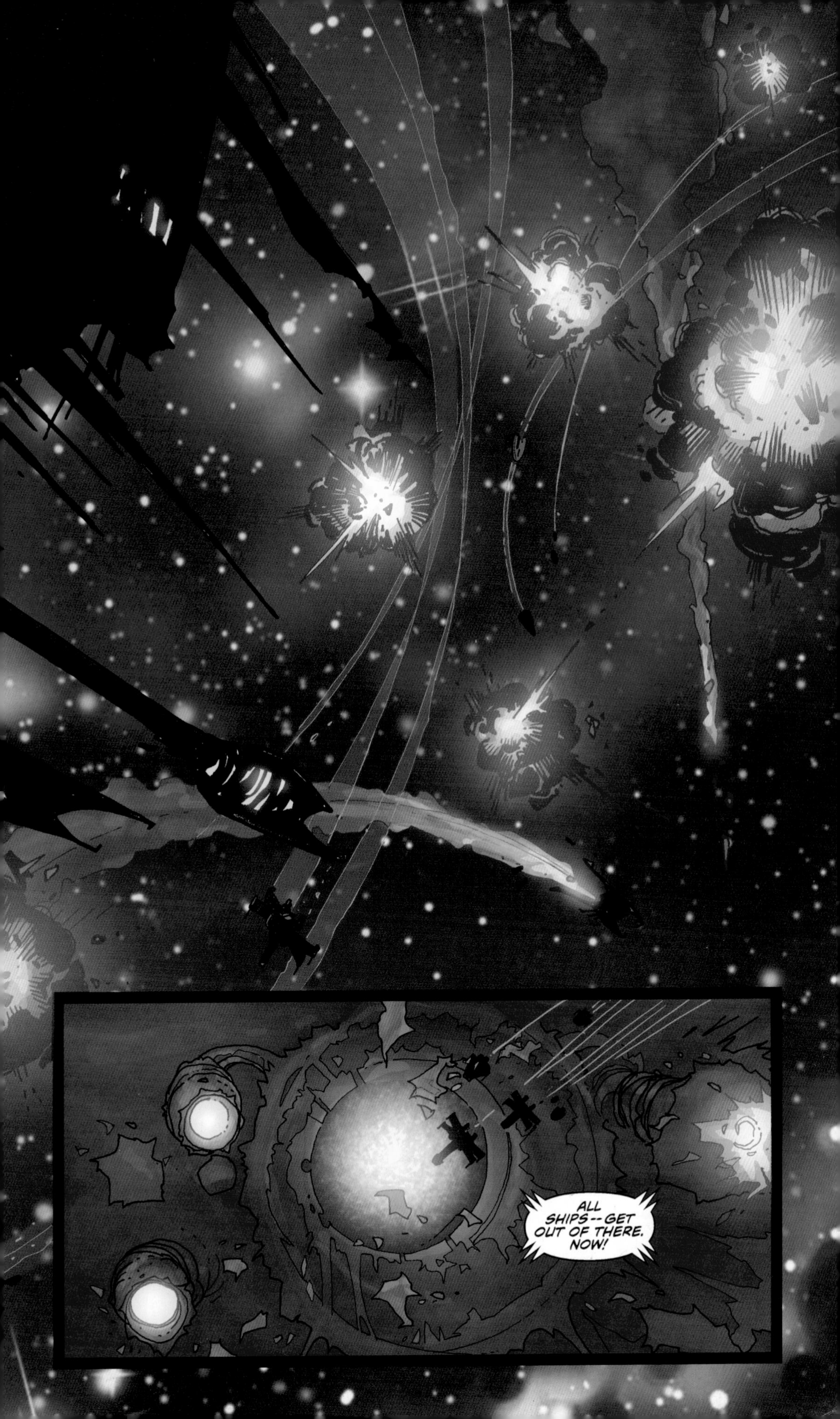
ALL SHIPS -- GET OUT OF THERE. NOW!

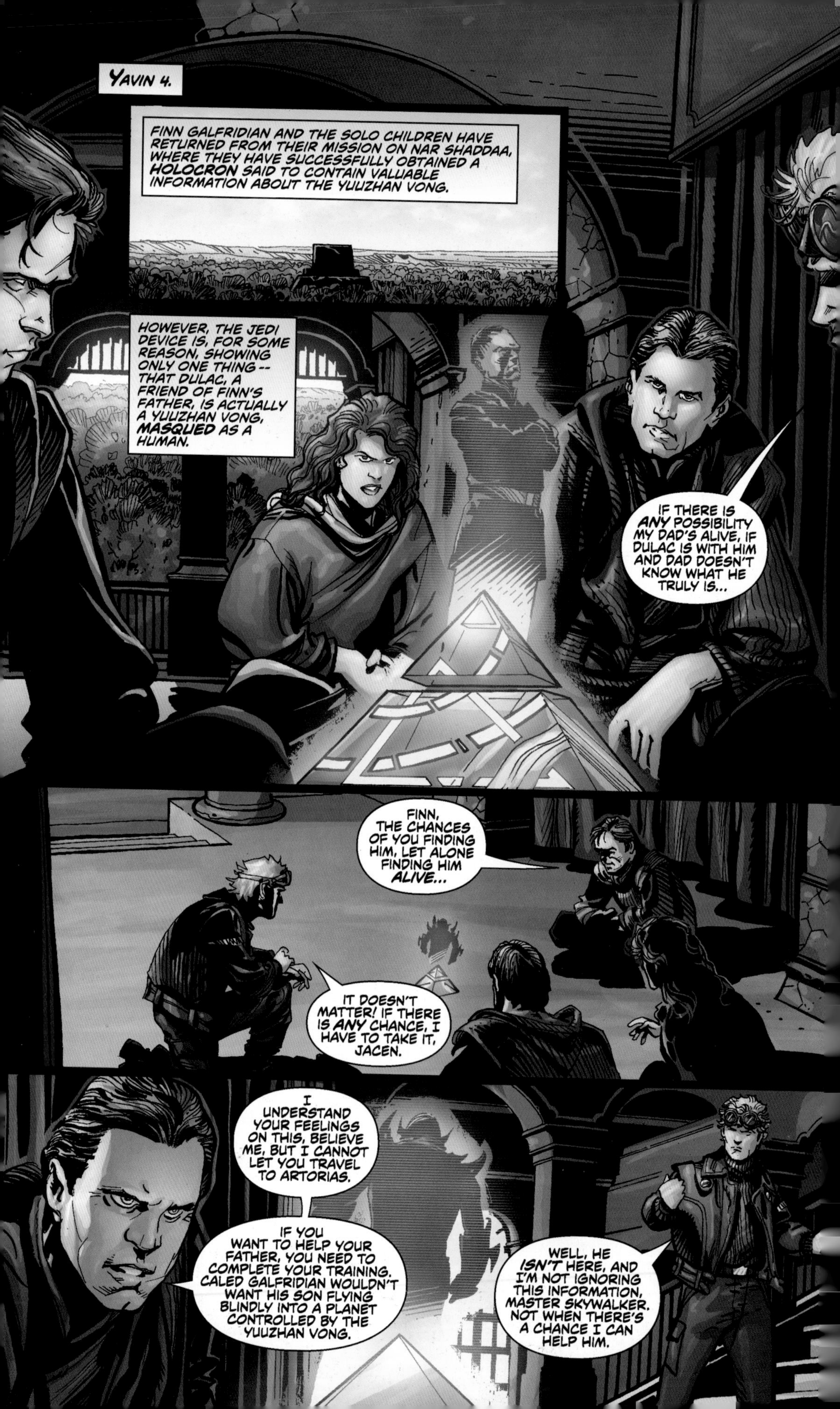
YAVIN 4.
FINN GALFRIDIAN AND THE SOLO CHILDREN HAVE RETURNED FROM THEIR MISSION ON NAR SHADDAA, WHERE THEY HAVE SUCCESSFULLY OBTAINED A HOLOCRON SAID TO CONTAIN VALUABLE INFORMATION ABOUT THE YUUZHAN VONG.
HOWEVER, THE JEDI DEVICE IS, FOR SOME REASON, SHOWING ONLY ONE THING -- THAT DULAC, A FRIEND OF FINN'S FATHER, IS ACTUALLY A YUUZHAN VONG, MASQUED AS A HUMAN.
IF THERE IS ANY POSSIBILITY MY DAD'S ALIVE, IF DULAC IS WITH HIM AND DAD DOESN'T KNOW WHAT HE TRULY IS...
FINN, THE CHANCES OF YOU FINDING HIM, LET ALONE FINDING HIM ALIVE...
IT DOESN'T MATTER! IF THERE IS ANY CHANCE, I HAVE TO TAKE IT, JACEN.
I UNDERSTAND YOUR FEELINGS ON THIS, BELIEVE ME, BUT I CANNOT LET YOU TRAVEL TO ARTORIAS.
IF YOU WANT TO HELP YOUR FATHER, YOU NEED TO COMPLETE YOUR TRAINING. CALED GALFRIDIAN WOULDN'T WANT HIS SON FLYING BLINDLY INTO A PLANET CONTROLLED BY THE YUUZHAN VONG.
WELL, HE ISN'T HERE, AND I'M NOT IGNORING THIS INFORMATION, MASTER SKYWALKER. NOT WHEN THERE'S A CHANCE I CAN HELP HIM.

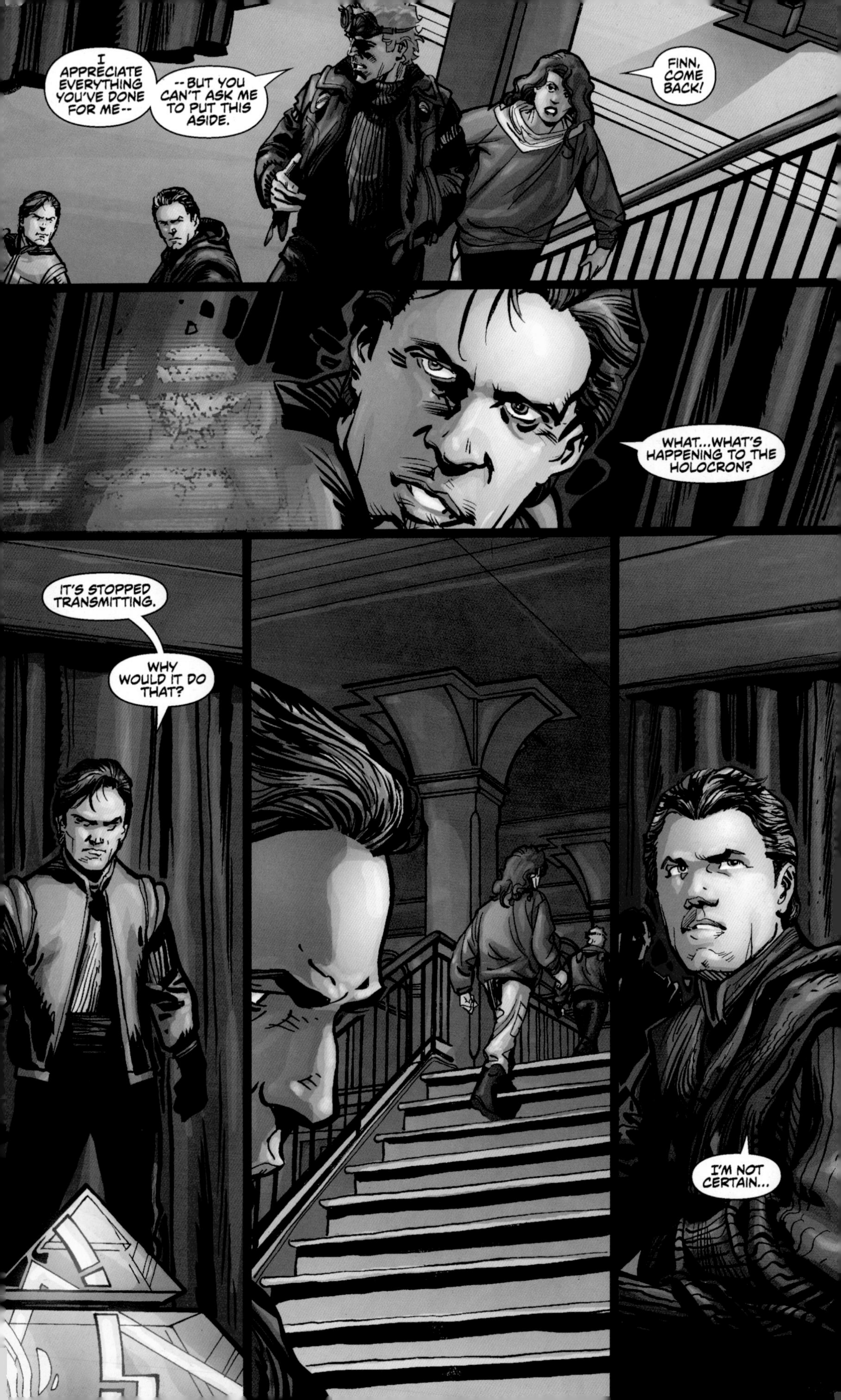
I APPRECIATE EVERYTHING YOU'VE DONE FOR ME--
--BUT YOU CAN'T ASK ME TO PUT THIS ASIDE.
FINN, COME BACK!
WHAT...WHAT'S HAPPENING TO THE HOLOCRON?
IT'S STOPPED TRANSMITTING.
WHY WOULD IT DO THAT?
I'M NOT CERTAIN...

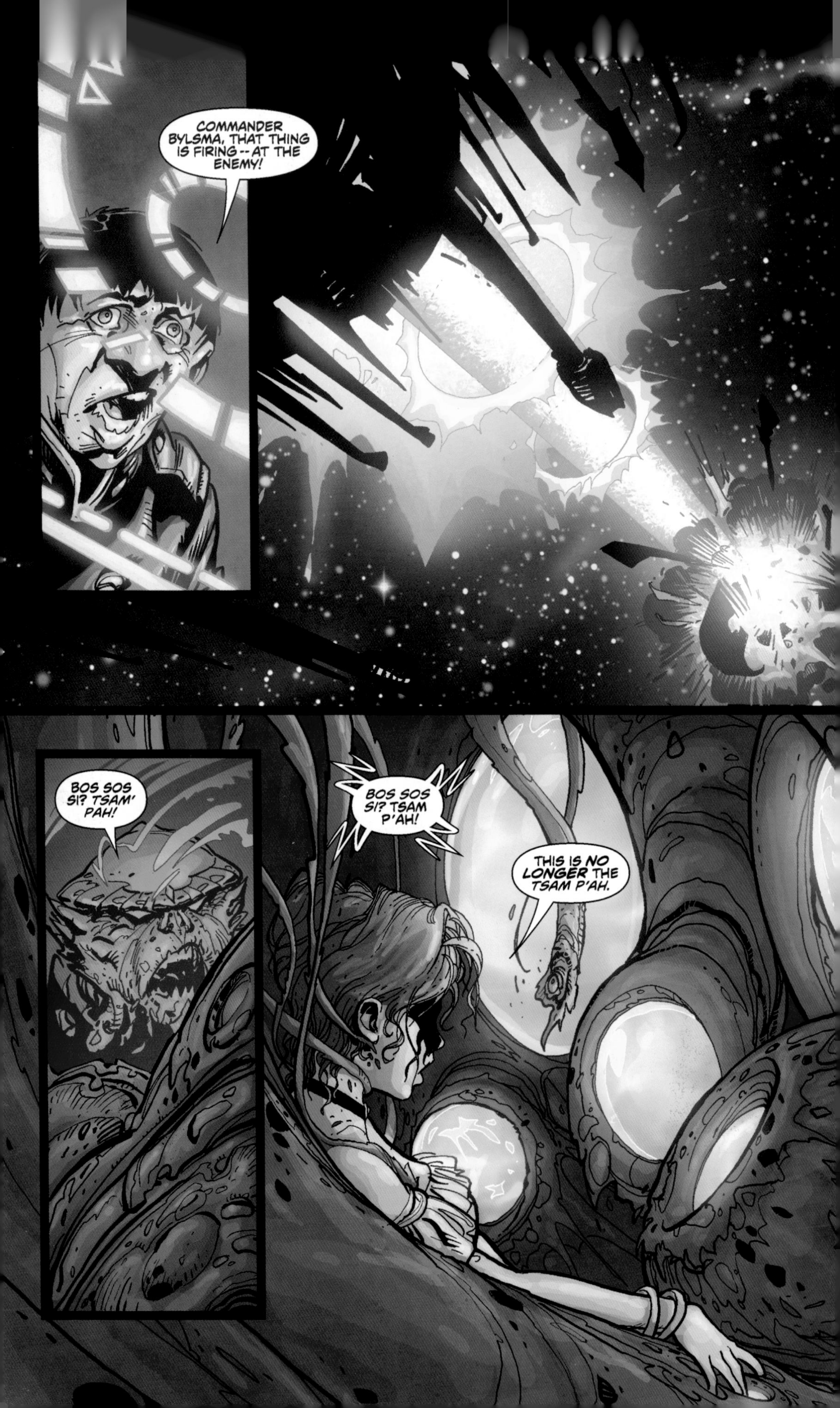
COMMANDER BYLSMA, THAT THING IS FIRING -- AT THE ENEMY!
BOS SOS SI? TSAM' PAH!
BOS SOS SI? TSAM P'AH!
THIS IS NO LONGER THE TSAM P'AH.

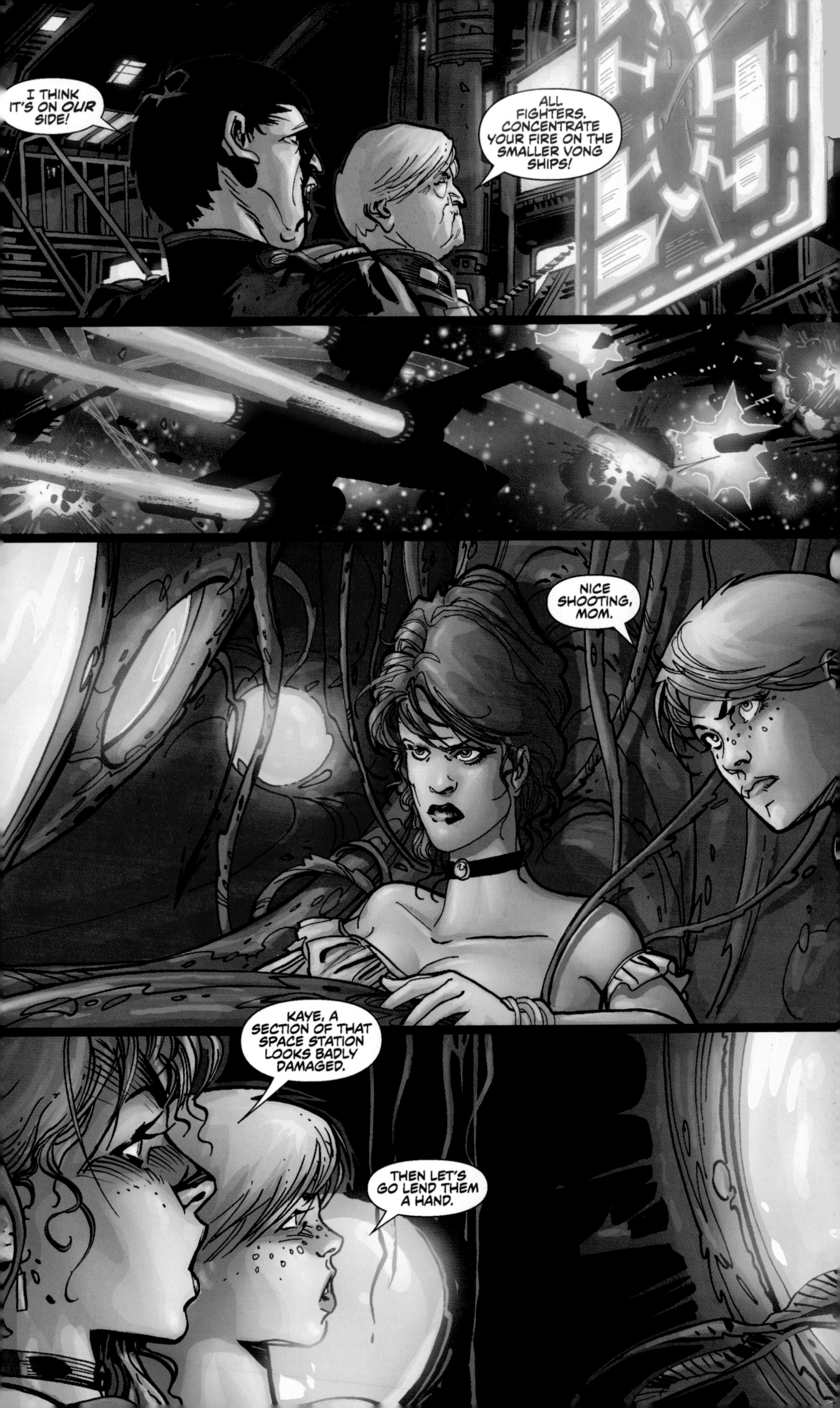
I THINK IT'S ON OUR SIDE!
ALL FIGHTERS. CONCENTRATE YOUR FIRE ON THE SMALLER VONG SHIPS!
NICE SHOOTING, MOM.
KAYE, A SECTION OF THAT SPACE STATION LOOKS BADLY DAMAGED.
THEN LET'S GO LEND THEM A HAND.

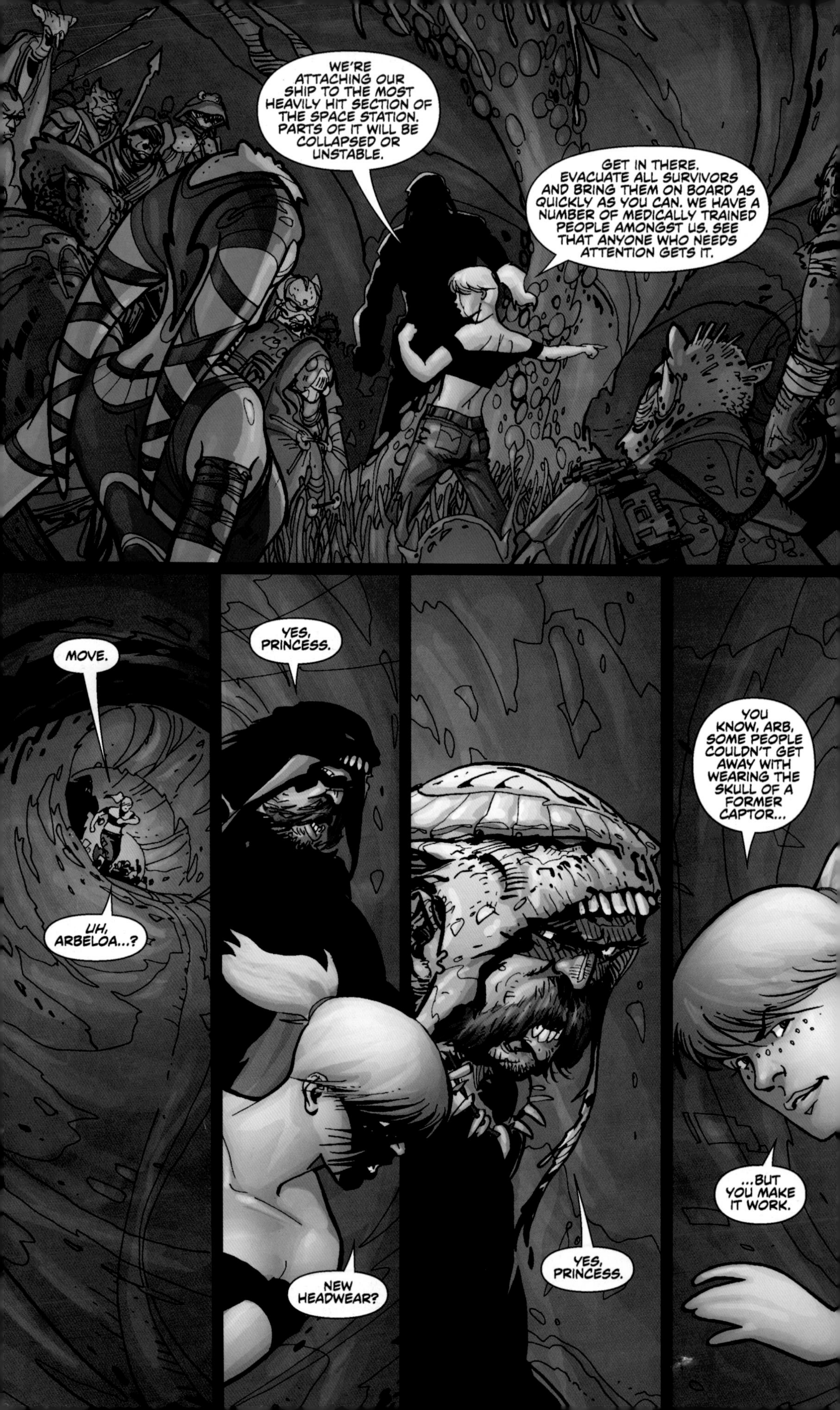
WE'RE ATTACHING OUR SHIP TO THE MOST HEAVILY HIT SECTION OF THE SPACE STATION. PARTS OF IT WILL BE COLLAPSED OR UNSTABLE.
GET IN THERE. EVACUATE ALL SURVIVORS AND BRING THEM ON BOARD AS QUICKLY AS YOU CAN. WE HAVE A NUMBER OF MEDICALLY TRAINED PEOPLE AMONGST US. SEE THAT ANYONE WHO NEEDS ATTENTION GETS IT.
MOVE.
UH, ARBELOA...?
YES, PRINCESS.
NEW HEADWEAR?
YES, PRINCESS.
YOU KNOW, ARB, SOME PEOPLE COULDN'T GET AWAY WITH WEARING THE SKULL OF A FORMER CAPTOR...
...BUT YOU MAKE IT WORK.

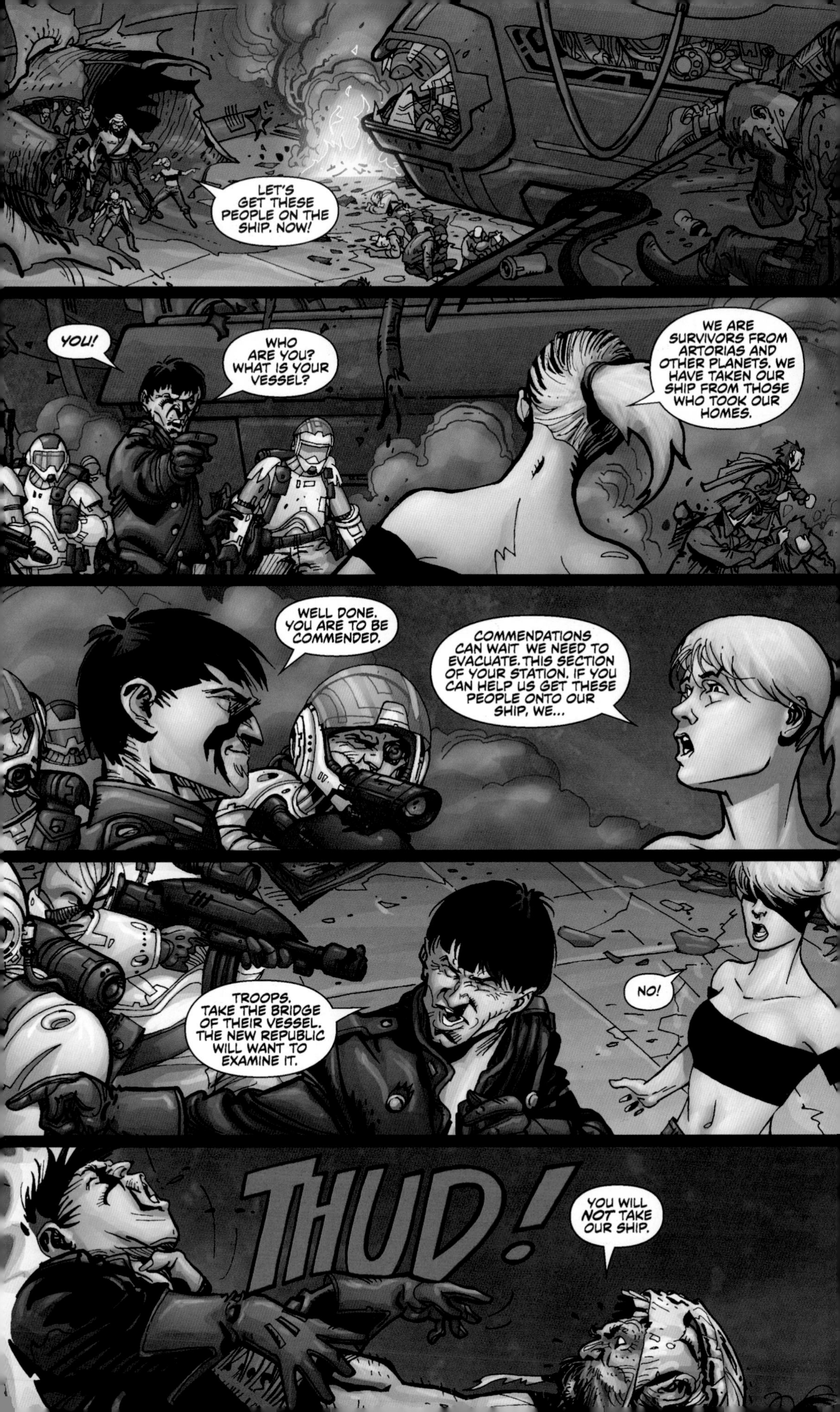
LET'S GET THESE PEOPLE ON THE SHIP. NOW!
YOU!
WHO ARE YOU? WHAT IS YOUR VESSEL?
WE ARE SURVIVORS FROM ARTORIAS AND OTHER PLANETS. WE HAVE TAKEN OUR SHIP FROM THOSE WHO TOOK OUR HOMES.
WELL DONE. YOU ARE TO BE COMMENDED.
COMMENDATIONS CAN WAIT WE NEED TO EVACUATE. THIS SECTION OF YOUR STATION. IF YOU CAN HELP US GET THESE PEOPLE ONTO OUR SHIP, WE...
TROOPS. TAKE THE BRIDGE OF THEIR VESSEL. THE NEW REPUBLIC WILL WANT TO EXAMINE IT.
NO!
THUD!
YOU WILL NOT TAKE OUR SHIP.

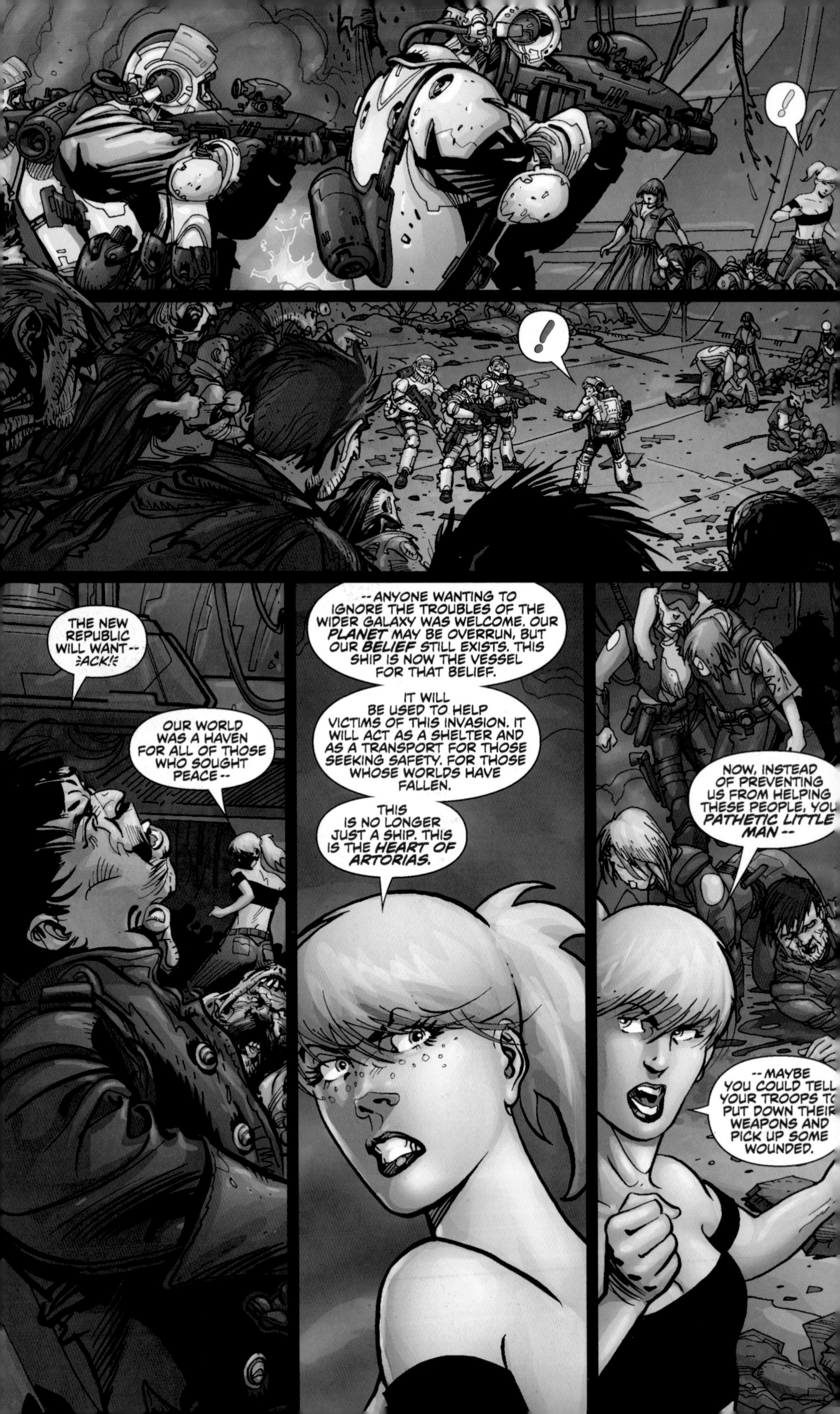
!
!
THE NEW REPUBLIC WILL WANT-- ACK!
OUR WORLD WAS A HAVEN FOR ALL OF THOSE WHO SOUGHT PEACE--
--ANYONE WANTING TO IGNORE THE TROUBLES OF THE WIDER GALAXY WAS WELCOME. OUR PLANET MAY BE OVERRUN, BUT OUR BELIEF STILL EXISTS. THIS SHIP IS NOW THE VESSEL FOR THAT BELIEF.
IT WILL BE USED TO HELP VICTIMS OF THIS INVASION. IT WILL ACT AS A SHELTER AND AS A TRANSPORT FOR THOSE SEEKING SAFETY. FOR THOSE WHOSE WORLDS HAVE FALLEN.
THIS IS NO LONGER JUST A SHIP. THIS IS THE HEART OF ARTORIAS.
NOW, INSTEAD OF PREVENTING US FROM HELPING THESE PEOPLE, YOU PATHETIC LITTLE MAN--
--MAYBE YOU COULD TELL YOUR TROOPS TO PUT DOWN THEIR WEAPONS AND PICK UP SOME WOUNDED.

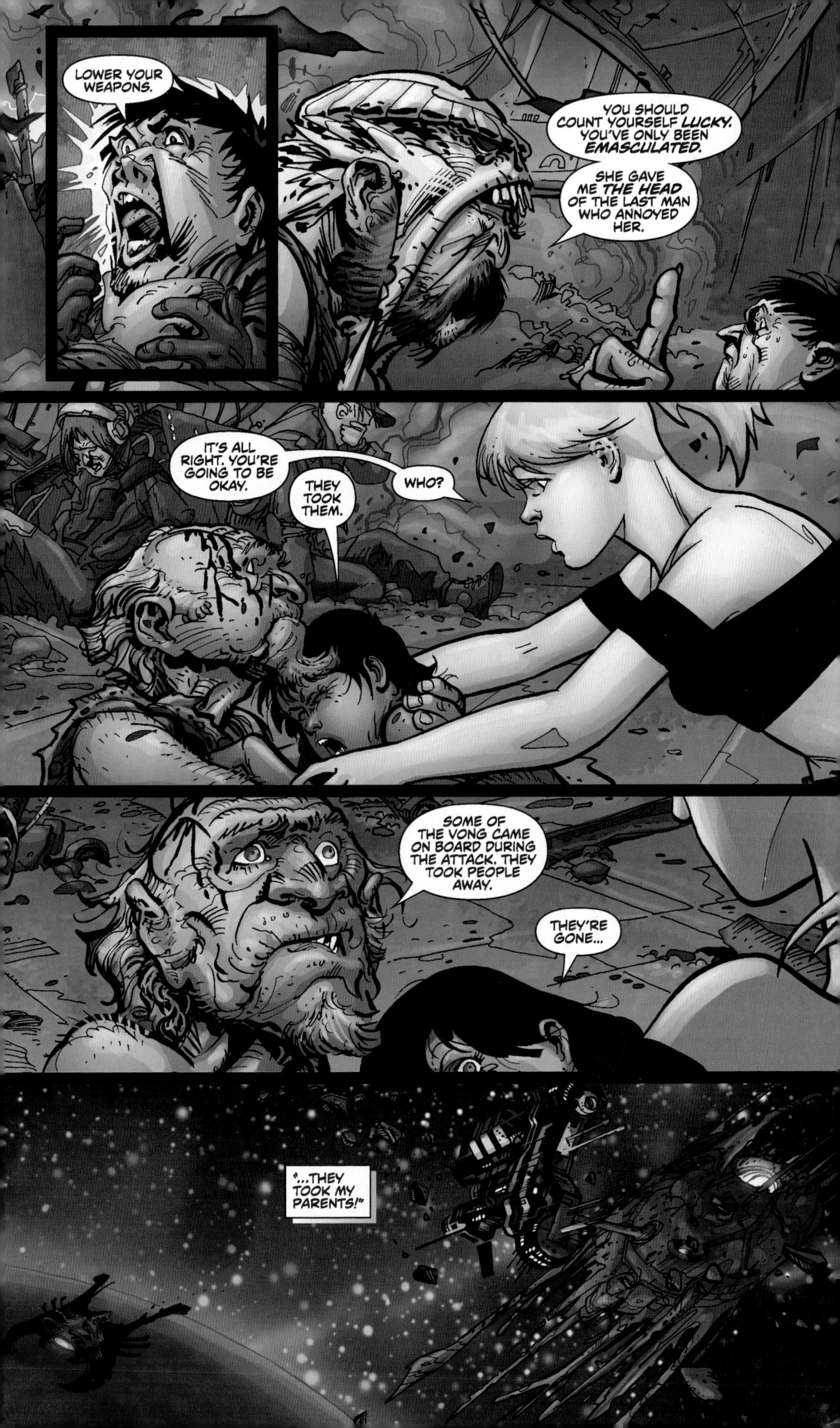
LOWER YOUR WEAPONS.
YOU SHOULD COUNT YOURSELF LUCKY. YOU'VE ONLY BEEN EMASCULATED.
SHE GAVE ME THE HEAD OF THE LAST MAN WHO ANNOYED HER.
IT'S ALL RIGHT. YOU'RE GOING TO BE OKAY.
THEY TOOK THEM.
WHO?
SOME OF THE VONG CAME ON BOARD DURING THE ATTACK. THEY TOOK PEOPLE AWAY.
THEY'RE GONE...
"...THEY TOOK MY PARENTS!"

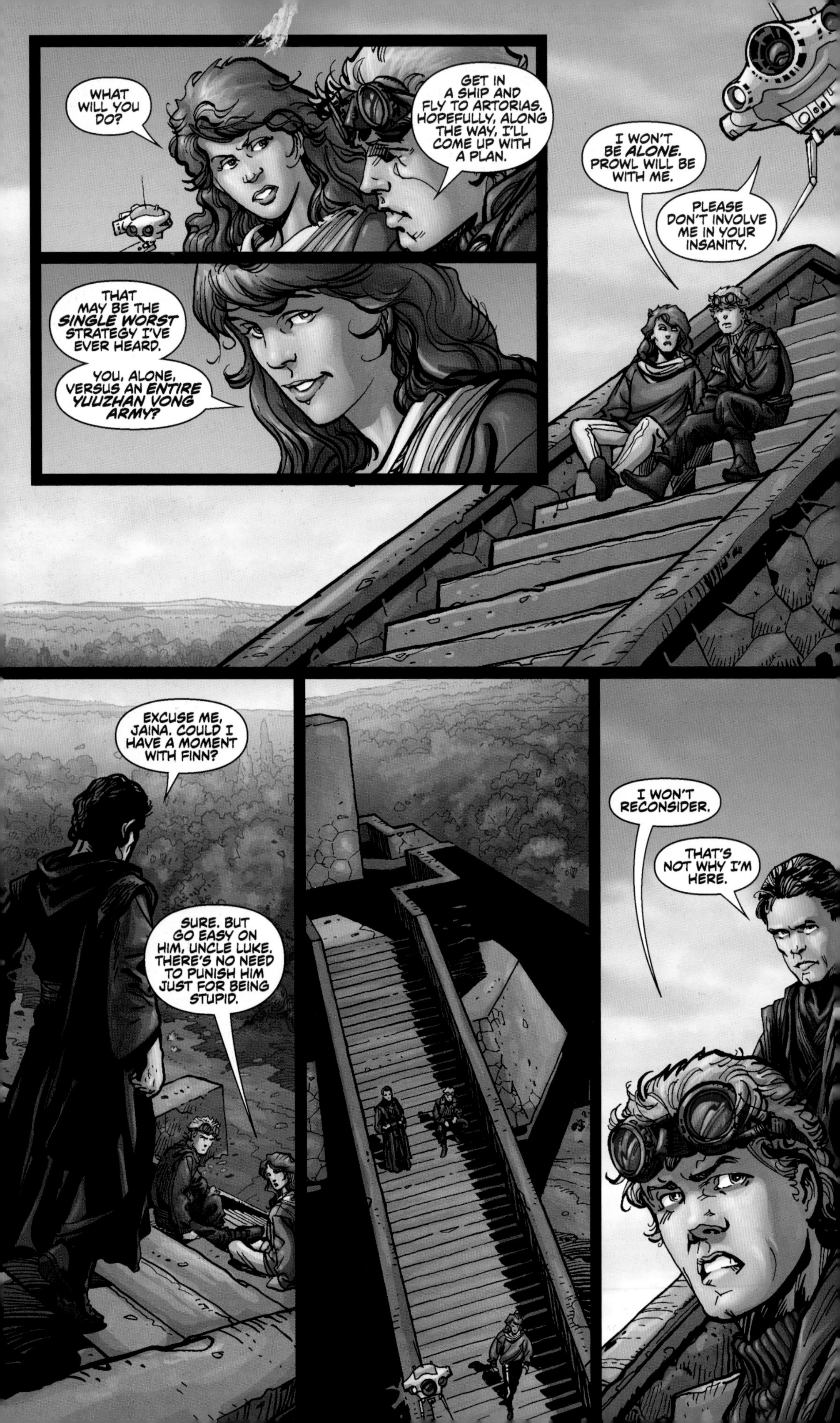
WHAT WILL YOU DO?
GET IN A SHIP AND FLY TO ARTORIAS. HOPEFULLY, ALONG THE WAY, I'LL COME UP WITH A PLAN.
THAT MAY BE THE SINGLE WORST STRATEGY I'VE EVER HEARD.
YOU, ALONE, VERSUS AN ENTIRE YUUZHAN VONG ARMY?
I WON'T BE ALONE. PROWL WILL BE WITH ME.
PLEASE DON'T INVOLVE ME IN YOUR INSANITY.
EXCUSE ME, JAINA. COULD I HAVE A MOMENT WITH FINN?
SURE. BUT GO EASY ON HIM, UNCLE LUKE. THERE'S NO NEED TO PUNISH HIM JUST FOR BEING STUPID.
I WON'T RECONSIDER.
THAT'S NOT WHY I'M HERE.

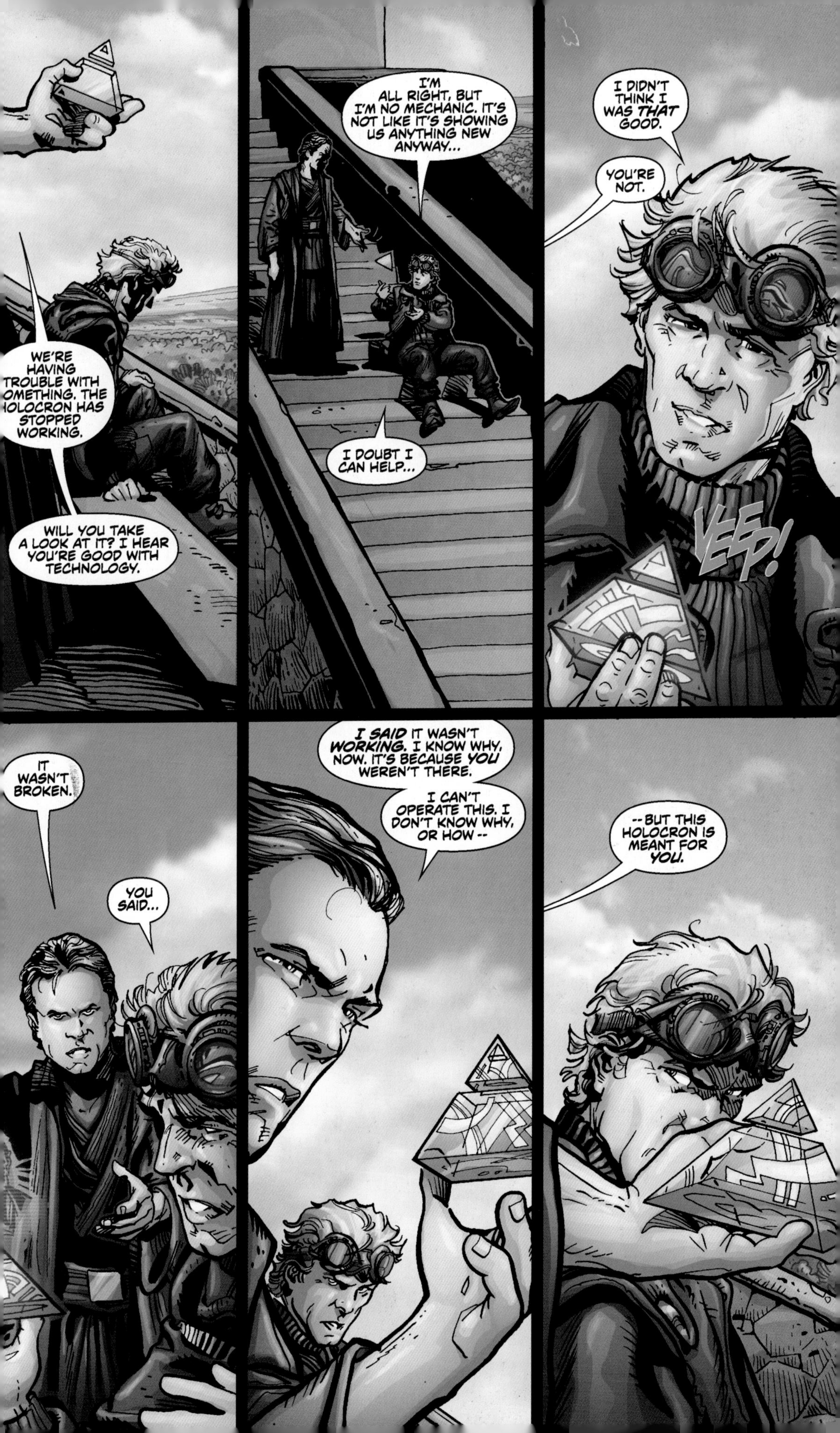
WE'RE HAVING TROUBLE WITH OMETHING. THE IOLOCRON HAS STOPPED WORKING.
WILL YOU TAKE A LOOK AT IT? I HEAR YOU'RE GOOD WITH TECHNOLOGY.
I'M ALL RIGHT, BUT I'M NO MECHANIC. IT'S NOT LIKE IT'S SHOWING US ANYTHING NEW ANYWAY...
I DOUBT I CAN HELP...
I DIDN'T THINK I WAS THAT GOOD.
YOU'RE NOT.
VEEEP!
IT WASN'T BROKEN.
YOU SAID...
I SAID IT WASN'T WORKING. I KNOW WHY, NOW. IT'S BECAUSE YOU WEREN'T THERE.
I CAN'T OPERATE THIS. I DON'T KNOW WHY, OR HOW --
-- BUT THIS HOLOCRON IS MEANT FOR YOU.

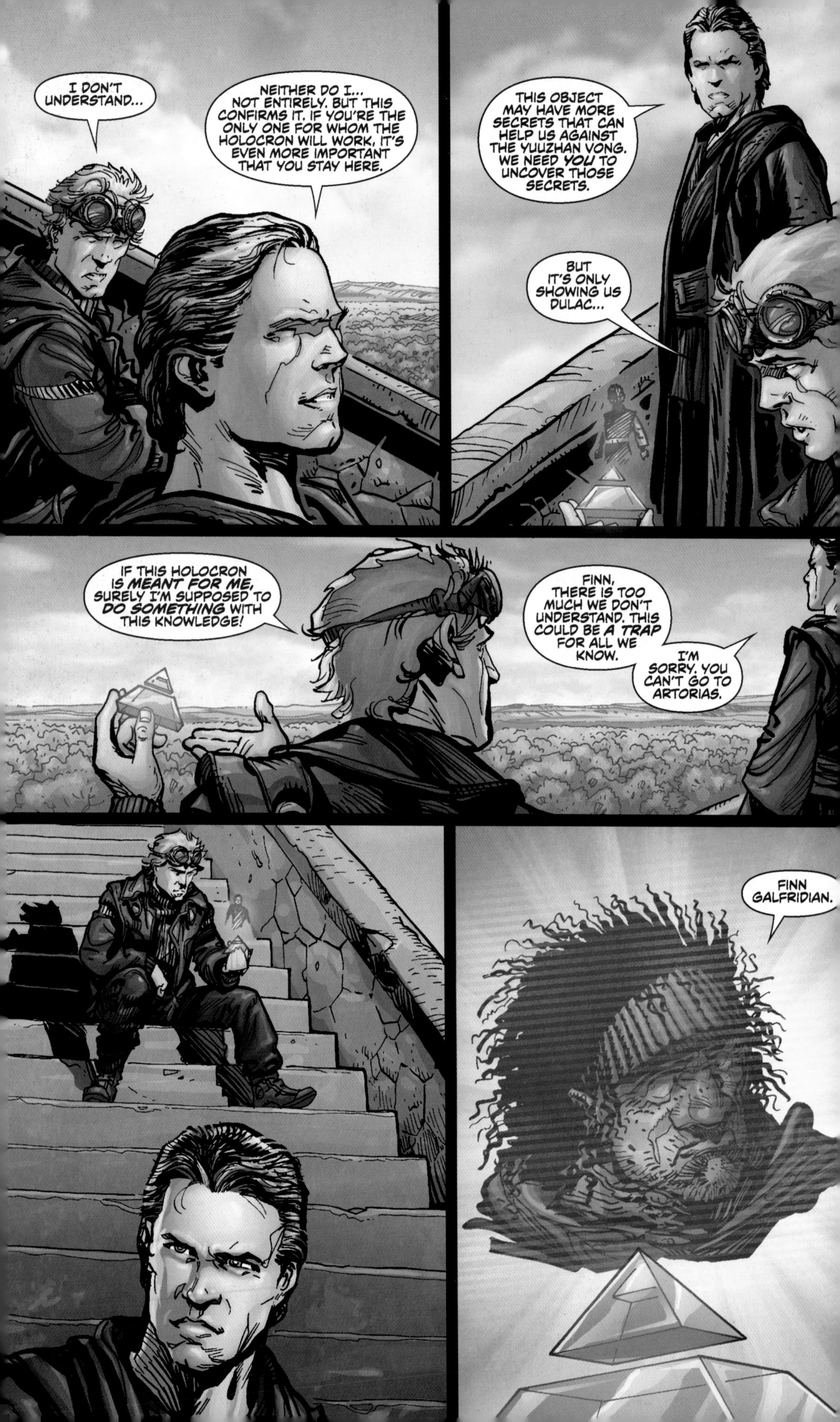
I DON'T UNDERSTAND...
NEITHER DO I... NOT ENTIRELY. BUT THIS CONFIRMS IT. IF YOU'RE THE ONLY ONE FOR WHOM THE HOLOCRON WILL WORK, IT'S EVEN MORE IMPORTANT THAT YOU STAY HERE.
THIS OBJECT MAY HAVE MORE SECRETS THAT CAN HELP US AGAINST THE YUUZHAN VONG. WE NEED YOU TO UNCOVER THOSE SECRETS.
BUT IT'S ONLY SHOWING US DULAC...
IF THIS HOLOCRON IS MEANT FOR ME, SURELY I'M SUPPOSED TO DO SOMETHING WITH THIS KNOWLEDGE!
FINN, THERE IS TOO MUCH WE DON'T UNDERSTAND. THIS COULD BE A TRAP FOR ALL WE KNOW.
I'M SORRY. YOU CAN'T GO TO ARTORIAS.
FINN GALFRIDIAN.

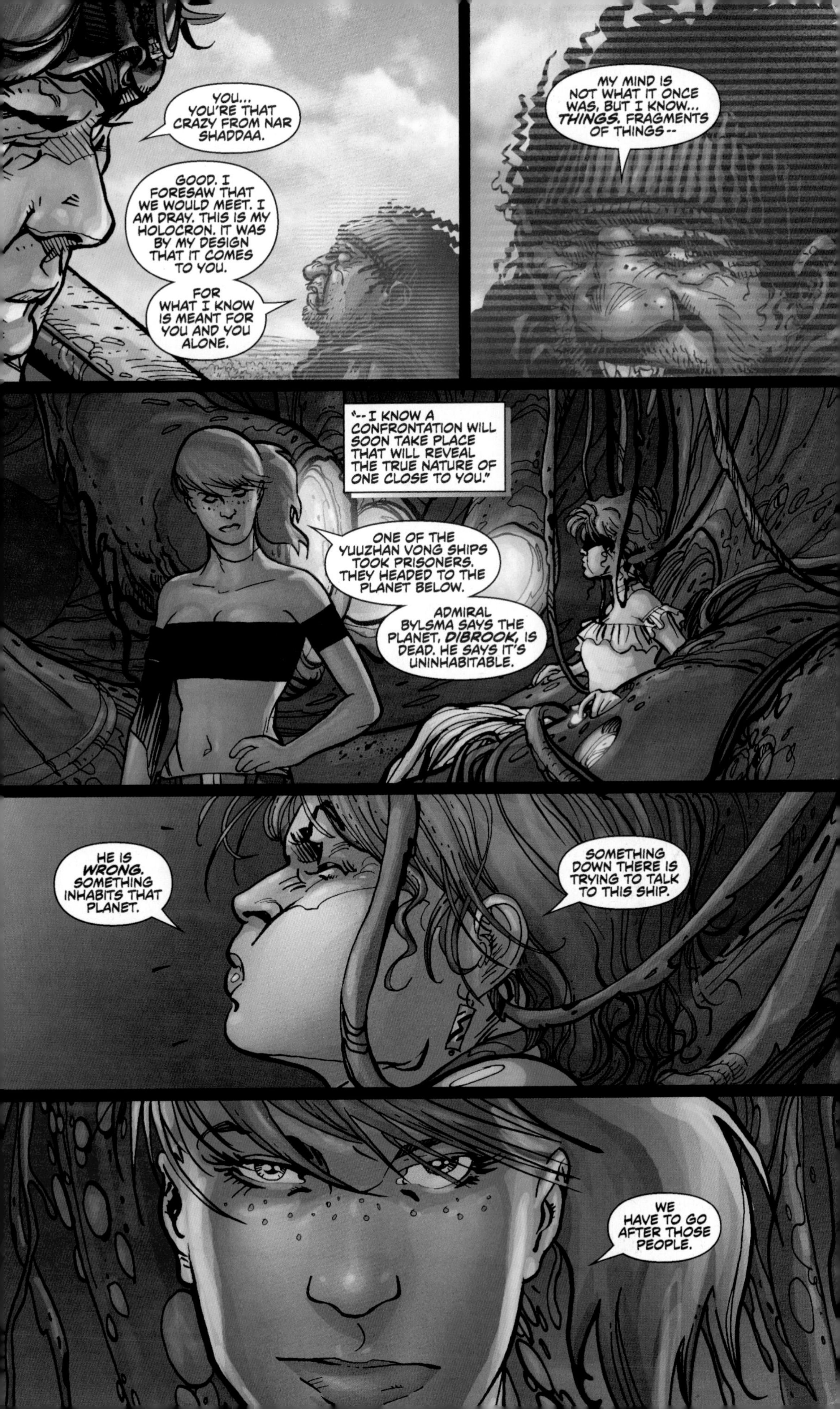
YOU... YOU'RE THAT CRAZY FROM NAR SHADDAA.
GOOD. I FORESAW THAT WE WOULD MEET. I AM DRAY. THIS IS MY HOLOCRON. IT WAS BY MY DESIGN THAT IT COMES TO YOU.
FOR WHAT I KNOW IS MEANT FOR YOU AND YOU ALONE.
MY MIND IS NOT WHAT IT ONCE WAS, BUT I KNOW... THINGS. FRAGMENTS OF THINGS--
"--I KNOW A CONFRONTATION WILL SOON TAKE PLACE THAT WILL REVEAL THE TRUE NATURE OF ONE CLOSE TO YOU."
ONE OF THE YUUZHAN VONG SHIPS TOOK PRISONERS. THEY HEADED TO THE PLANET BELOW.
ADMIRAL BYLSMA SAYS THE PLANET, DIBROOK, IS DEAD. HE SAYS IT'S UNINHABITABLE.
HE IS WRONG. SOMETHING INHABITS THAT PLANET.
SOMETHING DOWN THERE IS TRYING TO TALK TO THIS SHIP.
WE HAVE TO GO AFTER THOSE PEOPLE.

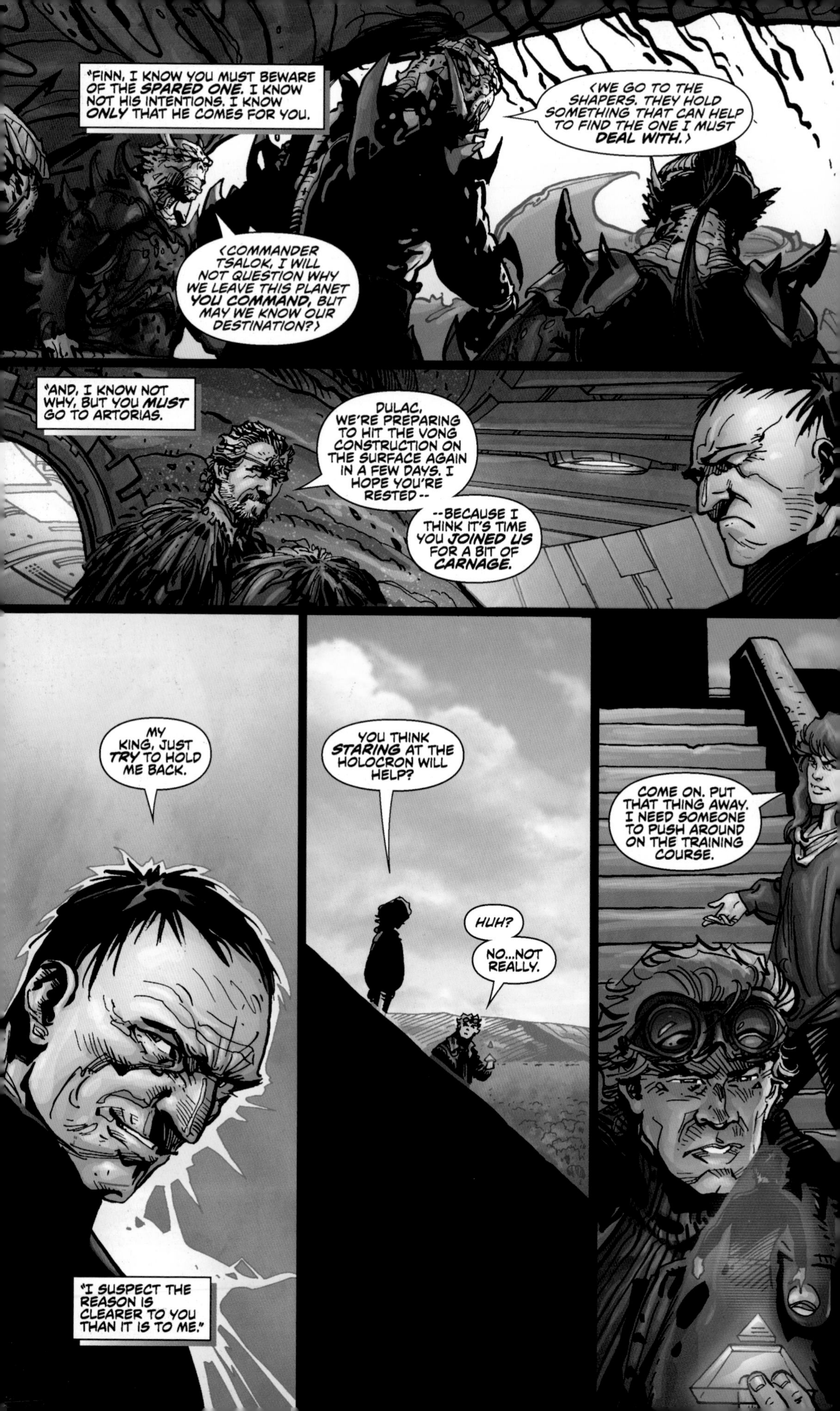
"FINN, I KNOW YOU MUST BEWARE OF THE SPARED ONE. I KNOW NOT HIS INTENTIONS. I KNOW ONLY THAT HE COMES FOR YOU.
‹COMMANDER TSALOK, I WILL NOT QUESTION WHY WE LEAVE THIS PLANET YOU COMMAND, BUT MAY WE KNOW OUR DESTINATION?›
‹WE GO TO THE SHAPERS. THEY HOLD SOMETHING THAT CAN HELP TO FIND THE ONE I MUST DEAL WITH.›
"AND, I KNOW NOT WHY, BUT YOU MUST GO TO ARTORIAS.
DULAC, WE'RE PREPARING TO HIT THE VONG CONSTRUCTION ON THE SURFACE AGAIN IN A FEW DAYS. I HOPE YOU'RE RESTED --
--BECAUSE I THINK IT'S TIME YOU JOINED US FOR A BIT OF CARNAGE.
MY KING, JUST TRY TO HOLD ME BACK.
"I SUSPECT THE REASON IS CLEARER TO YOU THAN IT IS TO ME."
YOU THINK STARING AT THE HOLOCRON WILL HELP?
HUH?
NO...NOT REALLY.
COME ON. PUT THAT THING AWAY. I NEED SOMEONE TO PUSH AROUND ON THE TRAINING COURSE.

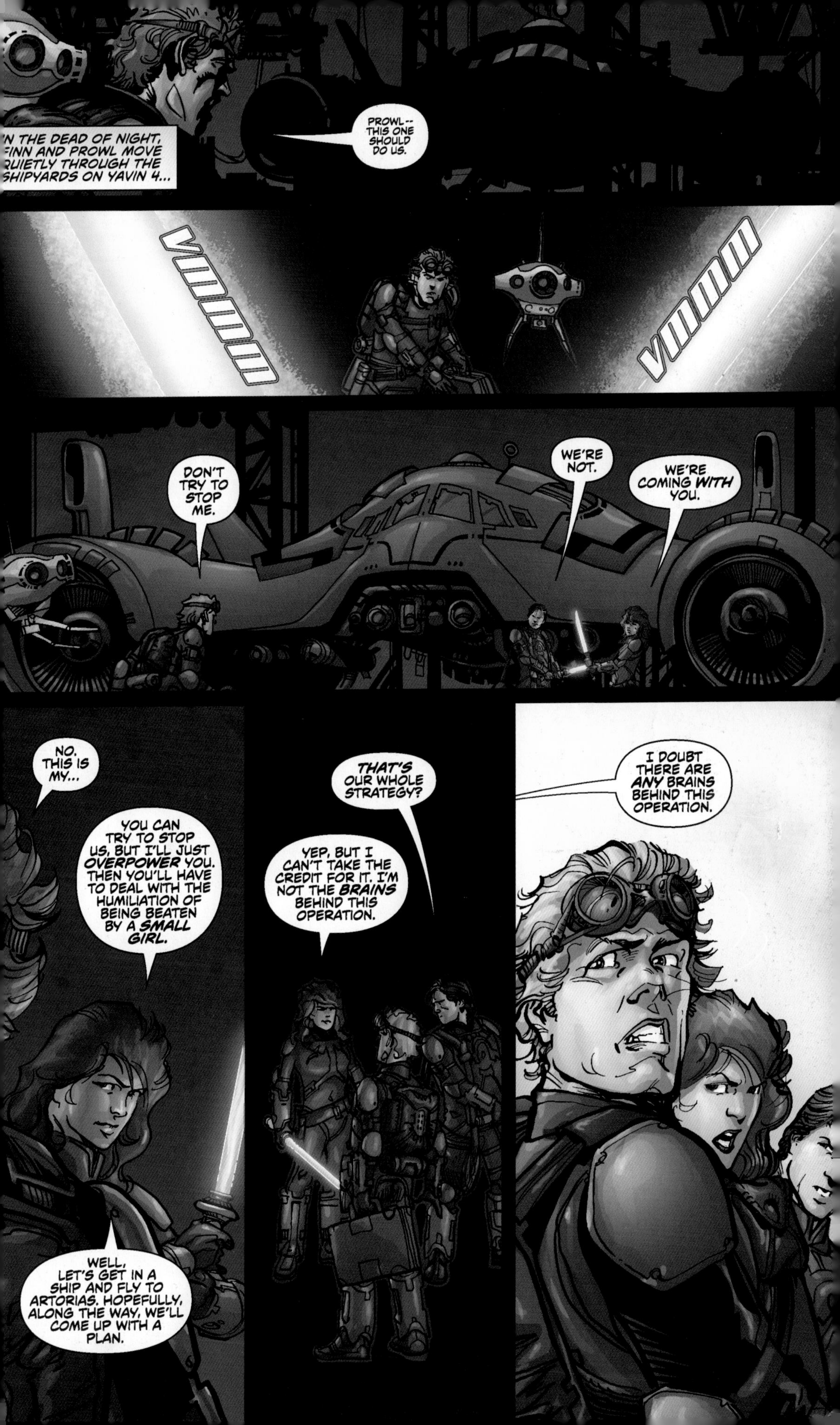

'N THE DEAD OF NIGHT, FINN AND PROWL MOVE QUIETLY THROUGH THE SHIPYARDS ON YAVIN 4...
PROWL-- THIS ONE SHOULD DO US.
VMMM
VMMM
DON'T TRY TO STOP ME.
WE'RE NOT.
WE'RE COMING WITH YOU.
NO. THIS IS MY...
YOU CAN TRY TO STOP US, BUT I'LL JUST OVERPOWER YOU. THEN YOU'LL HAVE TO DEAL WITH THE HUMILIATION OF BEING BEATEN BY A SMALL GIRL.
WELL, LET'S GET IN A SHIP AND FLY TO ARTORIAS. HOPEFULLY, ALONG THE WAY, WE'LL COME UP WITH A PLAN.
THAT'S OUR WHOLE STRATEGY?
YEP, BUT I CAN'T TAKE THE CREDIT FOR IT. I'M NOT THE BRAINS BEHIND THIS OPERATION.
I DOUBT THERE ARE ANY BRAINS BEHIND THIS OPERATION.

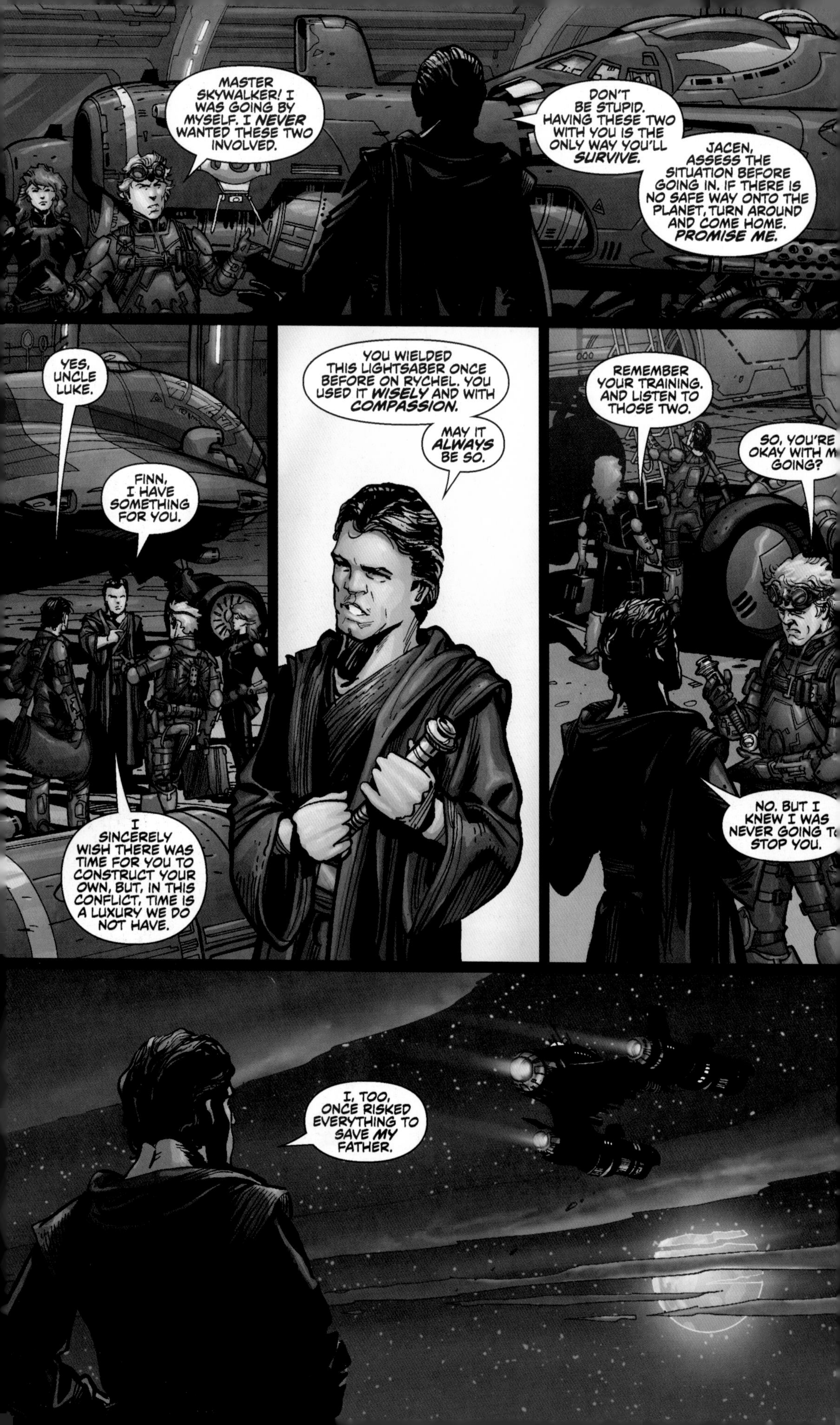
MASTER SKYWALKER! I WAS GOING BY MYSELF. I NEVER WANTED THESE TWO INVOLVED.
DON'T BE STUPID. HAVING THESE TWO WITH YOU IS THE ONLY WAY YOU'LL SURVIVE.
JACEN, ASSESS THE SITUATION BEFORE GOING IN. IF THERE IS NO SAFE WAY ONTO THE PLANET, TURN AROUND AND COME HOME. PROMISE ME.
YES, UNCLE LUKE.
FINN, I HAVE SOMETHING FOR YOU.
I SINCERELY WISH THERE WAS TIME FOR YOU TO CONSTRUCT YOUR OWN, BUT, IN THIS CONFLICT, TIME IS A LUXURY WE DO NOT HAVE.
YOU WIELDED THIS LIGHTSABER ONCE BEFORE ON RYCHEL. YOU USED IT WISELY AND WITH COMPASSION.
MAY IT ALWAYS BE SO.
REMEMBER YOUR TRAINING. AND LISTEN TO THOSE TWO.
NO. BUT I KNEW I WAS NEVER GOING TO STOP YOU.
I, TOO, ONCE RISKED EVERYTHING TO SAVE MY FATHER.

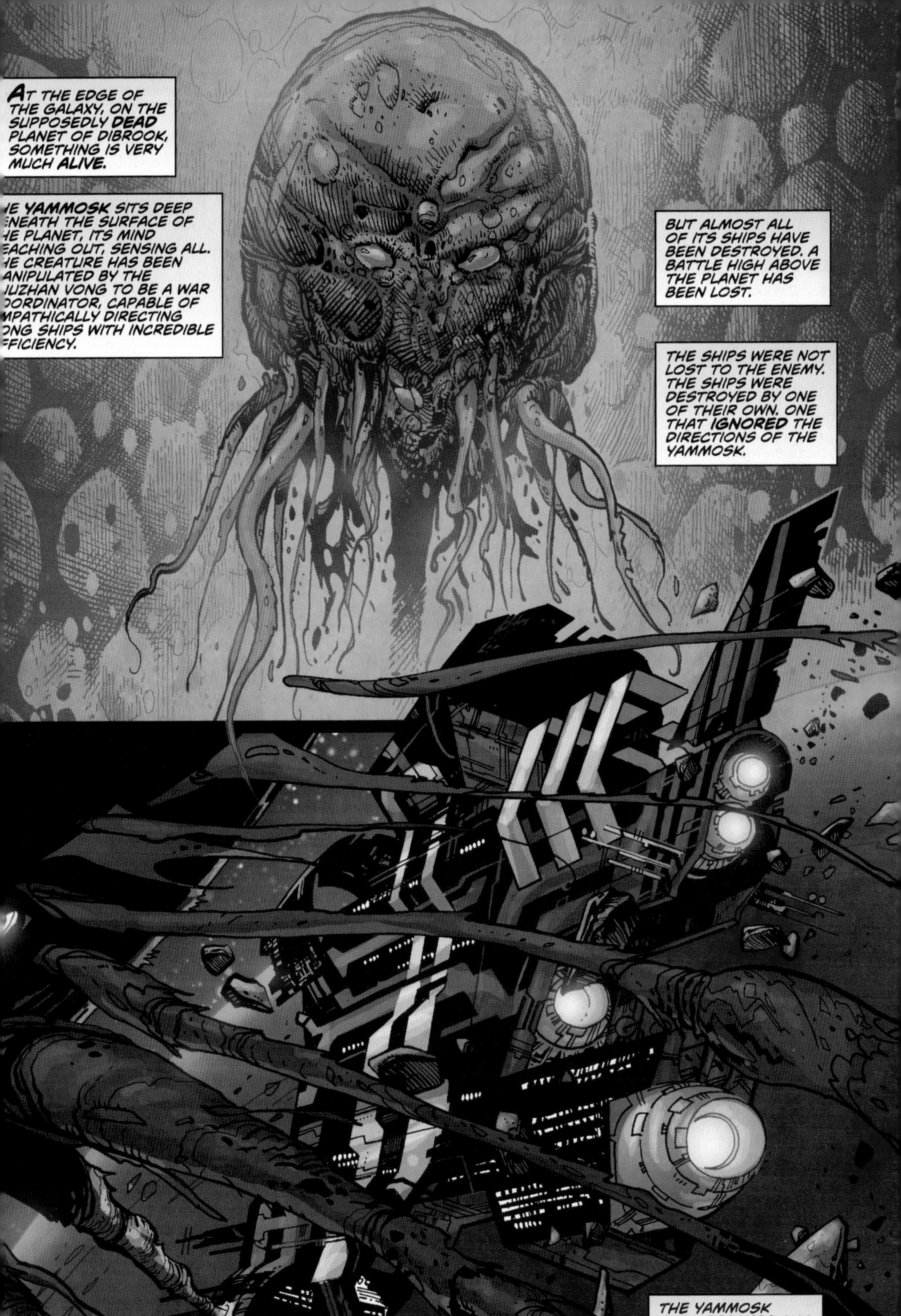
AT THE EDGE OF THE GALAXY, ON THE SUPPOSEDLY DEAD PLANET OF DIBROOK, SOMETHING IS VERY MUCH ALIVE.
IE YAMMOSK SITS DEEP ENEATH THE SURFACE OF IE PLANET, ITS MIND EACHING OUT, SENSING ALL. IE CREATURE HAS BEEN ANIPULATED BY THE IUZHAN VONG TO BE A WAR OORDINATOR, CAPABLE OF MPATHICALLY DIRECTING ONG SHIPS WITH INCREDIBLE FFICIENCY.
BUT ALMOST ALL OF ITS SHIPS HAVE BEEN DESTROYED. A BATTLE HIGH ABOVE THE PLANET HAS BEEN LOST.
THE SHIPS WERE NOT LOST TO THE ENEMY. THE SHIPS WERE DESTROYED BY ONE OF THEIR OWN. ONE THAT IGNORED THE DIRECTIONS OF THE YAMMOSK.
THE YAMMOSK STILL REACHES OUT TO THIS SHIP.

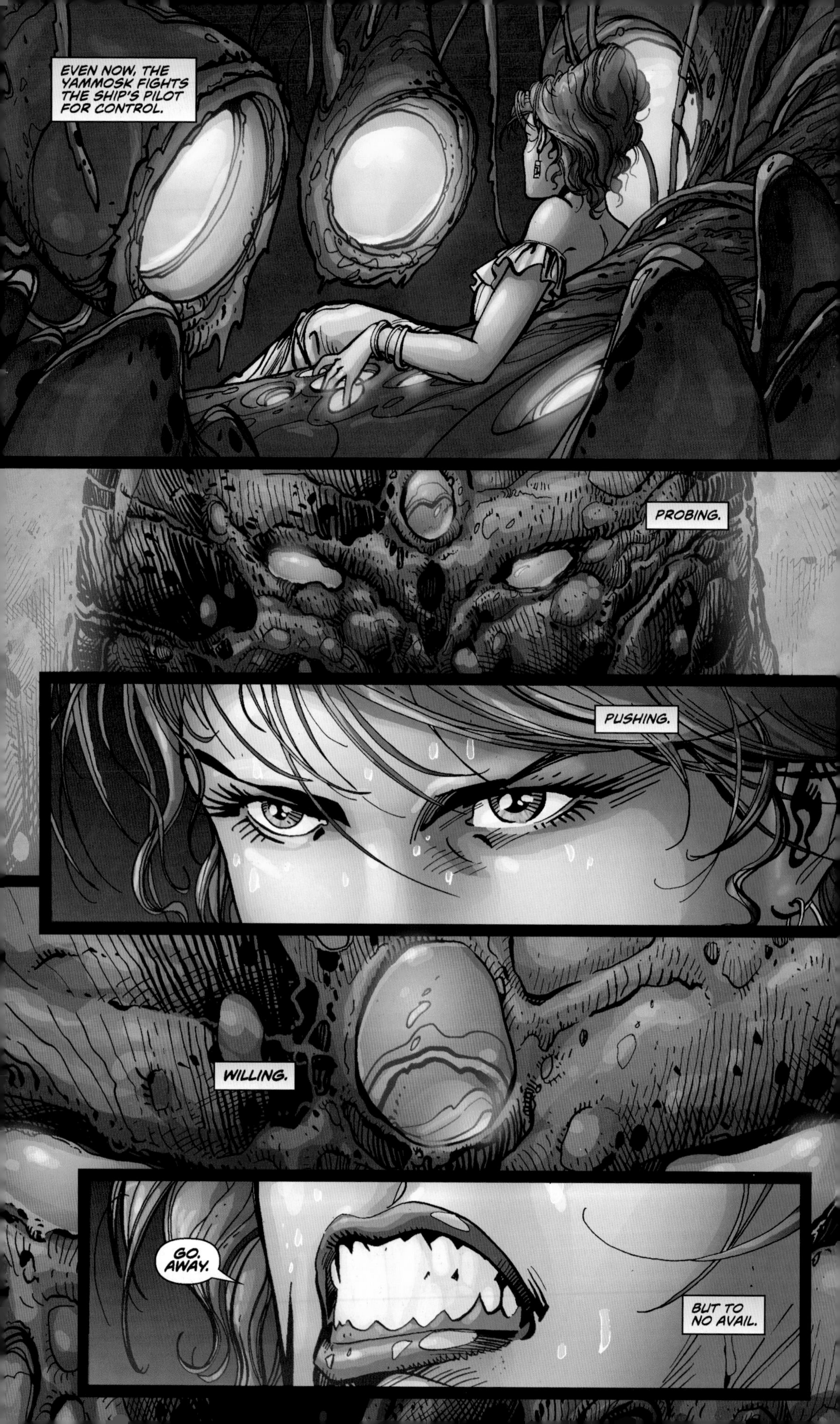
EVEN NOW, THE YAMMOSK FIGHTS THE SHIP'S PILOT FOR CONTROL.
PROBING.
PUSHING.
WILLING.
GO. AWAY.
BUT TO NO AVAIL.

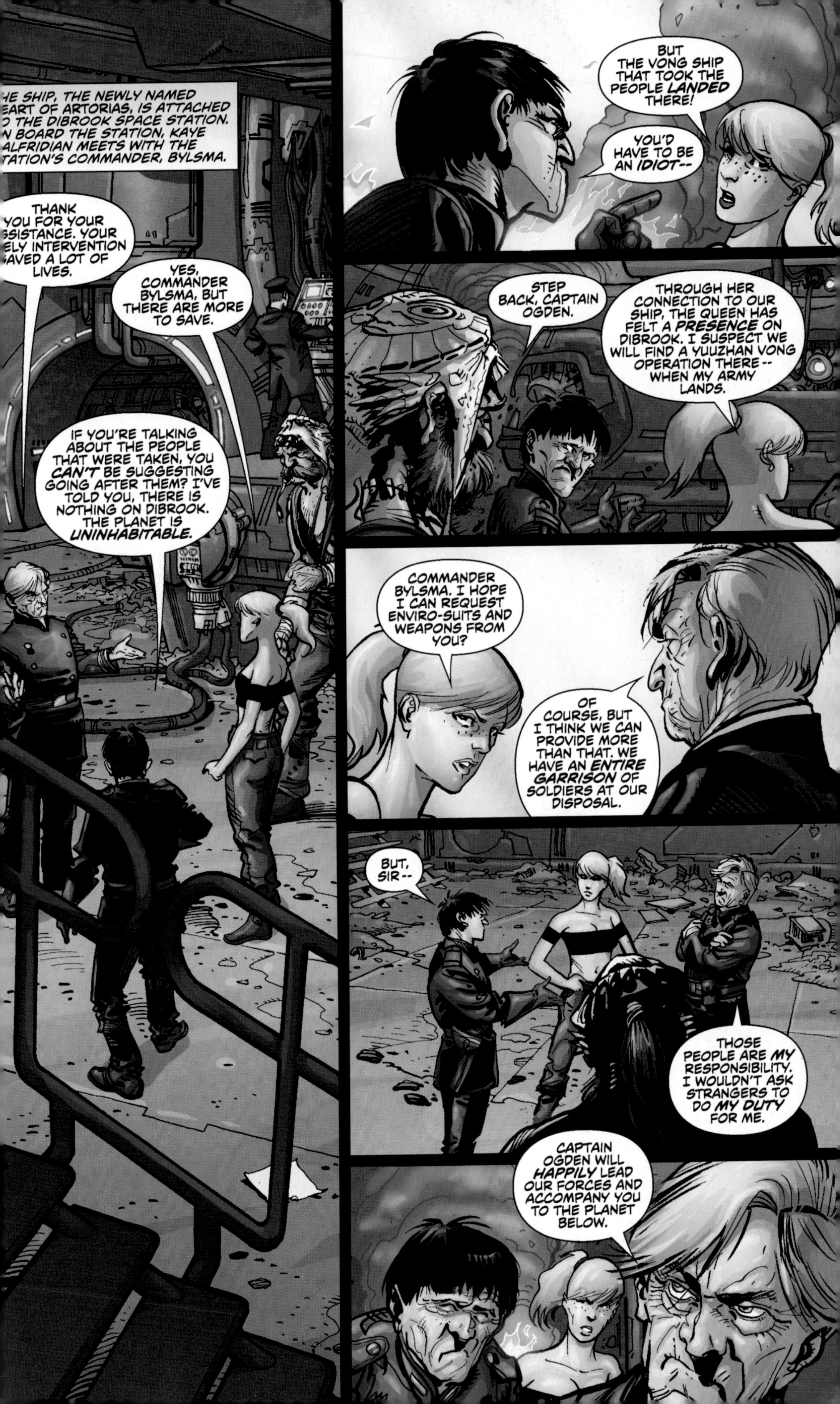

HE SHIP, THE NEWLY NAMED EART OF ARTORIAS, IS ATTACHED O THE DIBROOK SPACE STATION. N BOARD THE STATION, KAYE ALFRIDIAN MEETS WITH THE TATION'S COMMANDER, BYLSMA.
THANK YOU FOR YOUR SSISTANCE. YOUR ELY INTERVENTION AVED A LOT OF LIVES.
YES, COMMANDER BYLSMA, BUT THERE ARE MORE TO SAVE.
IF YOU'RE TALKING ABOUT THE PEOPLE THAT WERE TAKEN, YOU CAN'T BE SUGGESTING GOING AFTER THEM? I'VE TOLD YOU, THERE IS NOTHING ON DIBROOK. THE PLANET IS UNINHABITABLE.
BUT THE VONG SHIP THAT TOOK THE PEOPLE LANDED THERE!
YOU'D HAVE TO BE AN IDIOT--
STEP BACK, CAPTAIN OGDEN.
THROUGH HER CONNECTION TO OUR SHIP, THE QUEEN HAS FELT A PRESENCE ON DIBROOK. I SUSPECT WE WILL FIND A YUUZHAN VONG OPERATION THERE -- WHEN MY ARMY LANDS.
COMMANDER BYLSMA. I HOPE I CAN REQUEST ENVIRO-SUITS AND WEAPONS FROM YOU?
OF COURSE, BUT I THINK WE CAN PROVIDE MORE THAN THAT. WE HAVE AN ENTIRE GARRISON OF SOLDIERS AT OUR DISPOSAL.
BUT, SIR--
THOSE PEOPLE ARE MY RESPONSIBILITY. I WOULDN'T ASK STRANGERS TO DO MY DUTY FOR ME.
CAPTAIN OGDEN WILL HAPPILY LEAD OUR FORCES AND ACCOMPANY YOU TO THE PLANET BELOW.

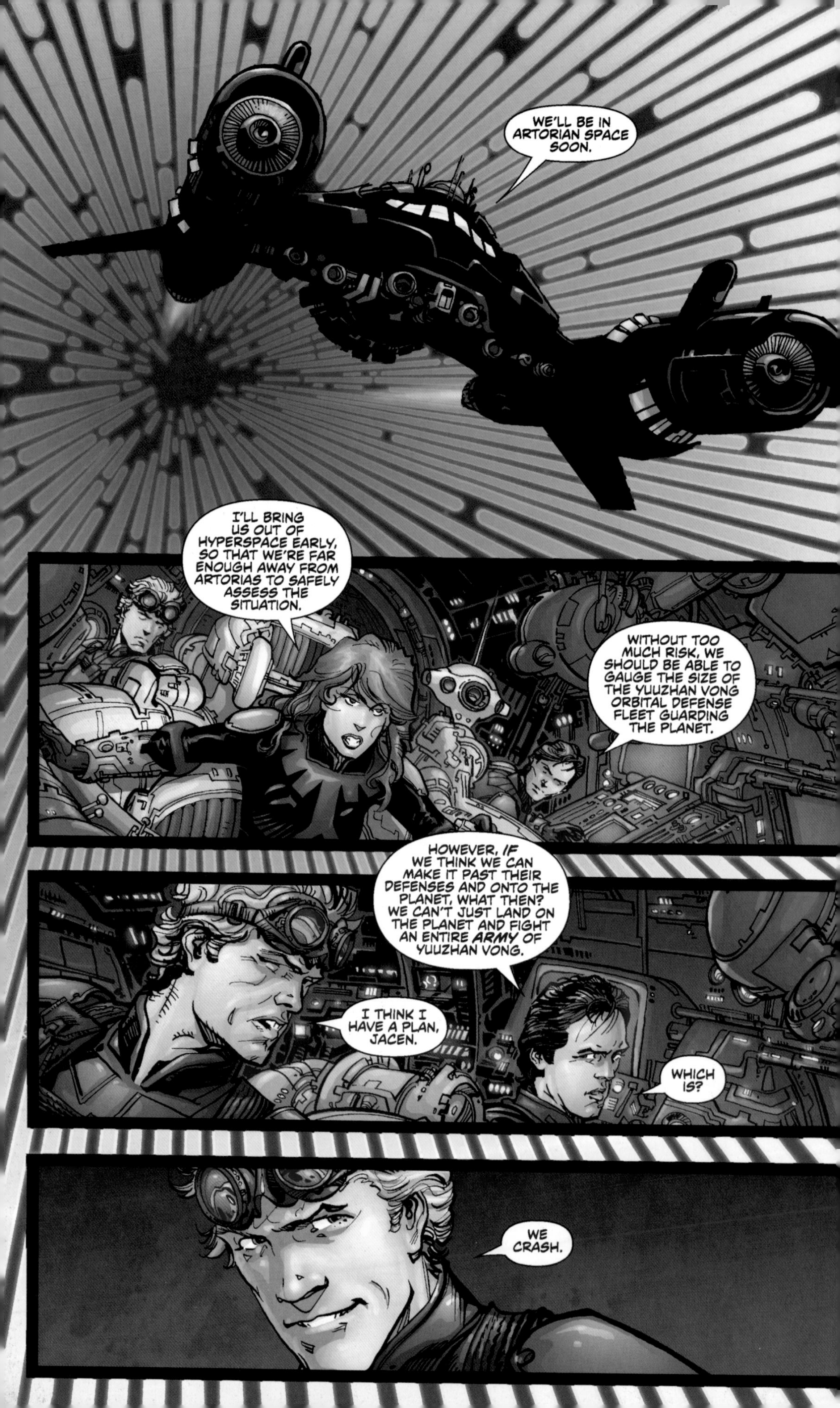
WE'LL BE IN ARTORIAN SPACE SOON.
I'LL BRING US OUT OF HYPERSPACE EARLY, SO THAT WE'RE FAR ENOUGH AWAY FROM ARTORIAS TO SAFELY ASSESS THE SITUATION.
WITHOUT TOO MUCH RISK, WE SHOULD BE ABLE TO GAUGE THE SIZE OF THE YUUZHAN VONG ORBITAL DEFENSE FLEET GUARDING THE PLANET.
HOWEVER, IF WE THINK WE CAN MAKE IT PAST THEIR DEFENSES AND ONTO THE PLANET, WHAT THEN? WE CAN'T JUST LAND ON THE PLANET AND FIGHT AN ENTIRE ARMY OF YUUZHAN VONG.
I THINK I HAVE A PLAN, JACEN.
WHICH IS?
WE CRASH.

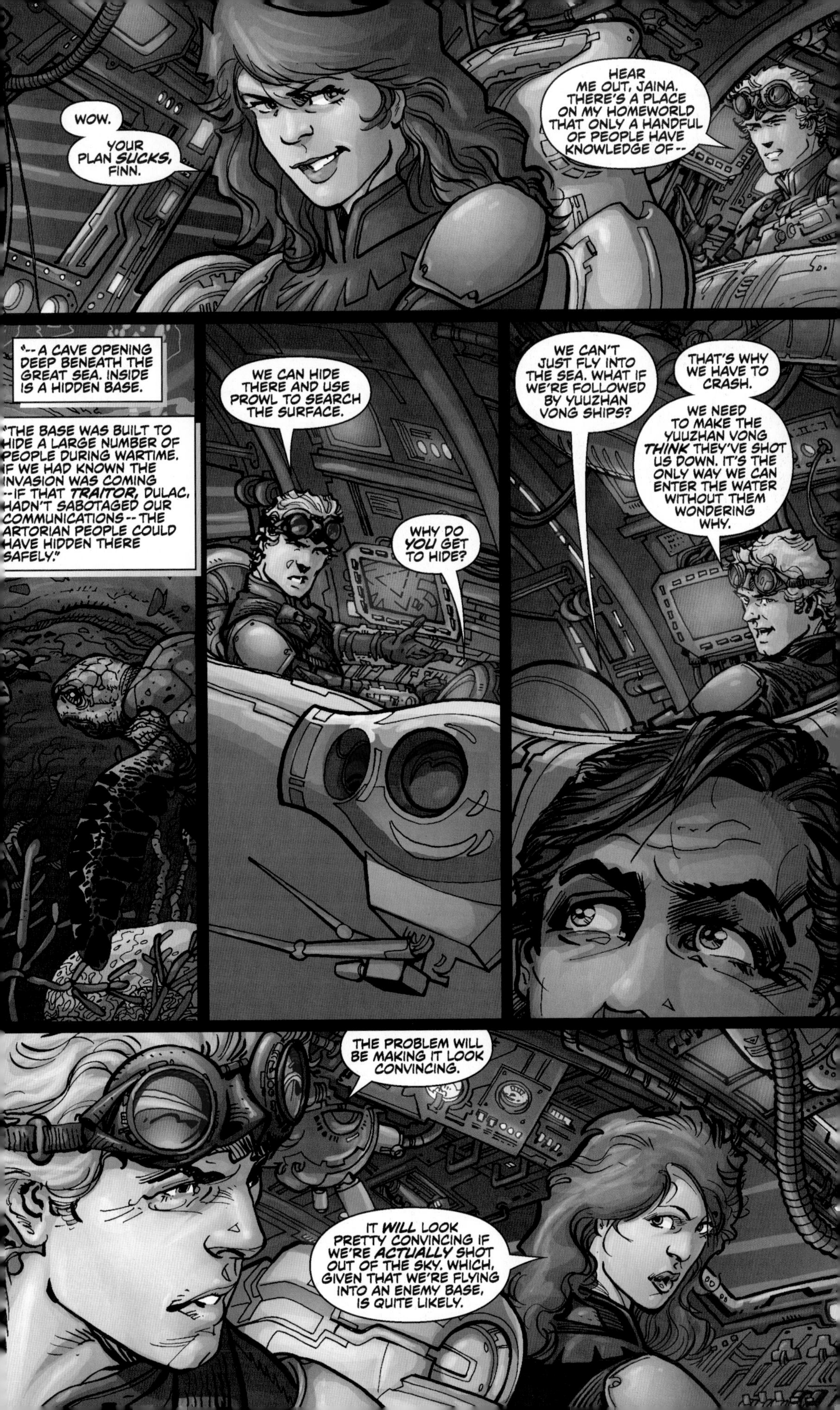
WOW.
YOUR PLAN SUCKS, FINN.
HEAR ME OUT, JAINA. THERE'S A PLACE ON MY HOMEWORLD THAT ONLY A HANDFUL OF PEOPLE HAVE KNOWLEDGE OF --
"-- A CAVE OPENING DEEP BENEATH THE GREAT SEA. INSIDE IS A HIDDEN BASE.
"THE BASE WAS BUILT TO HIDE A LARGE NUMBER OF PEOPLE DURING WARTIME. IF WE HAD KNOWN THE INVASION WAS COMING --IF THAT TRAITOR, DULAC, HADN'T SABOTAGED OUR COMMUNICATIONS -- THE ARTORIAN PEOPLE COULD HAVE HIDDEN THERE SAFELY."
WE CAN HIDE THERE AND USE PROWL TO SEARCH THE SURFACE.
WHY DO YOU GET TO HIDE?
WE CAN'T JUST FLY INTO THE SEA. WHAT IF WE'RE FOLLOWED BY YUUZHAN VONG SHIPS?
THAT'S WHY WE HAVE TO CRASH.
WE NEED TO MAKE THE YUUZHAN VONG THINK THEY'VE SHOT US DOWN. IT'S THE ONLY WAY WE CAN ENTER THE WATER WITHOUT THEM WONDERING WHY.
THE PROBLEM WILL BE MAKING IT LOOK CONVINCING.
IT WILL LOOK PRETTY CONVINCING IF WE'RE ACTUALLY SHOT OUT OF THE SKY. WHICH, GIVEN THAT WE'RE FLYING INTO AN ENEMY BASE, IS QUITE LIKELY.

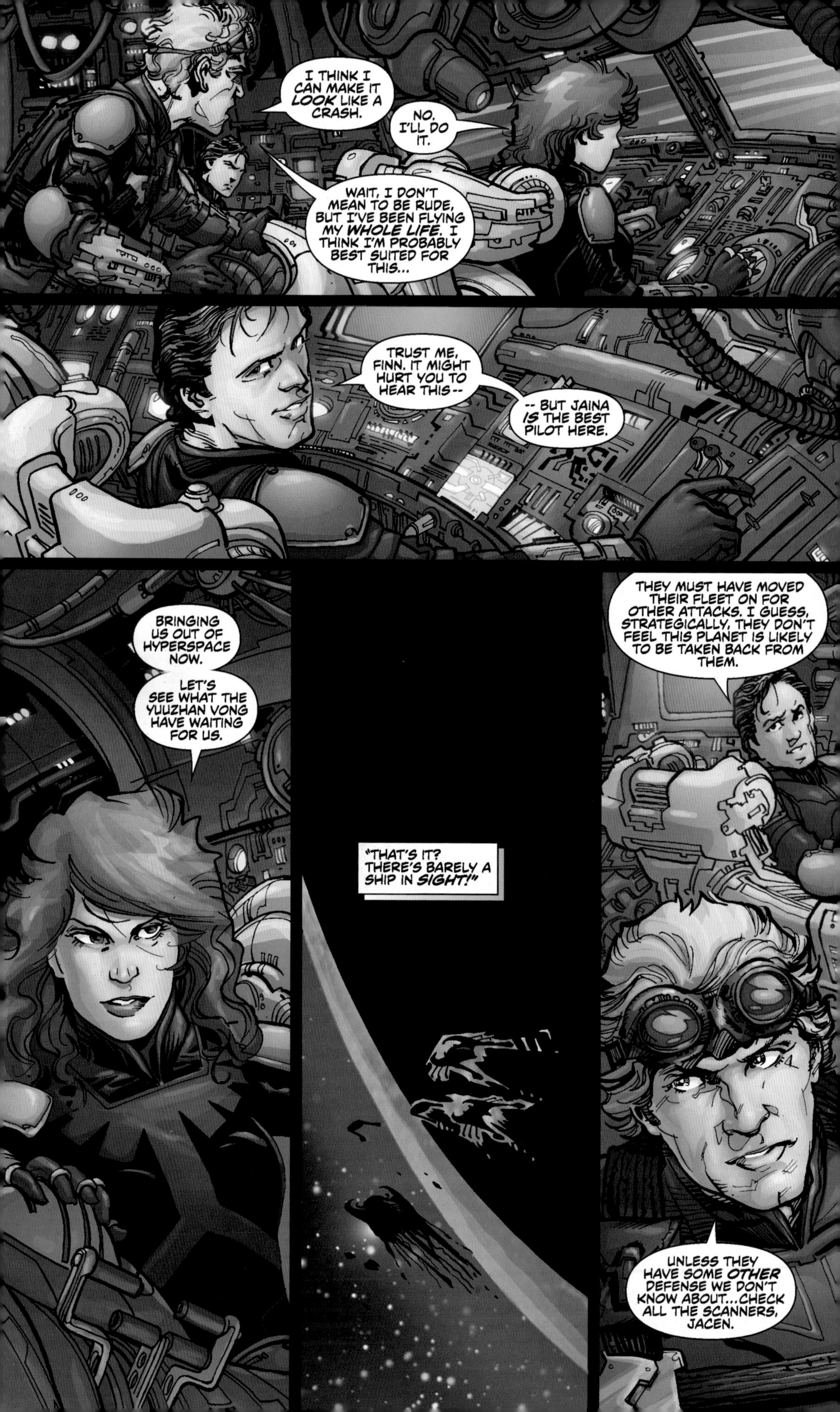
I THINK I CAN MAKE IT LOOK LIKE A CRASH.
NO. I'LL DO IT.
WAIT, I DON'T MEAN TO BE RUDE, BUT I'VE BEEN FLYING MY WHOLE LIFE. I THINK I'M PROBABLY BEST SUITED FOR THIS...
TRUST ME, FINN. IT MIGHT HURT YOU TO HEAR THIS--
-- BUT JAINA IS THE BEST PILOT HERE.
BRINGING US OUT OF HYPERSPACE NOW.
LET'S SEE WHAT THE YUUZHAN VONG HAVE WAITING FOR US.
"THAT'S IT? THERE'S BARELY A SHIP IN SIGHT!"
THEY MUST HAVE MOVED THEIR FLEET ON FOR OTHER ATTACKS. I GUESS, STRATEGICALLY, THEY DON'T FEEL THIS PLANET IS LIKELY TO BE TAKEN BACK FROM THEM.
UNLESS THEY HAVE SOME OTHER DEFENSE WE DON'T KNOW ABOUT...CHECK ALL THE SCANNERS, JACEN.

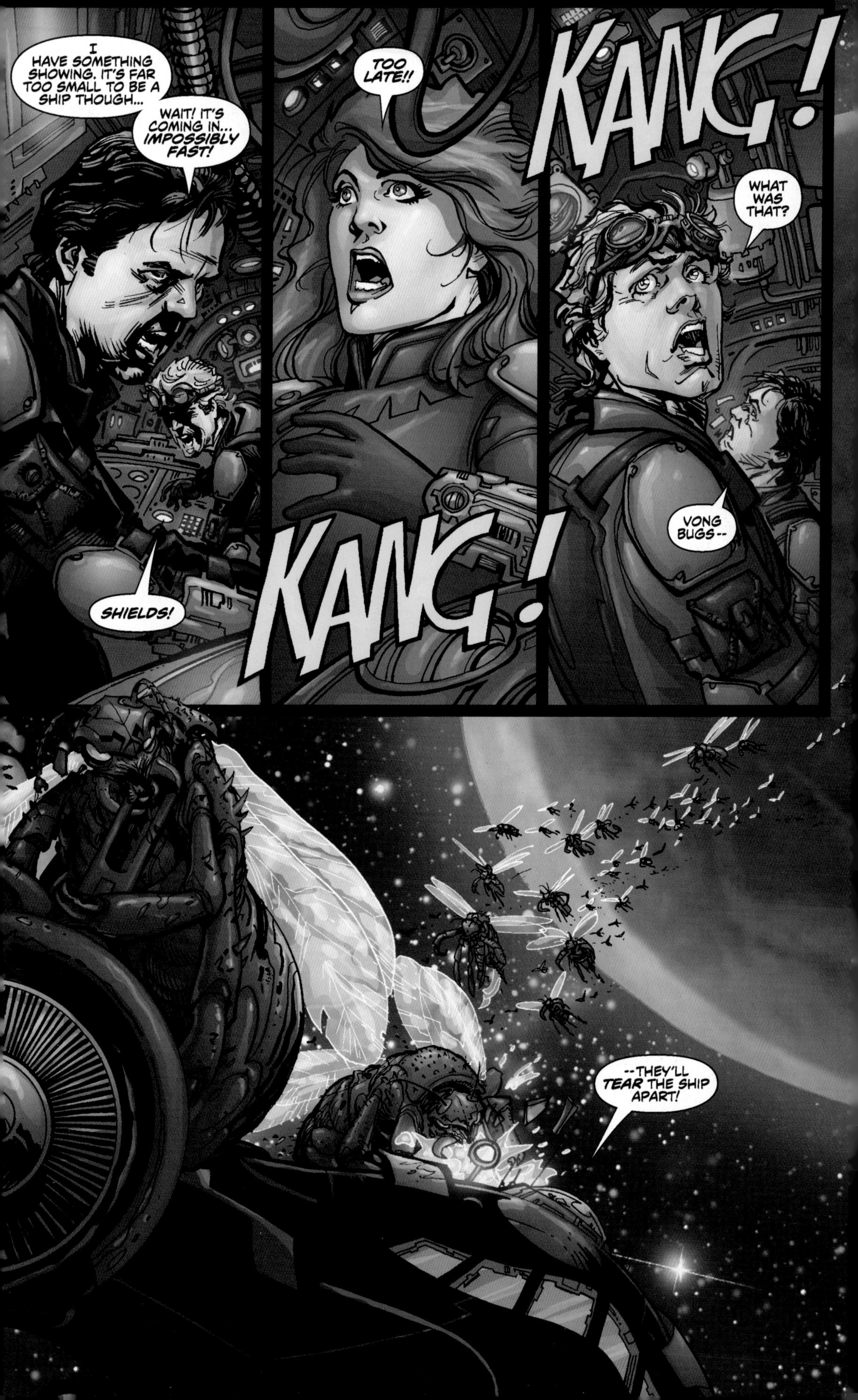
I HAVE SOMETHING SHOWING. IT'S FAR TOO SMALL TO BE A SHIP THOUGH...
WAIT! IT'S COMING IN... IMPOSSIBLY FAST!
SHIELDS!
TOO LATE!!
KANG!
KANG!
WHAT WAS THAT?
VONG BUGS--
--THEY'LL TEAR THE SHIP APART!

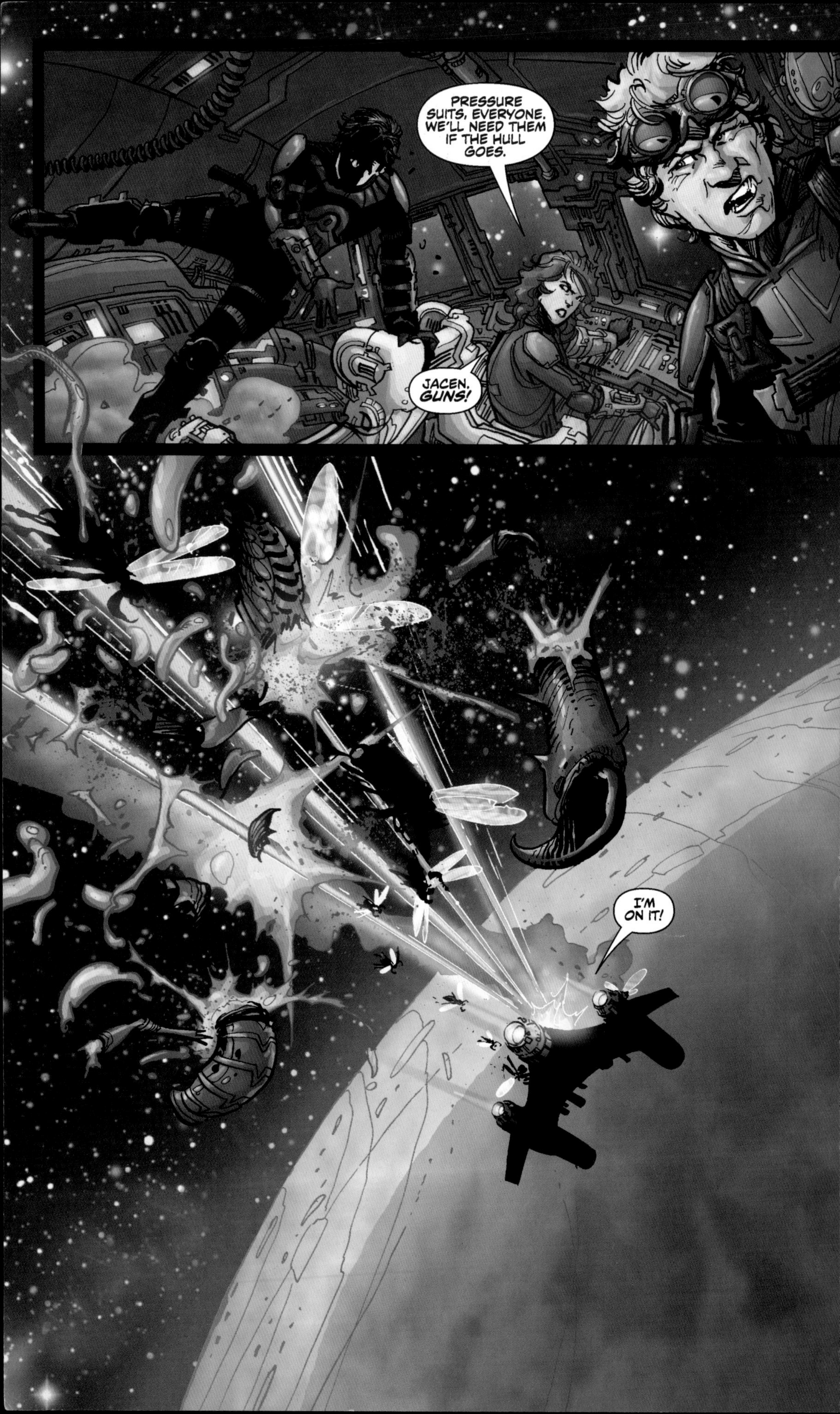
PRESSURE SUITS, EVERYONE. WE'LL NEED THEM IF THE HULL GOES.
JACEN, GUNS!
I'M ON IT!

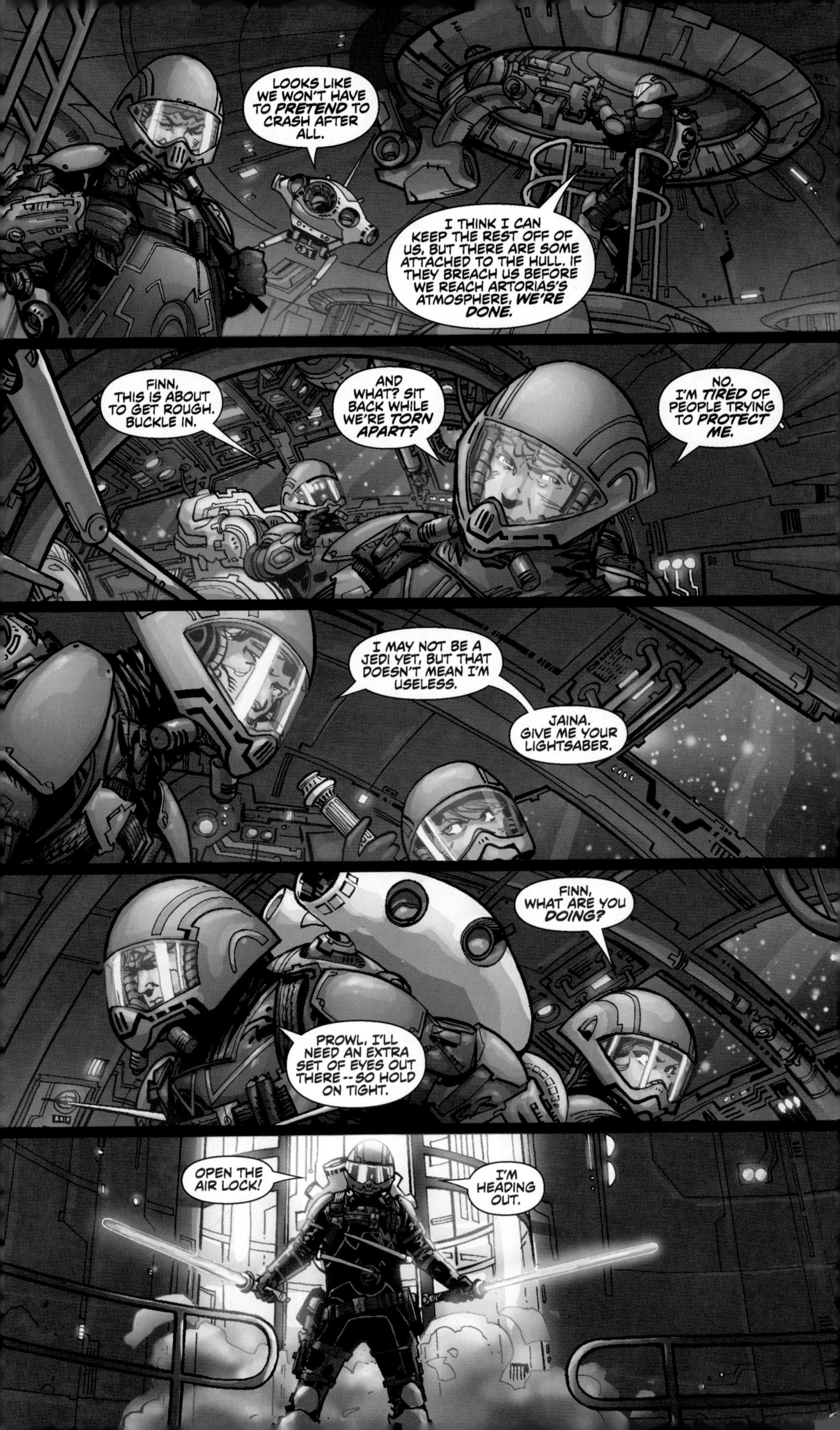
LOOKS LIKE WE WON'T HAVE TO *PRETEND* TO CRASH AFTER ALL.
I THINK I CAN KEEP THE REST OFF OF US, BUT THERE ARE SOME ATTACHED TO THE HULL. IF THEY BREACH US BEFORE WE REACH ARTORIAS'S ATMOSPHERE, *WE'RE DONE.*
FINN, THIS IS ABOUT TO GET ROUGH. BUCKLE IN.
AND WHAT? SIT BACK WHILE WE'RE *TORN APART?*
NO. I'M *TIRED* OF PEOPLE TRYING TO *PROTECT ME.*
I MAY NOT BE A JEDI YET, BUT THAT DOESN'T MEAN I'M USELESS.
JAINA. GIVE ME YOUR LIGHTSABER.
FINN, WHAT ARE YOU *DOING?*
PROWL, I'LL NEED AN EXTRA SET OF EYES OUT THERE -- SO HOLD ON TIGHT.
OPEN THE AIR LOCK!
I'M HEADING OUT.

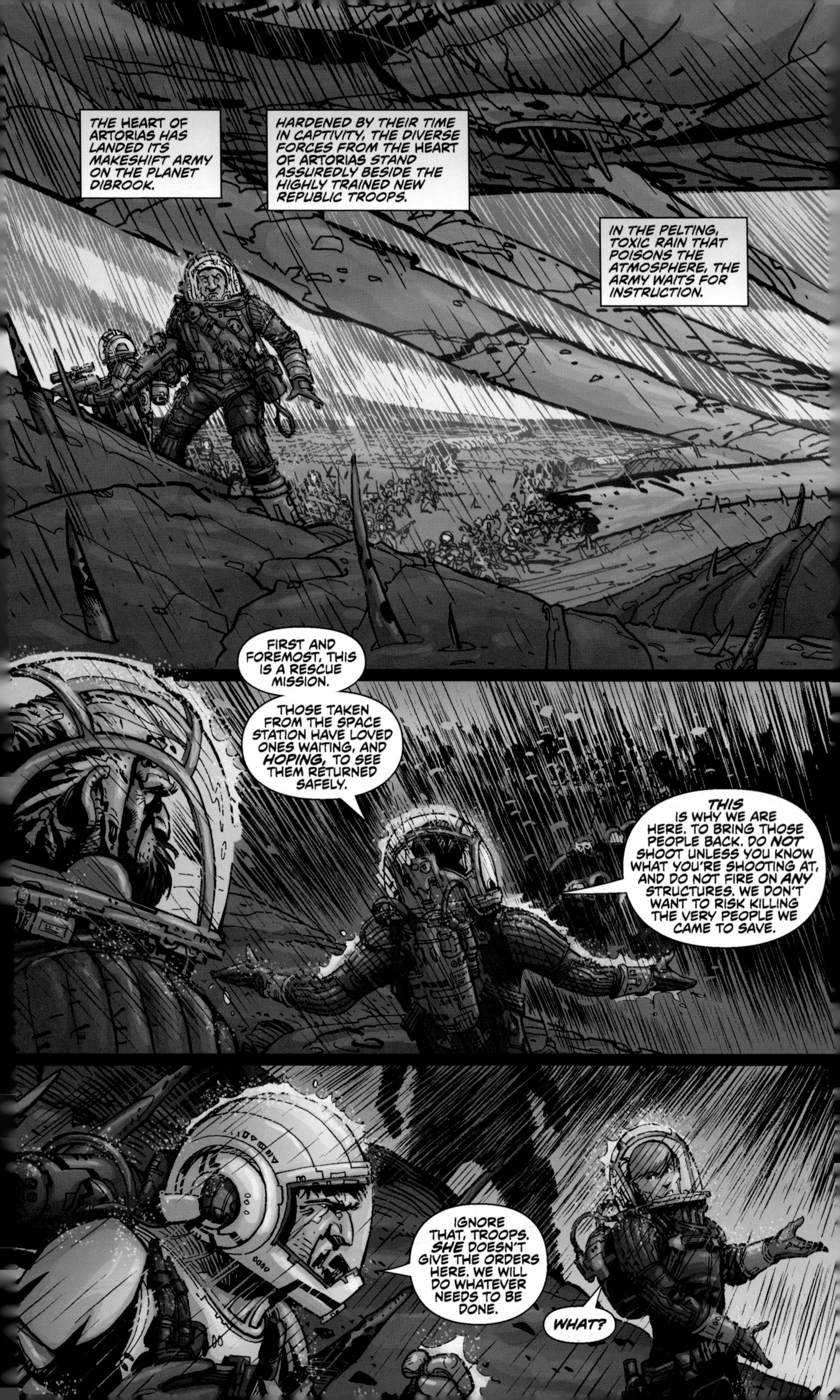
THE HEART OF ARTORIAS HAS LANDED ITS MAKESHIFT ARMY ON THE PLANET DIBROOK.
HARDENED BY THEIR TIME IN CAPTIVITY, THE DIVERSE FORCES FROM THE HEART OF ARTORIAS STAND ASSUREDLY BESIDE THE HIGHLY TRAINED NEW REPUBLIC TROOPS.
IN THE PELTING, TOXIC RAIN THAT POISONS THE ATMOSPHERE, THE ARMY WAITS FOR INSTRUCTION.
FIRST AND FOREMOST, THIS IS A RESCUE MISSION.
THOSE TAKEN FROM THE SPACE STATION HAVE LOVED ONES WAITING, AND *HOPING*, TO SEE THEM RETURNED SAFELY.
THIS IS WHY WE ARE HERE, TO BRING THOSE PEOPLE BACK. DO *NOT* SHOOT UNLESS YOU KNOW WHAT YOU'RE SHOOTING AT, AND DO NOT FIRE ON *ANY* STRUCTURES. WE DON'T WANT TO RISK KILLING THE VERY PEOPLE WE CAME TO SAVE.
IGNORE THAT, TROOPS. *SHE* DOESN'T GIVE THE ORDERS HERE. WE WILL DO WHATEVER NEEDS TO BE DONE.
WHAT?

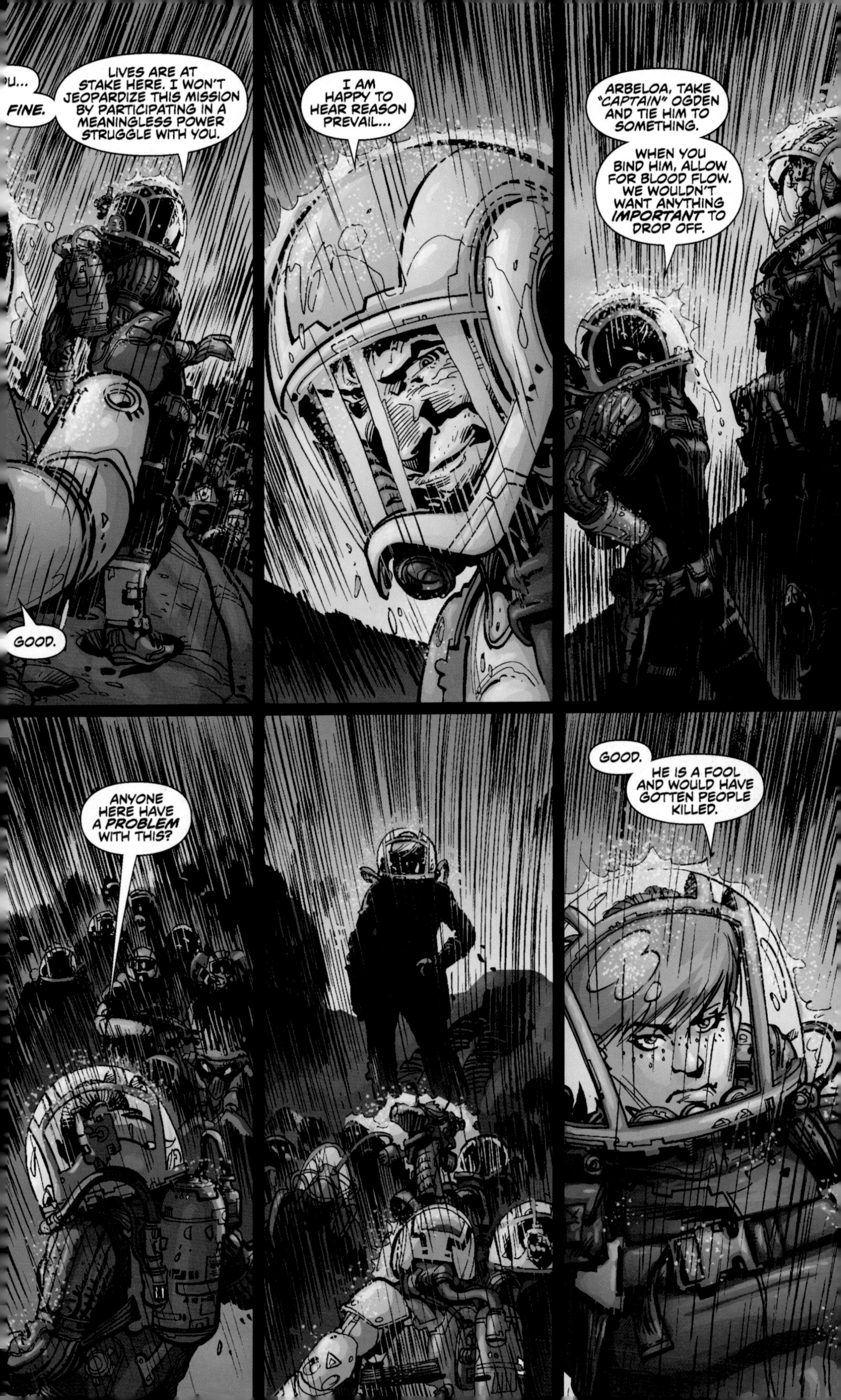

...OU...
FINE.
LIVES ARE AT STAKE HERE. I WON'T JEOPARDIZE THIS MISSION BY PARTICIPATING IN A MEANINGLESS POWER STRUGGLE WITH YOU.
GOOD.
I AM HAPPY TO HEAR REASON PREVAIL...
ARBELOA, TAKE "CAPTAIN" OGDEN AND TIE HIM TO SOMETHING.
WHEN YOU BIND HIM, ALLOW FOR BLOOD FLOW. WE WOULDN'T WANT ANYTHING IMPORTANT TO DROP OFF.
ANYONE HERE HAVE A PROBLEM WITH THIS?
GOOD.
HE IS A FOOL AND WOULD HAVE GOTTEN PEOPLE KILLED.

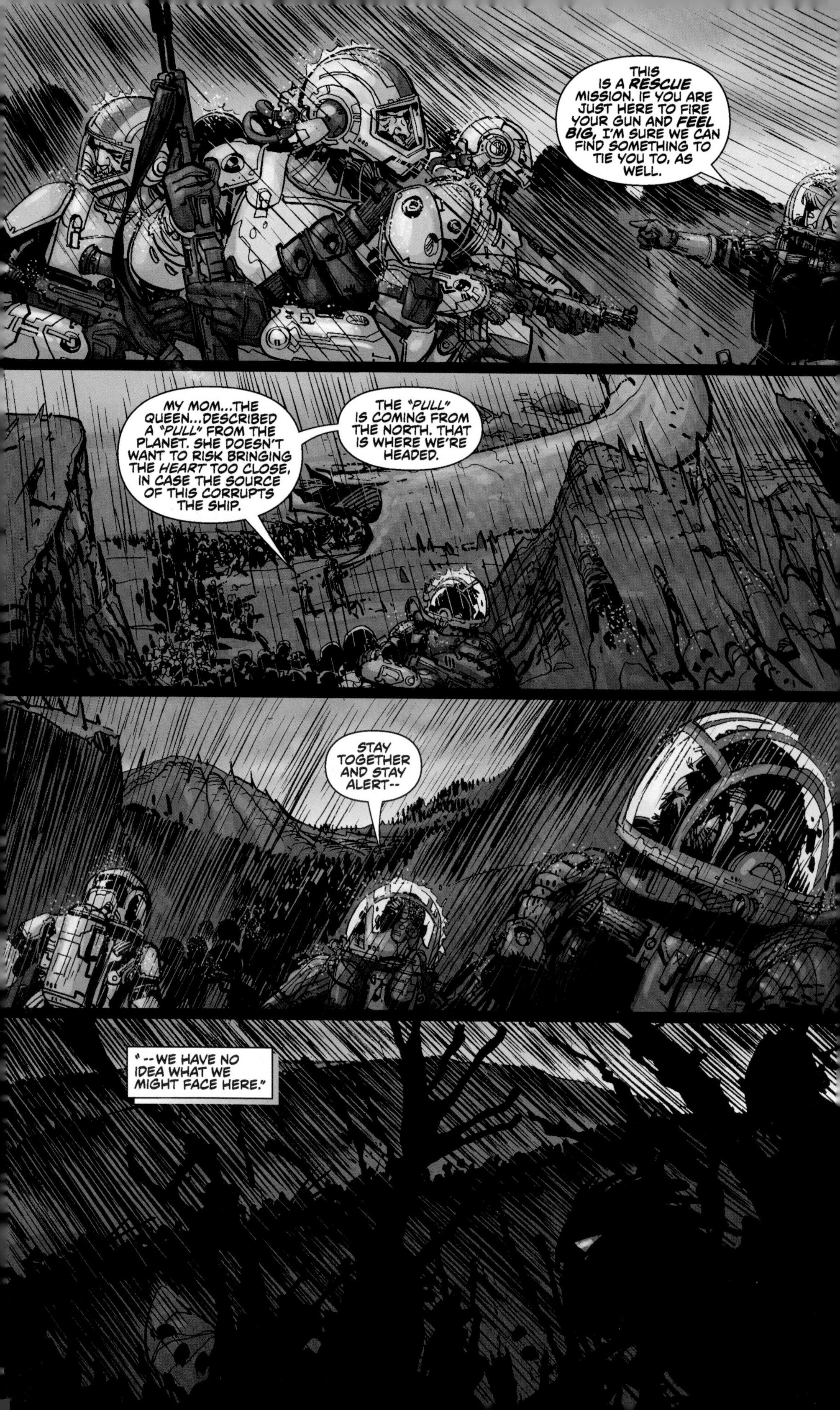
THIS IS A RESCUE MISSION. IF YOU ARE JUST HERE TO FIRE YOUR GUN AND FEEL BIG, I'M SURE WE CAN FIND SOMETHING TO TIE YOU TO, AS WELL.
MY MOM...THE QUEEN...DESCRIBED A "PULL" FROM THE PLANET. SHE DOESN'T WANT TO RISK BRINGING THE HEART TOO CLOSE, IN CASE THE SOURCE OF THIS CORRUPTS THE SHIP.
THE "PULL" IS COMING FROM THE NORTH. THAT IS WHERE WE'RE HEADED.
STAY TOGETHER AND STAY ALERT--
"--WE HAVE NO IDEA WHAT WE MIGHT FACE HERE."

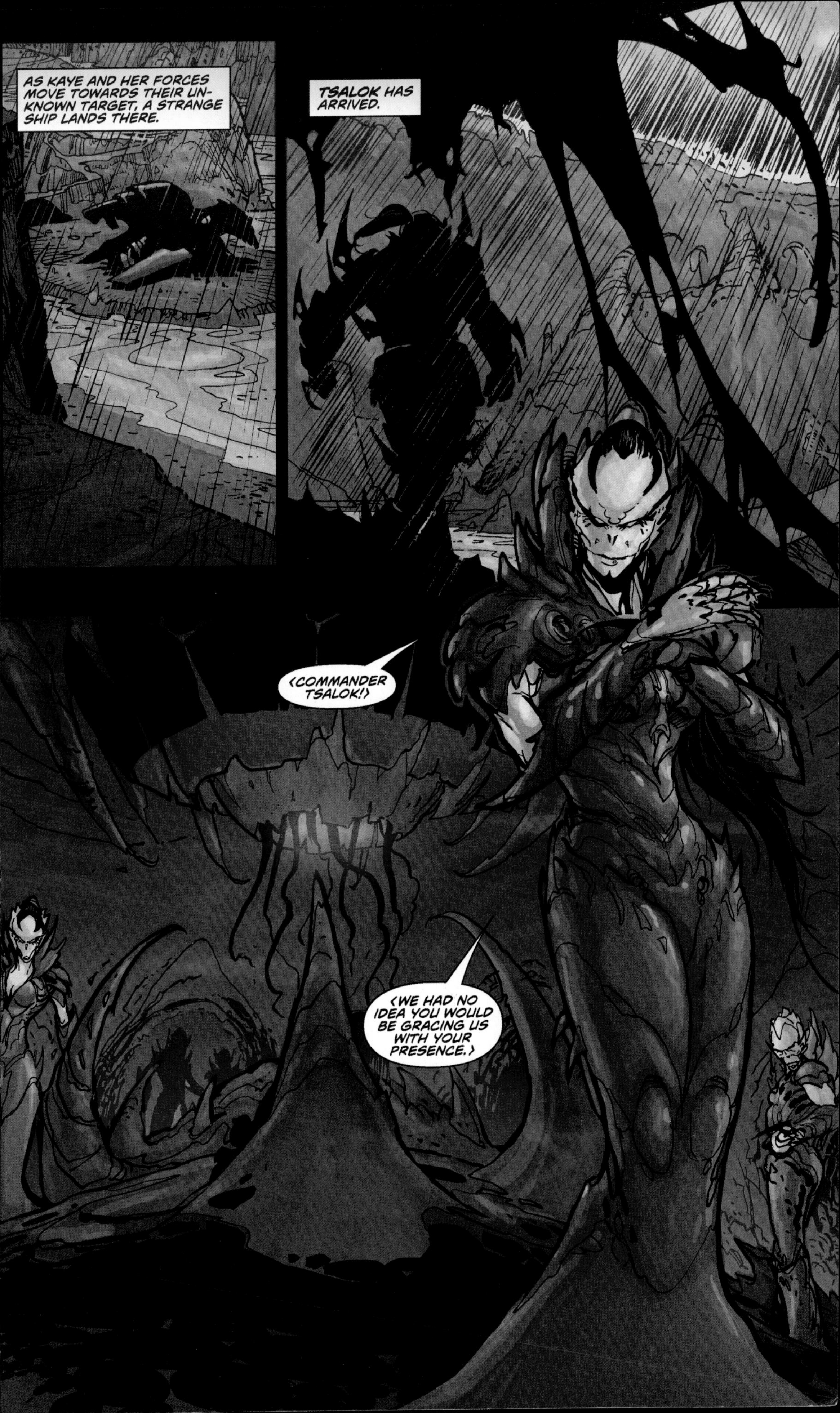
AS KAYE AND HER FORCES MOVE TOWARDS THEIR UN-KNOWN TARGET, A STRANGE SHIP LANDS THERE.
TSALOK HAS ARRIVED.
‹COMMANDER TSALOK!›
‹WE HAD NO IDEA YOU WOULD BE GRACING US WITH YOUR PRESENCE.›

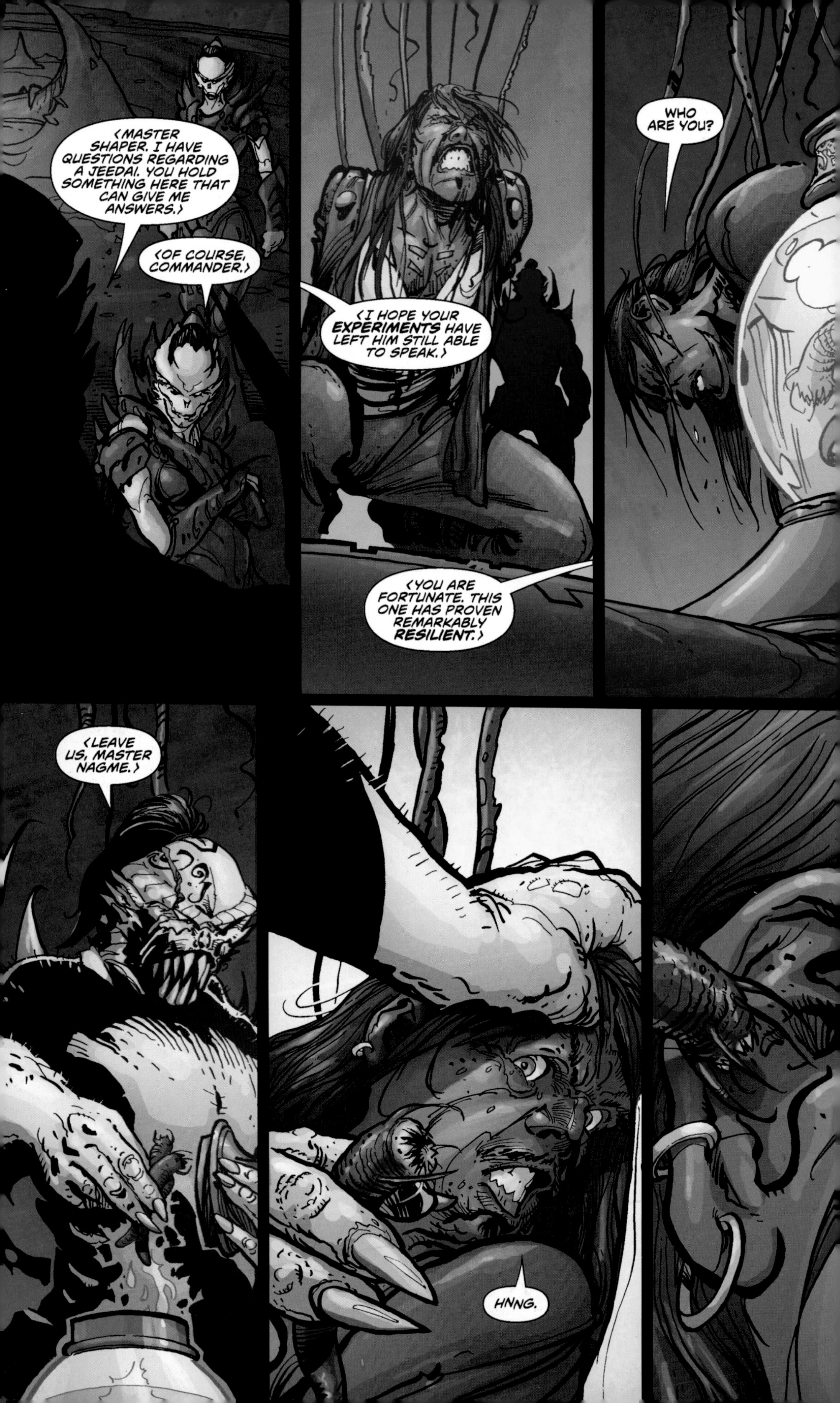

‹MASTER SHAPER. I HAVE QUESTIONS REGARDING A JEEDAI. YOU HOLD SOMETHING HERE THAT CAN GIVE ME ANSWERS.›
‹OF COURSE, COMMANDER.›
‹I HOPE YOUR EXPERIMENTS HAVE LEFT HIM STILL ABLE TO SPEAK.›
‹YOU ARE FORTUNATE. THIS ONE HAS PROVEN REMARKABLY RESILIENT.›
WHO ARE YOU?
‹LEAVE US, MASTER NAGME.›
HNNG.

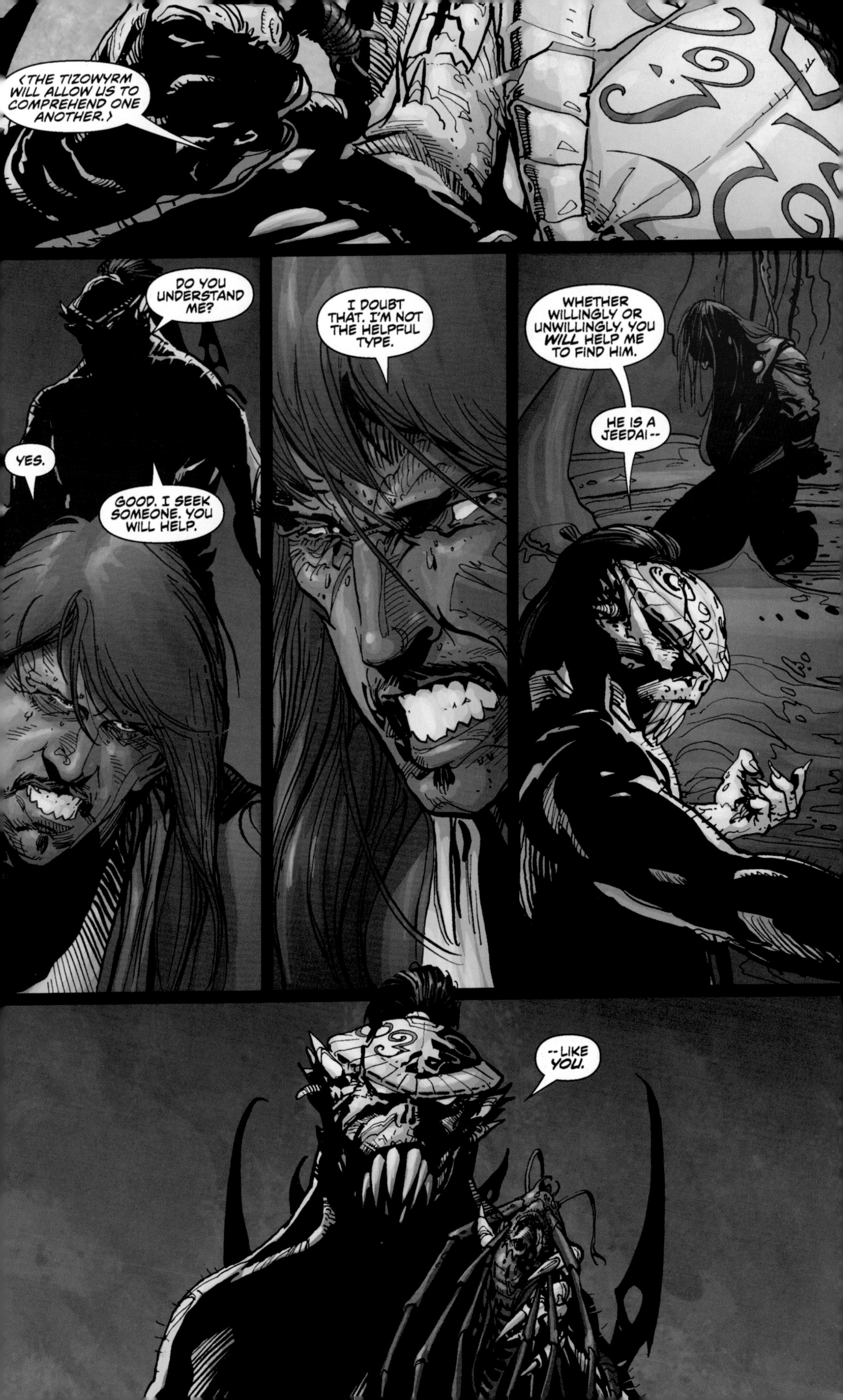
‹THE TIZOWYRM WILL ALLOW US TO COMPREHEND ONE ANOTHER.›
DO YOU UNDERSTAND ME?
YES.
GOOD. I SEEK SOMEONE. YOU WILL HELP.
I DOUBT THAT. I'M NOT THE HELPFUL TYPE.
WHETHER WILLINGLY OR UNWILLINGLY, YOU WILL HELP ME TO FIND HIM.
HE IS A JEEDAI --
-- LIKE YOU.

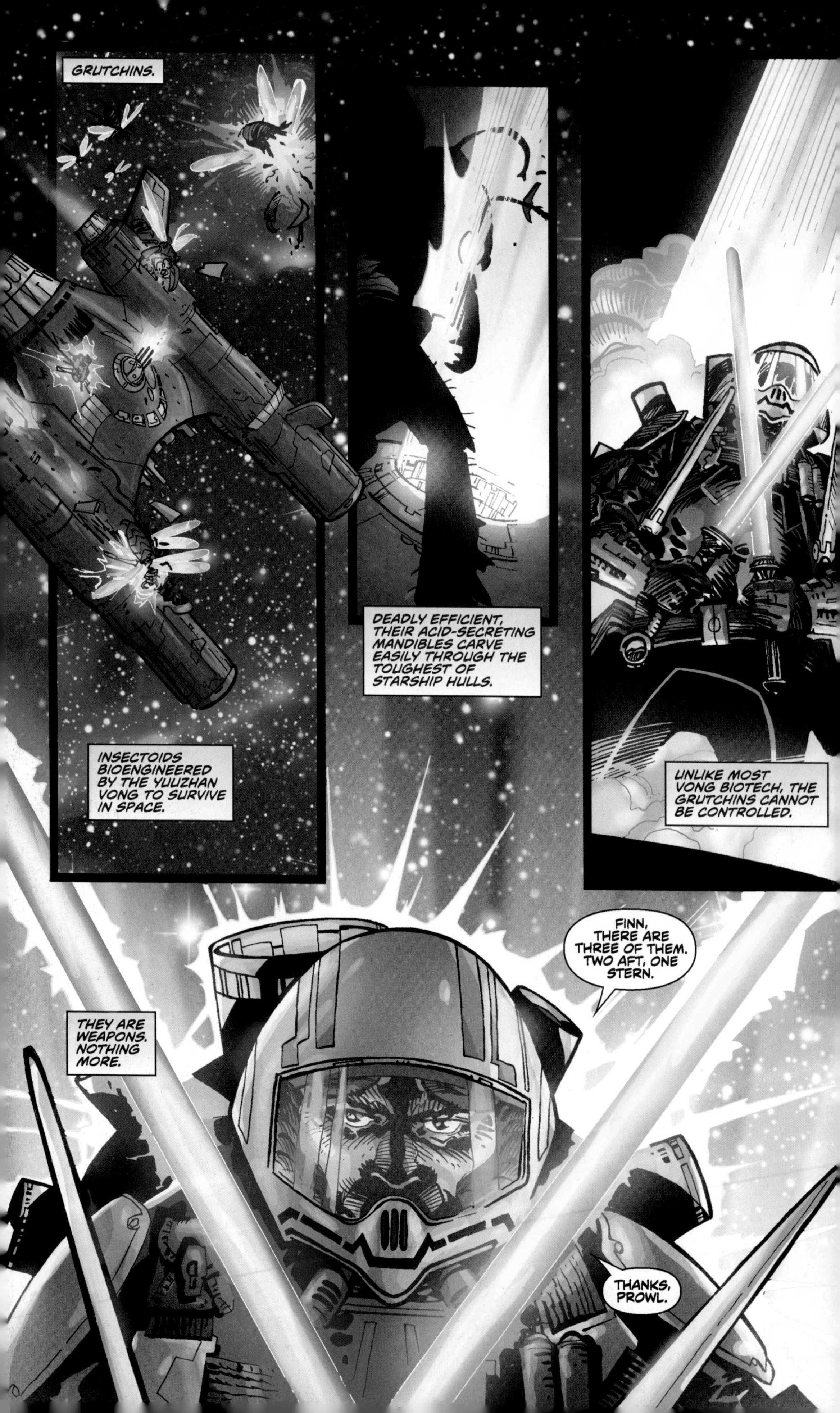
GRUTCHINS.
INSECTOIDS BIOENGINEERED BY THE YUUZHAN VONG TO SURVIVE IN SPACE.
DEADLY EFFICIENT, THEIR ACID-SECRETING MANDIBLES CARVE EASILY THROUGH THE TOUGHEST OF STARSHIP HULLS.
UNLIKE MOST VONG BIOTECH, THE GRUTCHINS CANNOT BE CONTROLLED.
THEY ARE WEAPONS. NOTHING MORE.
FINN, THERE ARE THREE OF THEM. TWO AFT, ONE STERN.
THANKS, PROWL.

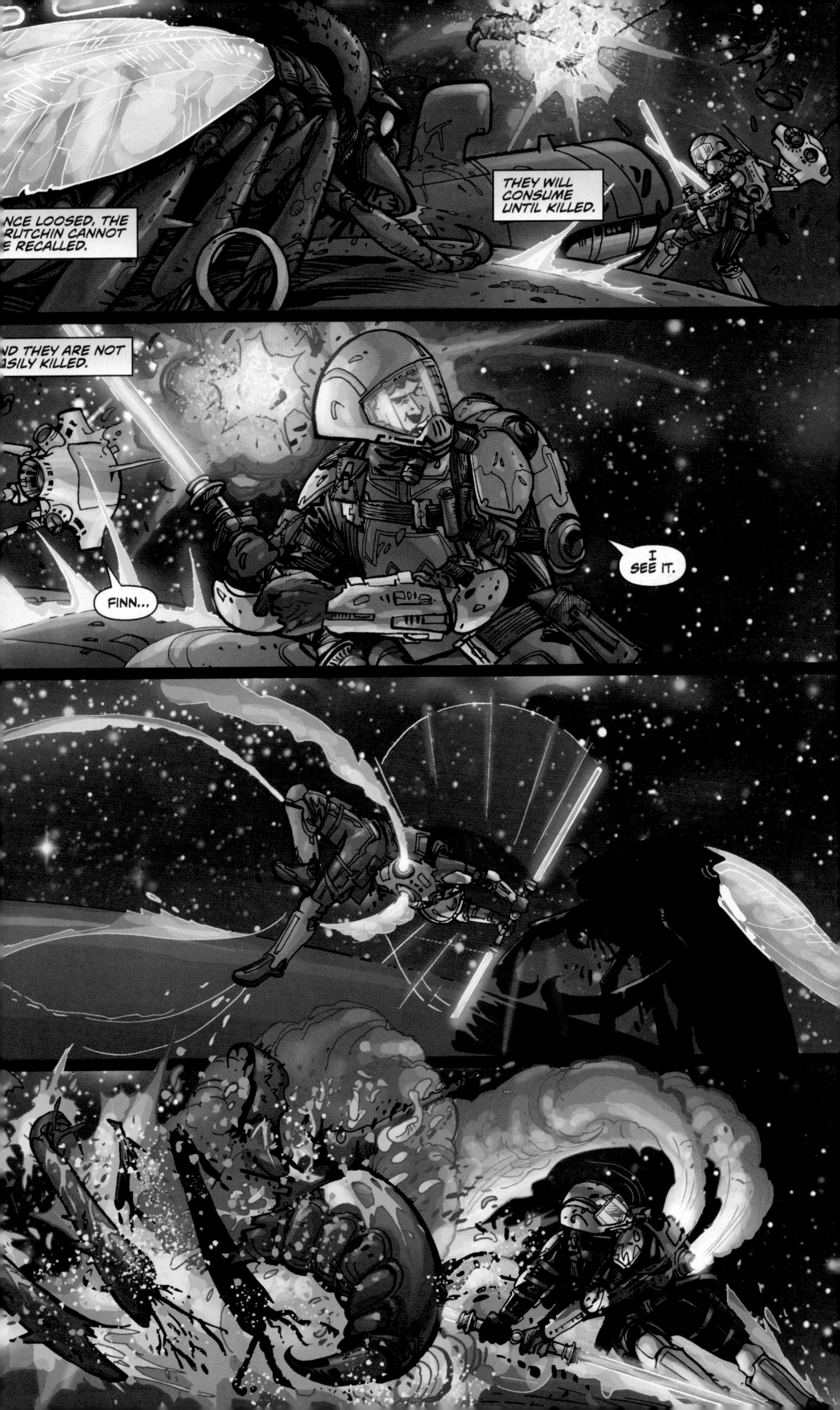
NCE LOOSED, THE
RUTCHIN CANNOT
E RECALLED.
THEY WILL
CONSUME
UNTIL KILLED.
ND THEY ARE NOT
ASILY KILLED.
FINN...
I
SEE IT.

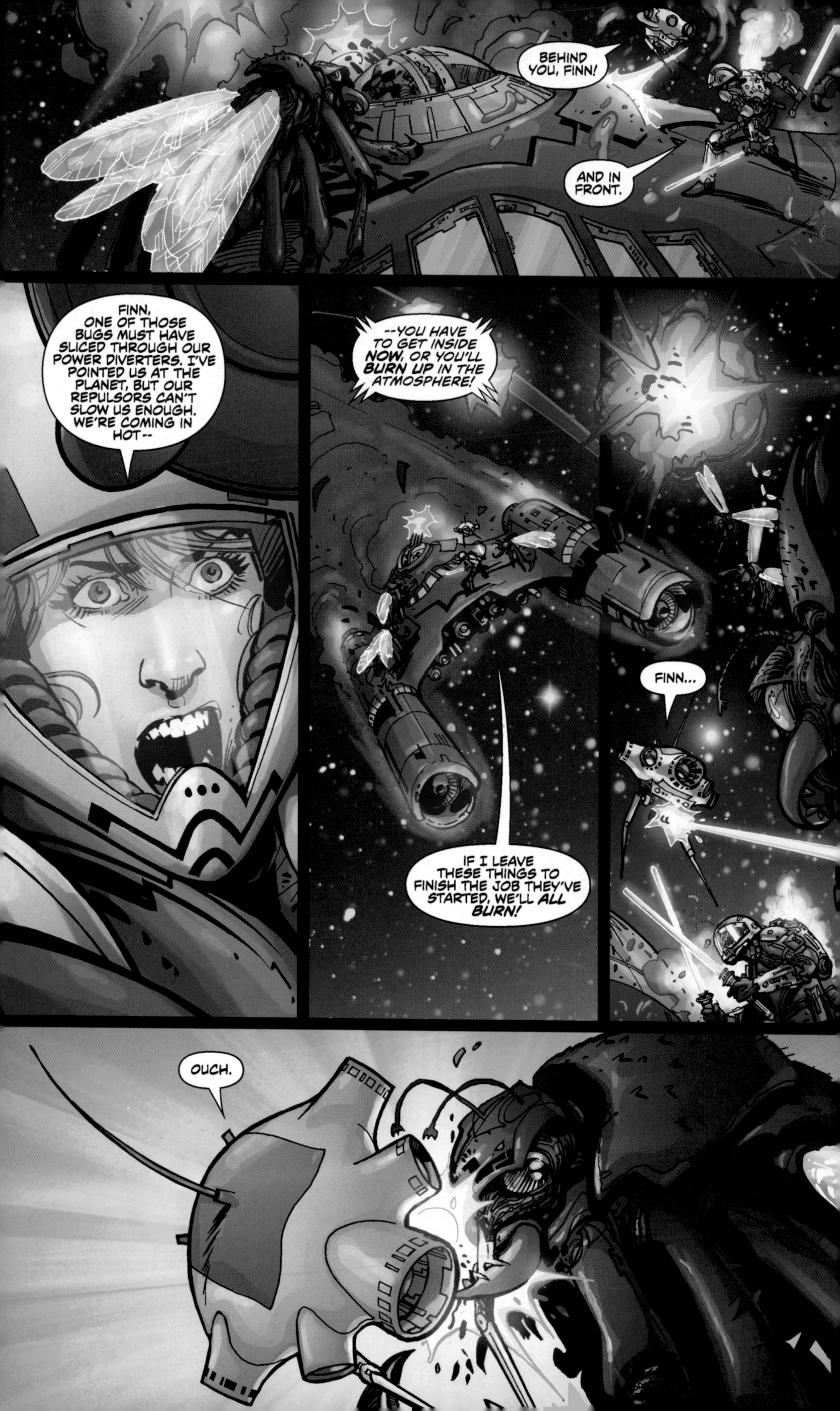
BEHIND YOU, FINN!
AND IN FRONT.
FINN, ONE OF THOSE BUGS MUST HAVE SLICED THROUGH OUR POWER DIVERTERS. I'VE POINTED US AT THE PLANET, BUT OUR REPULSORS CAN'T SLOW US ENOUGH. WE'RE COMING IN HOT--
--YOU HAVE TO GET INSIDE NOW, OR YOU'LL BURN UP IN THE ATMOSPHERE!
IF I LEAVE THESE THINGS TO FINISH THE JOB THEY'VE STARTED, WE'LL ALL BURN!
FINN...
OUCH.

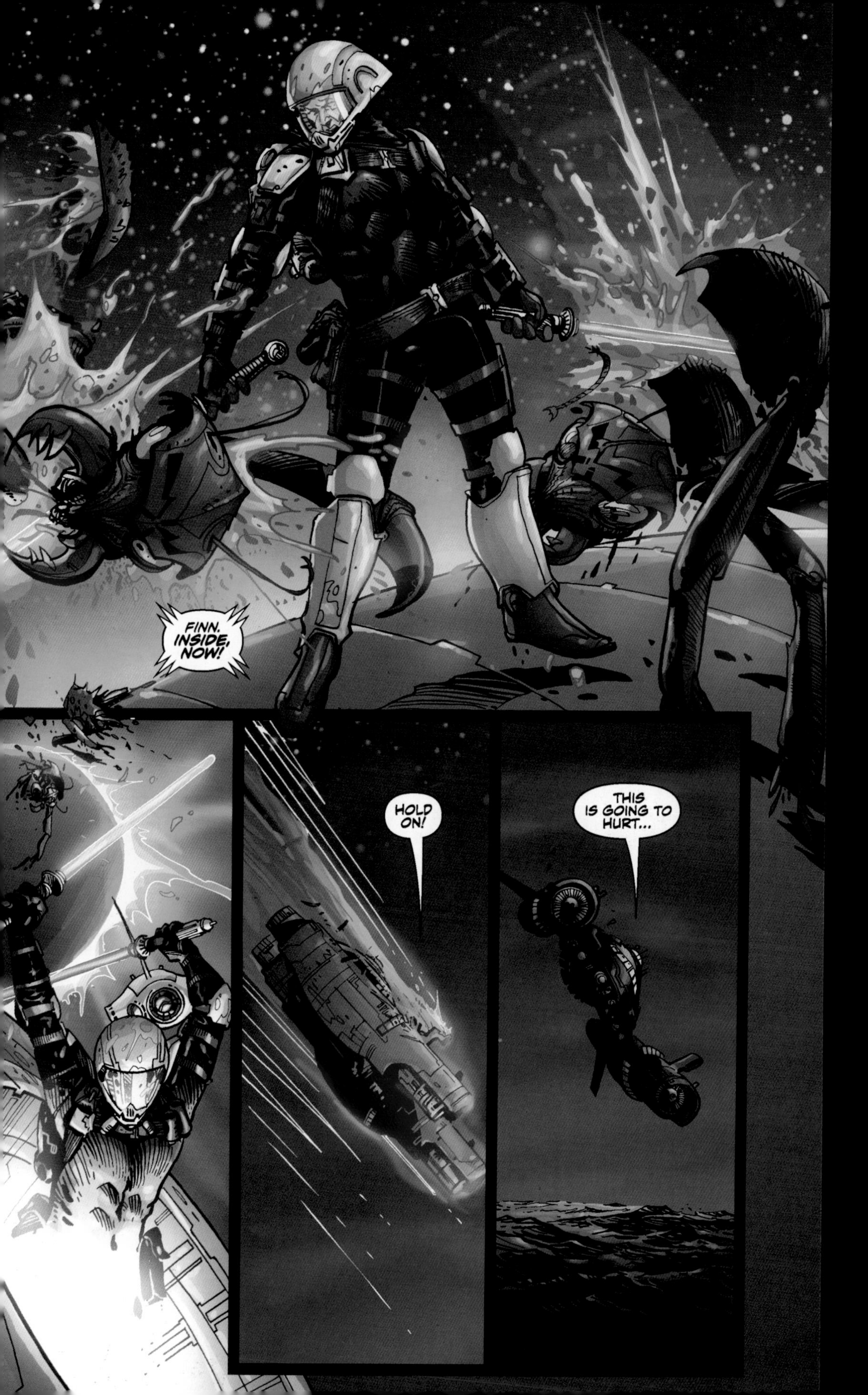
FINN. INSIDE, NOW!
HOLD ON!
THIS IS GOING TO HURT...

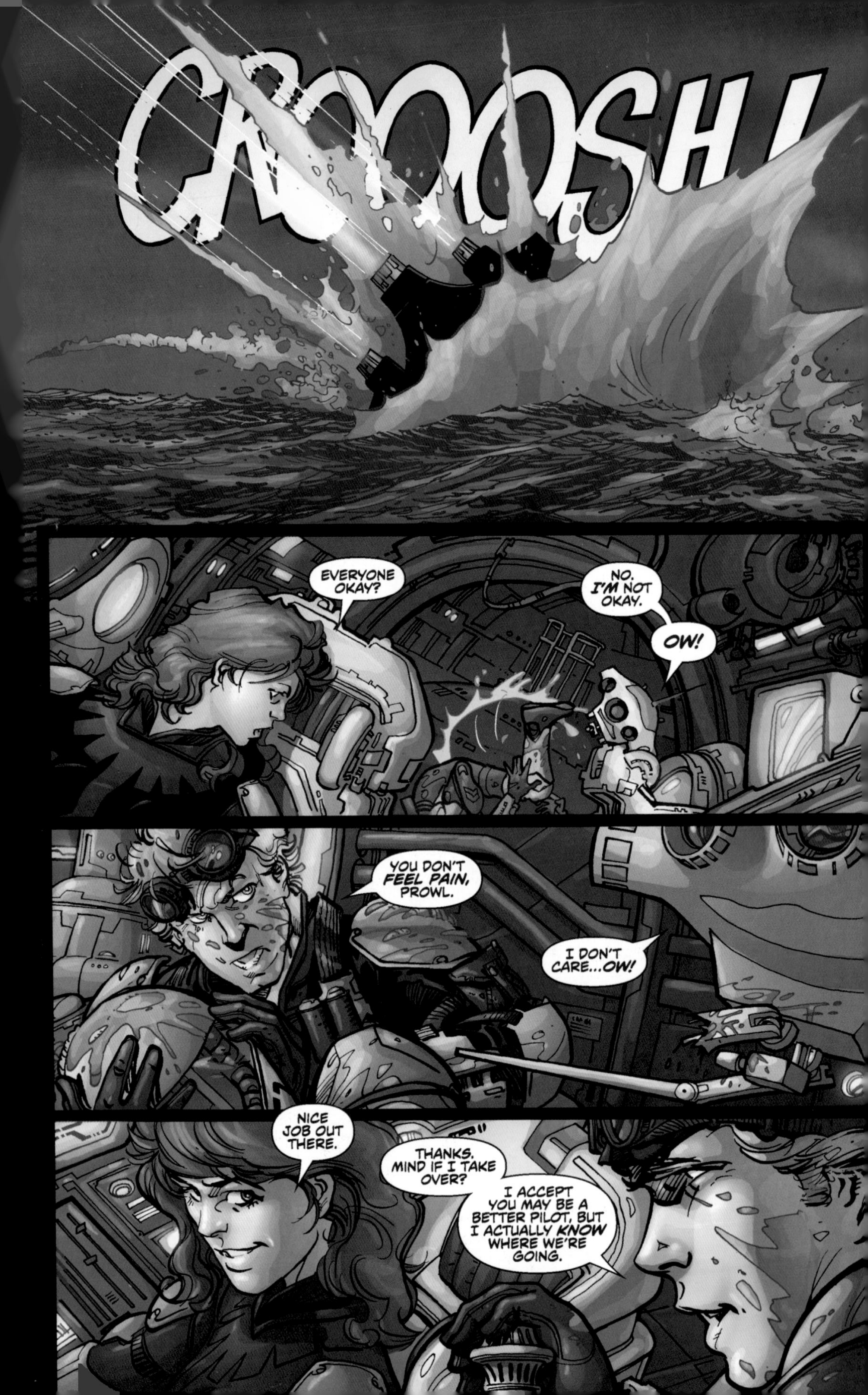

CRSSSH!!
EVERYONE OKAY?
NO. I'M NOT OKAY.
OW!
YOU DON'T FEEL PAIN, PROWL.
I DON'T CARE...OW!
NICE JOB OUT THERE.
THANKS. MIND IF I TAKE OVER?
I ACCEPT YOU MAY BE A BETTER PILOT, BUT I ACTUALLY KNOW WHERE WE'RE GOING.

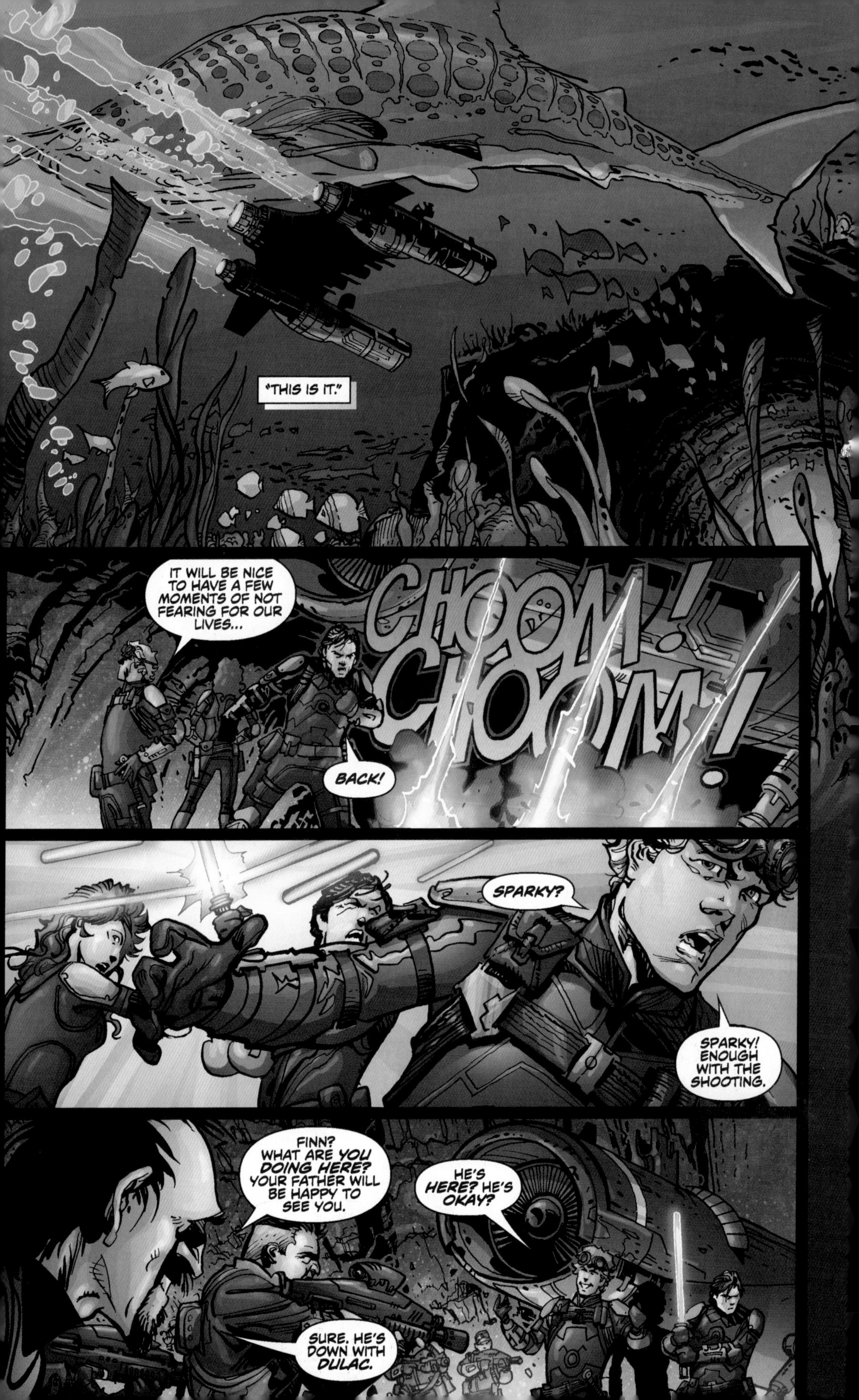
"THIS IS IT."
IT WILL BE NICE TO HAVE A FEW MOMENTS OF NOT FEARING FOR OUR LIVES...
CHOOM! CHOOM!
BACK!
SPARKY?
SPARKY! ENOUGH WITH THE SHOOTING.
FINN? WHAT ARE YOU DOING HERE? YOUR FATHER WILL BE HAPPY TO SEE YOU.
HE'S HERE? HE'S OKAY?
SURE. HE'S DOWN WITH DULAC.

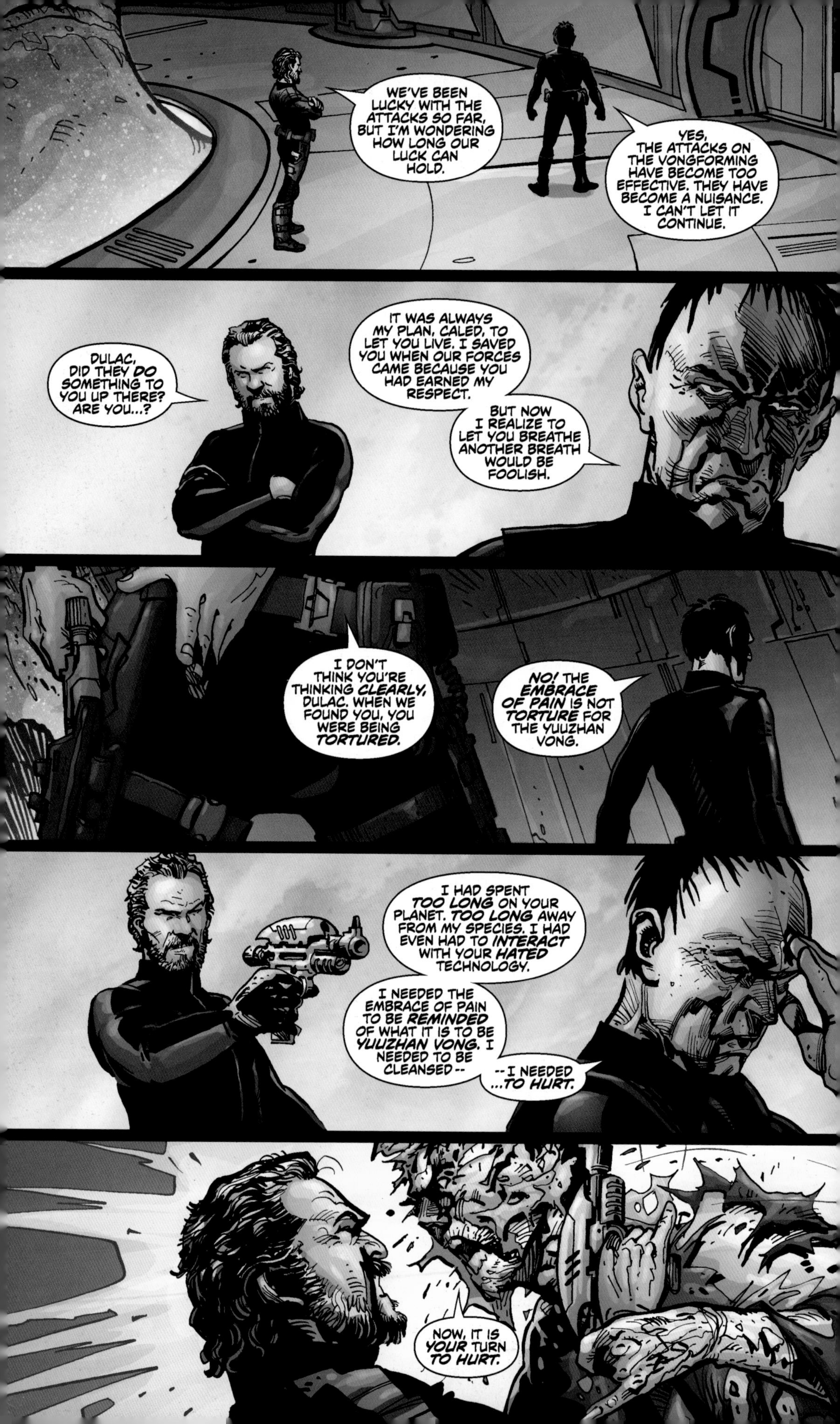
WE'VE BEEN LUCKY WITH THE ATTACKS SO FAR, BUT I'M WONDERING HOW LONG OUR LUCK CAN HOLD.
YES, THE ATTACKS ON THE VONGFORMING HAVE BECOME TOO EFFECTIVE. THEY HAVE BECOME A NUISANCE. I CAN'T LET IT CONTINUE.
DULAC, DID THEY *DO* SOMETHING TO YOU UP THERE? ARE YOU...?
IT WAS ALWAYS MY PLAN, CALED, TO LET YOU LIVE. I SAVED YOU WHEN OUR FORCES CAME BECAUSE YOU HAD EARNED MY RESPECT.
BUT NOW I REALIZE TO LET YOU BREATHE ANOTHER BREATH WOULD BE FOOLISH.
I DON'T THINK YOU'RE THINKING *CLEARLY,* DULAC. WHEN WE FOUND YOU, YOU WERE BEING *TORTURED.*
NO! THE *EMBRACE OF PAIN* IS NOT *TORTURE* FOR THE YUUZHAN VONG.
I HAD SPENT *TOO LONG* ON YOUR PLANET. *TOO LONG* AWAY FROM MY SPECIES. I HAD EVEN HAD TO *INTERACT* WITH YOUR *HATED* TECHNOLOGY.
I NEEDED THE EMBRACE OF PAIN TO BE *REMINDED* OF WHAT IT IS TO BE *YUUZHAN VONG.* I NEEDED TO BE CLEANSED --
-- I NEEDED ...*TO HURT.*
NOW, IT IS *YOUR* TURN *TO HURT.*

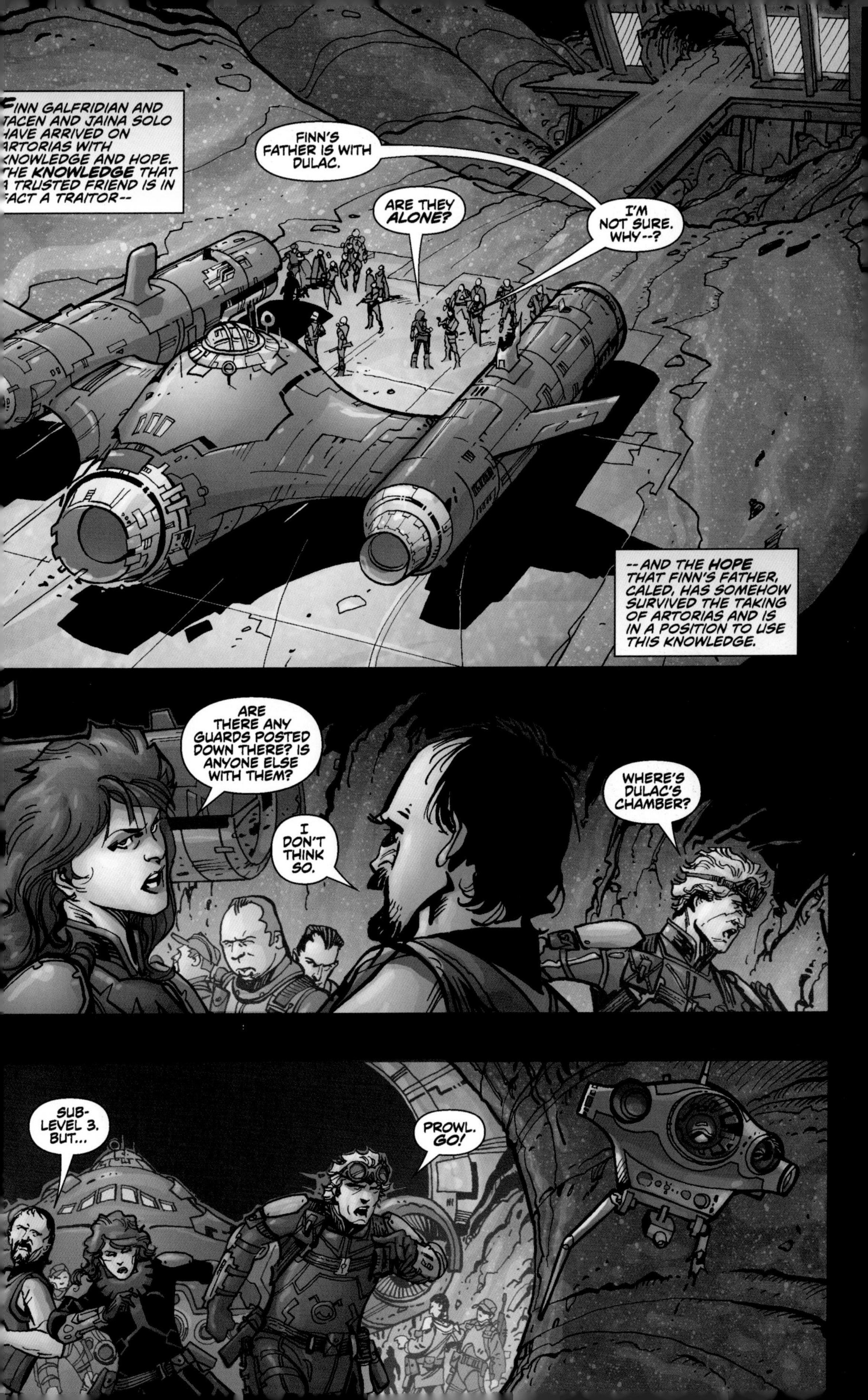
FINN GALFRIDIAN AND TACEN AND JAINA SOLO HAVE ARRIVED ON ARTORIAS WITH KNOWLEDGE AND HOPE. THE KNOWLEDGE THAT A TRUSTED FRIEND IS IN FACT A TRAITOR--
FINN'S FATHER IS WITH DULAC.
ARE THEY ALONE?
I'M NOT SURE. WHY--?
--AND THE HOPE THAT FINN'S FATHER, CALED, HAS SOMEHOW SURVIVED THE TAKING OF ARTORIAS AND IS IN A POSITION TO USE THIS KNOWLEDGE.
ARE THERE ANY GUARDS POSTED DOWN THERE? IS ANYONE ELSE WITH THEM?
I DON'T THINK SO.
WHERE'S DULAC'S CHAMBER?
SUB-LEVEL 3. BUT...
PROWL. GO!

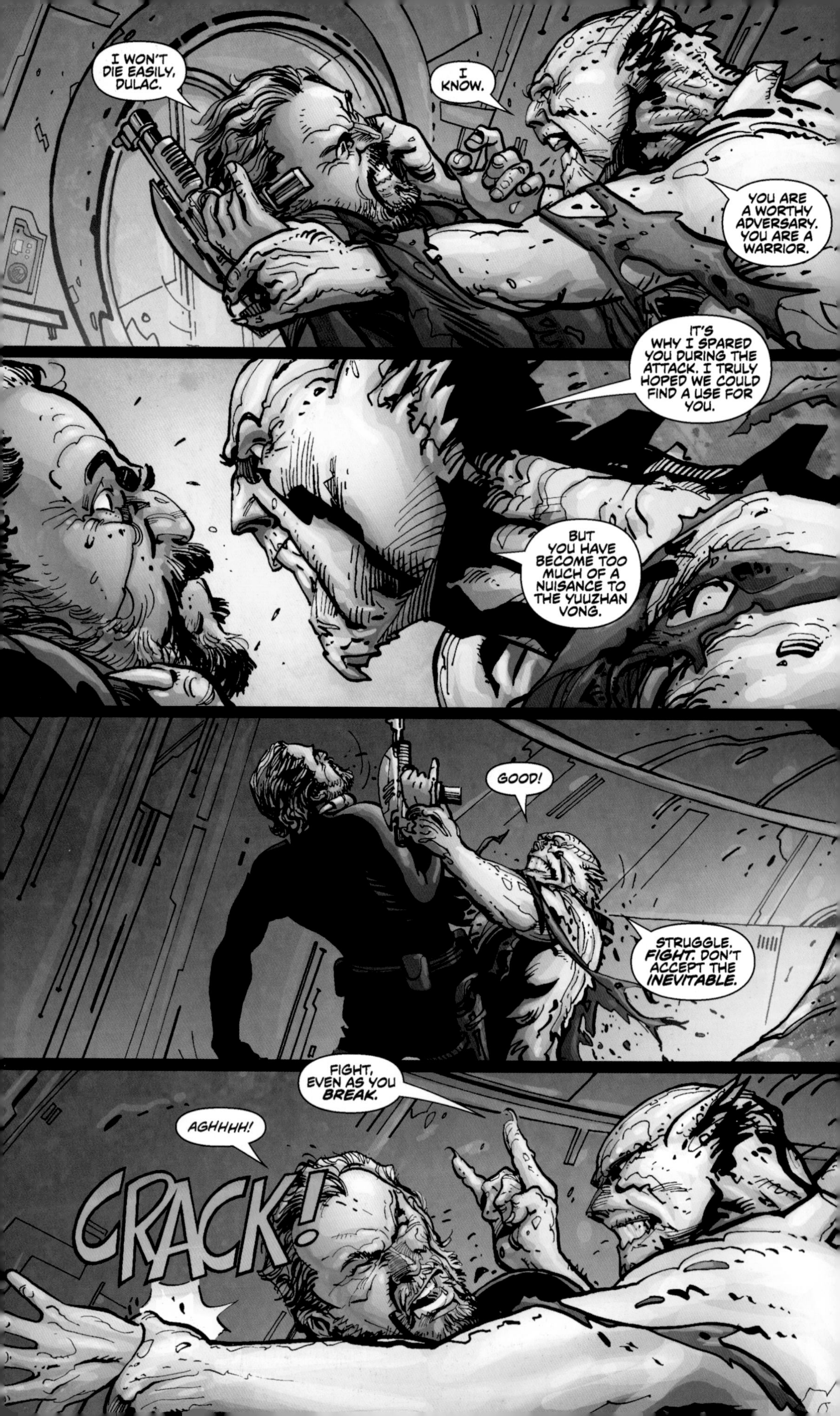

I WON'T DIE EASILY, DULAC.
I KNOW.
YOU ARE A WORTHY ADVERSARY. YOU ARE A WARRIOR.
IT'S WHY I SPARED YOU DURING THE ATTACK. I TRULY HOPED WE COULD FIND A USE FOR YOU.
BUT YOU HAVE BECOME TOO MUCH OF A NUISANCE TO THE YUUZHAN VONG.
GOOD!
STRUGGLE. FIGHT. DON'T ACCEPT THE INEVITABLE.
FIGHT, EVEN AS YOU BREAK.
AGHHHH!
CRACK!

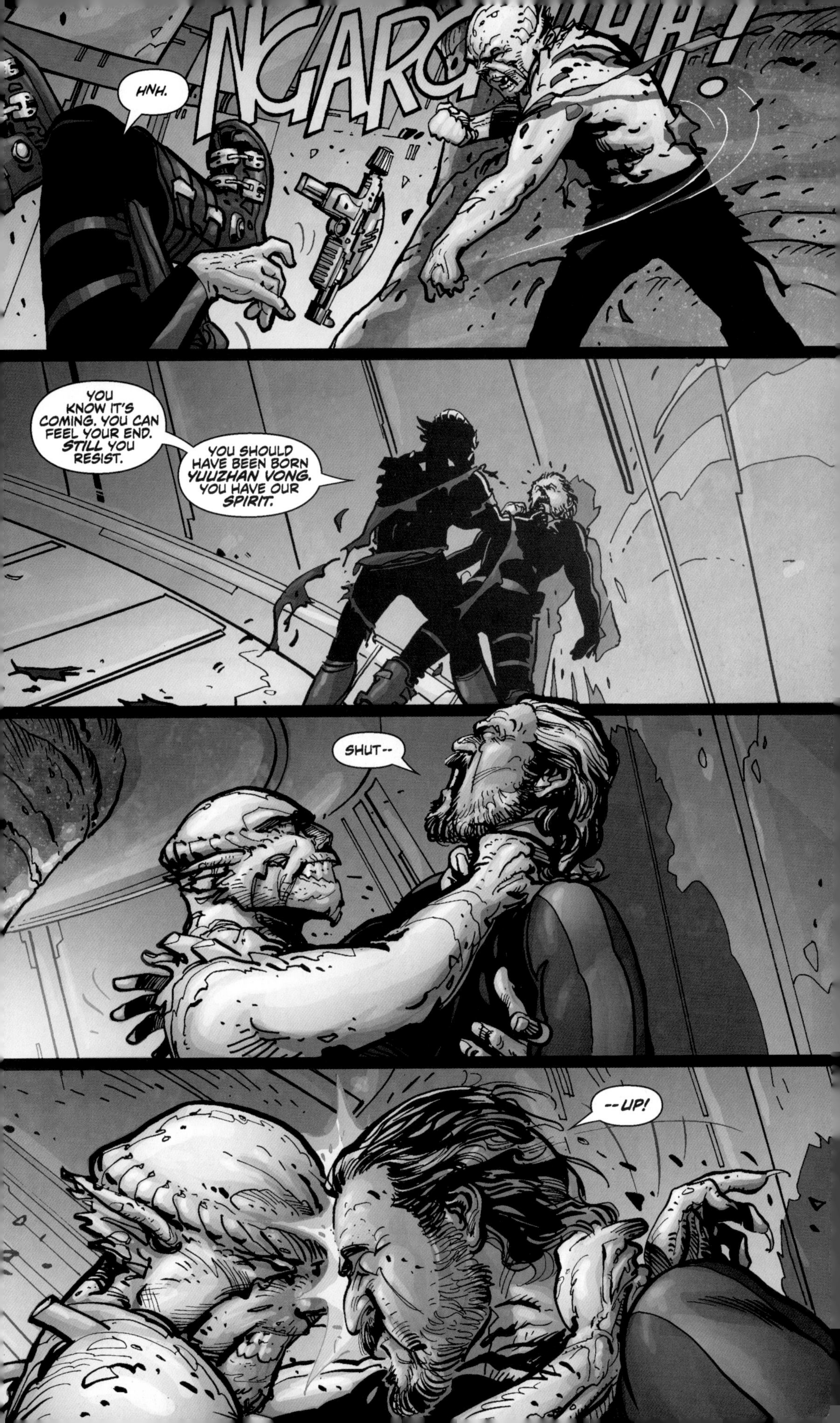
NGARGHHH!
HNH.
YOU KNOW IT'S COMING. YOU CAN FEEL YOUR END. STILL YOU RESIST.
YOU SHOULD HAVE BEEN BORN YUUZHAN VONG. YOU HAVE OUR SPIRIT.
SHUT--
--UP!

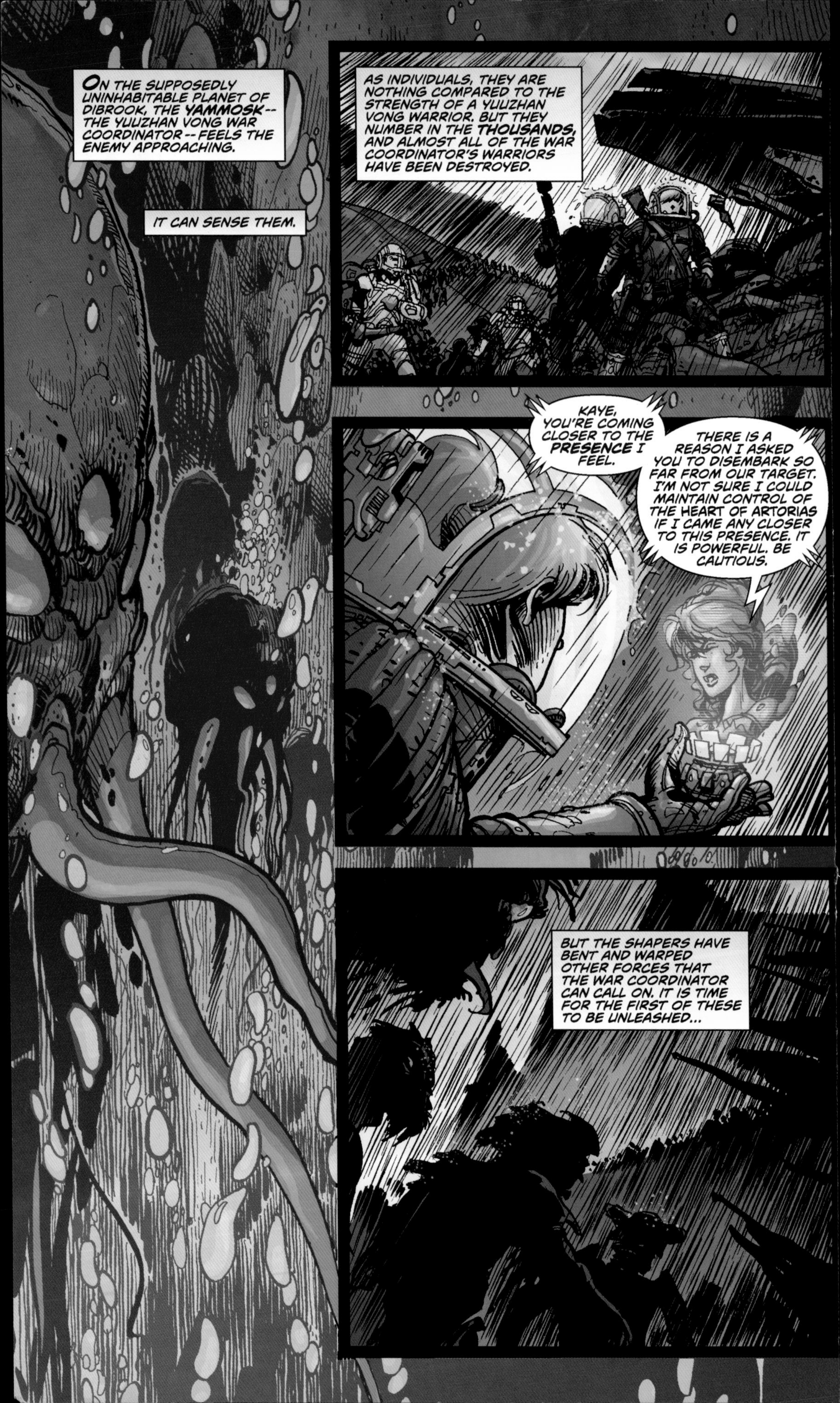
ON THE SUPPOSEDLY UNINHABITABLE PLANET OF DIBROOK, THE **YAMMOSK**-- THE YUUZHAN VONG WAR COORDINATOR--FEELS THE ENEMY APPROACHING.
IT CAN SENSE THEM.
AS INDIVIDUALS, THEY ARE NOTHING COMPARED TO THE STRENGTH OF A YUUZHAN VONG WARRIOR. BUT THEY NUMBER IN THE **THOUSANDS**, AND ALMOST ALL OF THE WAR COORDINATOR'S WARRIORS HAVE BEEN DESTROYED.
KAYE, YOU'RE COMING CLOSER TO THE **PRESENCE** I FEEL.
THERE IS A REASON I ASKED YOU TO DISEMBARK SO FAR FROM OUR TARGET. I'M NOT SURE I COULD MAINTAIN CONTROL OF THE HEART OF ARTORIAS IF I CAME ANY CLOSER TO THIS PRESENCE. IT IS POWERFUL. BE CAUTIOUS.
BUT THE SHAPERS HAVE BENT AND WARPED OTHER FORCES THAT THE WAR COORDINATOR CAN CALL ON. IT IS TIME FOR THE FIRST OF THESE TO BE UNLEASHED...

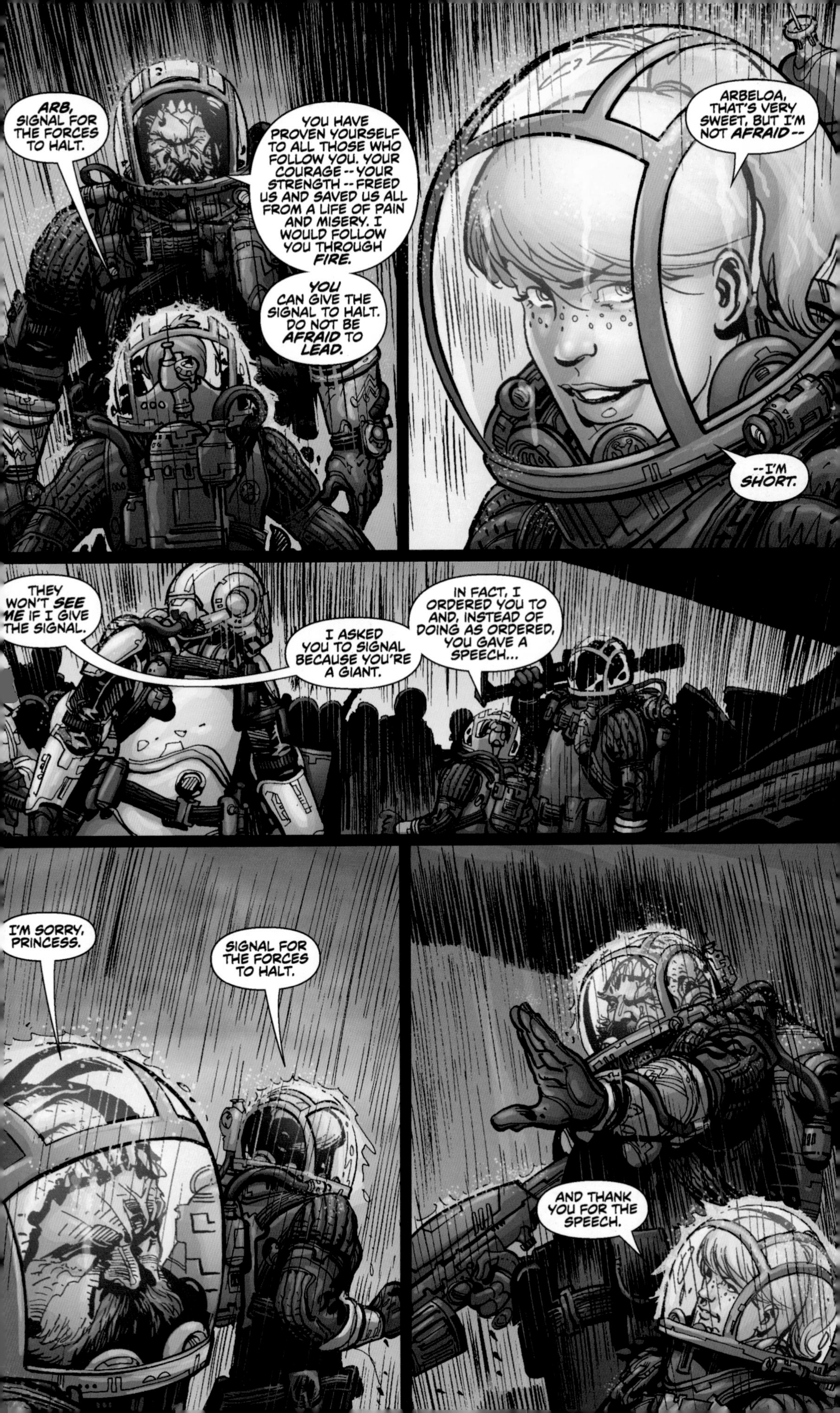
ARB, SIGNAL FOR THE FORCES TO HALT.
YOU HAVE PROVEN YOURSELF TO ALL THOSE WHO FOLLOW YOU. YOUR COURAGE--YOUR STRENGTH--FREED US AND SAVED US ALL FROM A LIFE OF PAIN AND MISERY. I WOULD FOLLOW YOU THROUGH FIRE.
YOU CAN GIVE THE SIGNAL TO HALT. DO NOT BE AFRAID TO LEAD.
ARBELOA, THAT'S VERY SWEET, BUT I'M NOT AFRAID--
--I'M SHORT.
THEY WON'T SEE ME IF I GIVE THE SIGNAL.
I ASKED YOU TO SIGNAL BECAUSE YOU'RE A GIANT.
IN FACT, I ORDERED YOU TO AND, INSTEAD OF DOING AS ORDERED, YOU GAVE A SPEECH...
I'M SORRY, PRINCESS.
SIGNAL FOR THE FORCES TO HALT.
AND THANK YOU FOR THE SPEECH.

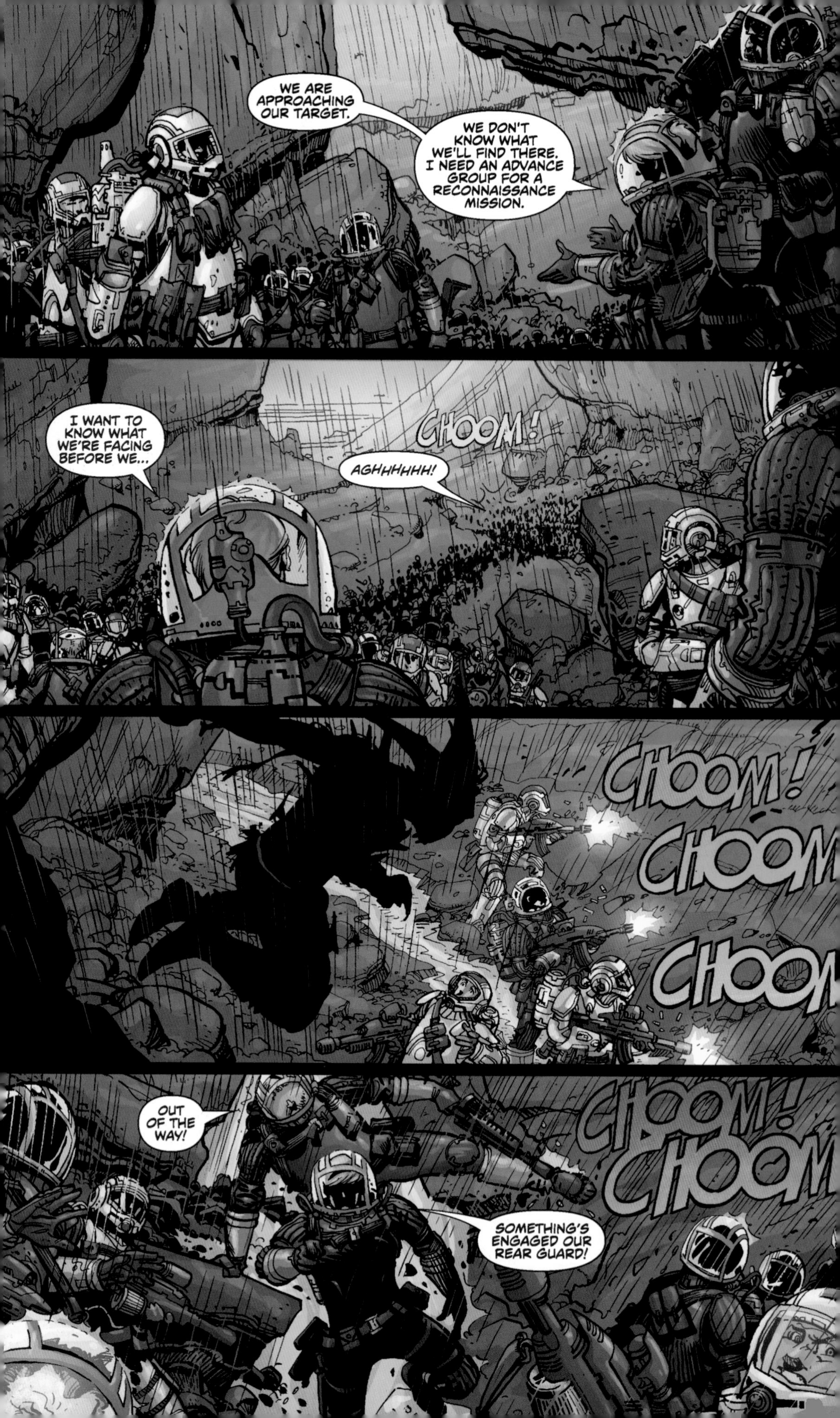
WE ARE APPROACHING OUR TARGET.
WE DON'T KNOW WHAT WE'LL FIND THERE. I NEED AN ADVANCE GROUP FOR A RECONNAISSANCE MISSION.
I WANT TO KNOW WHAT WE'RE FACING BEFORE WE...
CHOOM!
AGHHHHHH!
CHOOM!
CHOOM!
OUT OF THE WAY!
CHOOM!
SOMETHING'S ENGAGED OUR REAR GUARD!

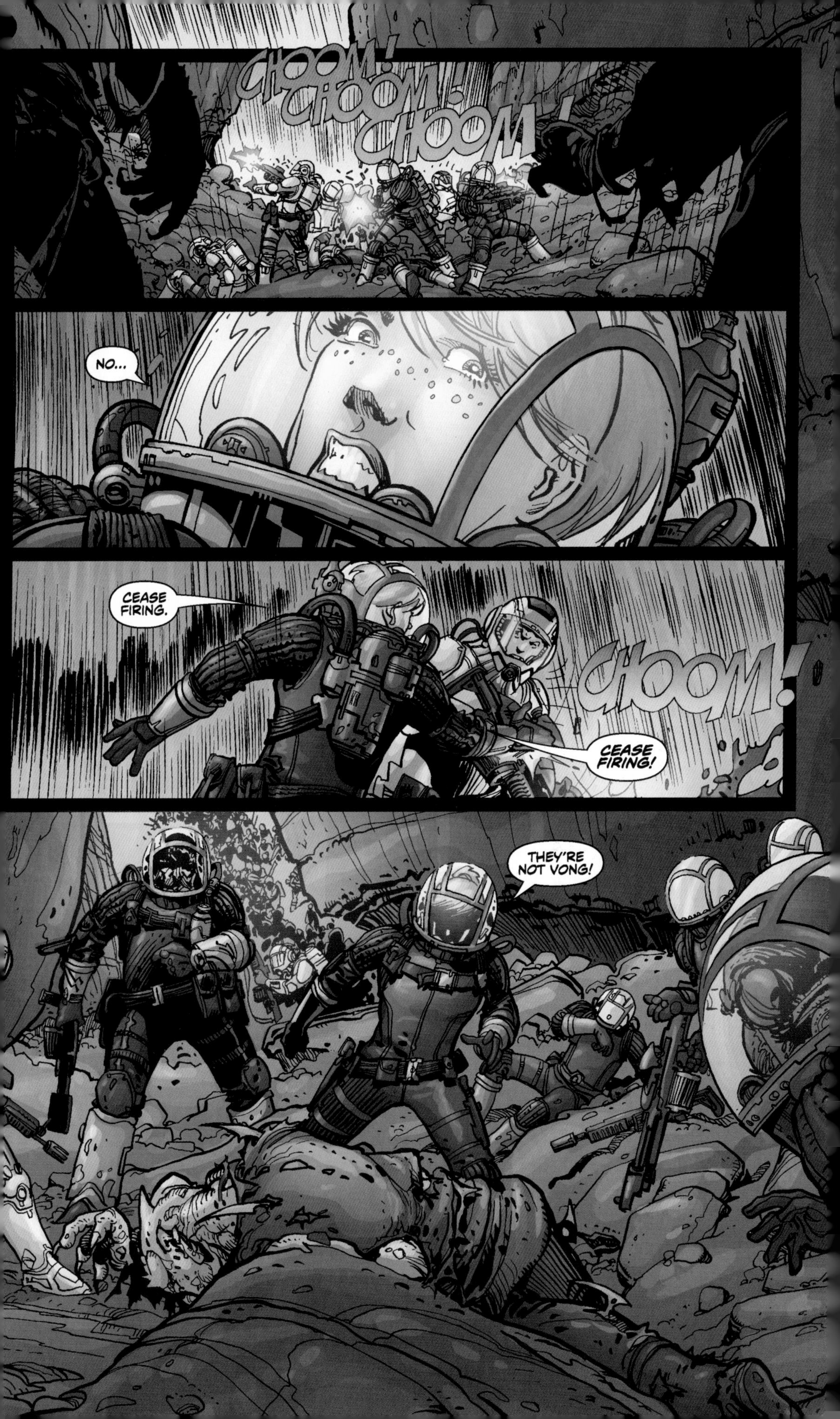
CHOOM! CHOOM! CHOOM!
NO...
CEASE FIRING.
CHOOM!
CEASE FIRING!
THEY'RE NOT VONG!

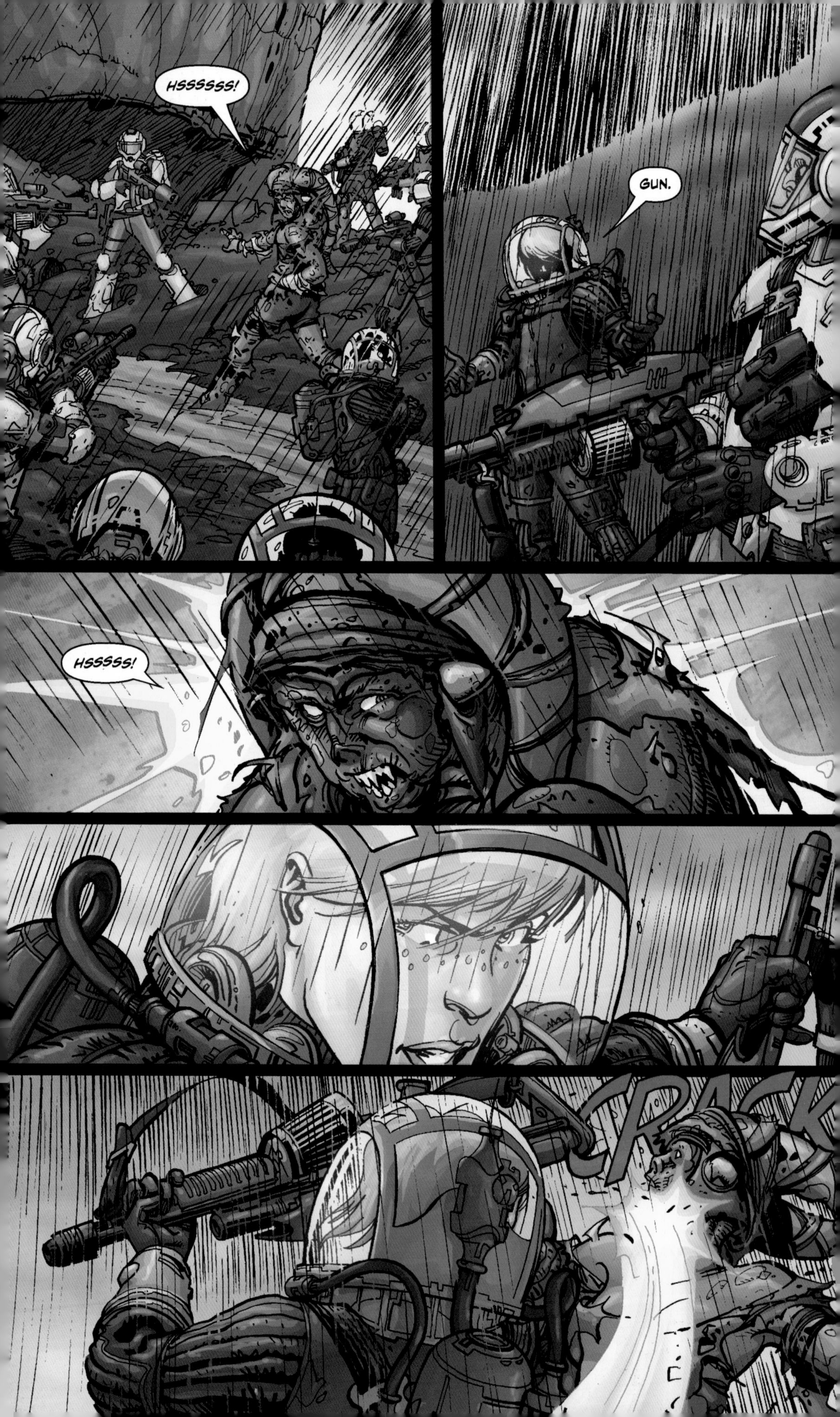
HSSSSSS!
GUN.
HSSSSS!
CRACK

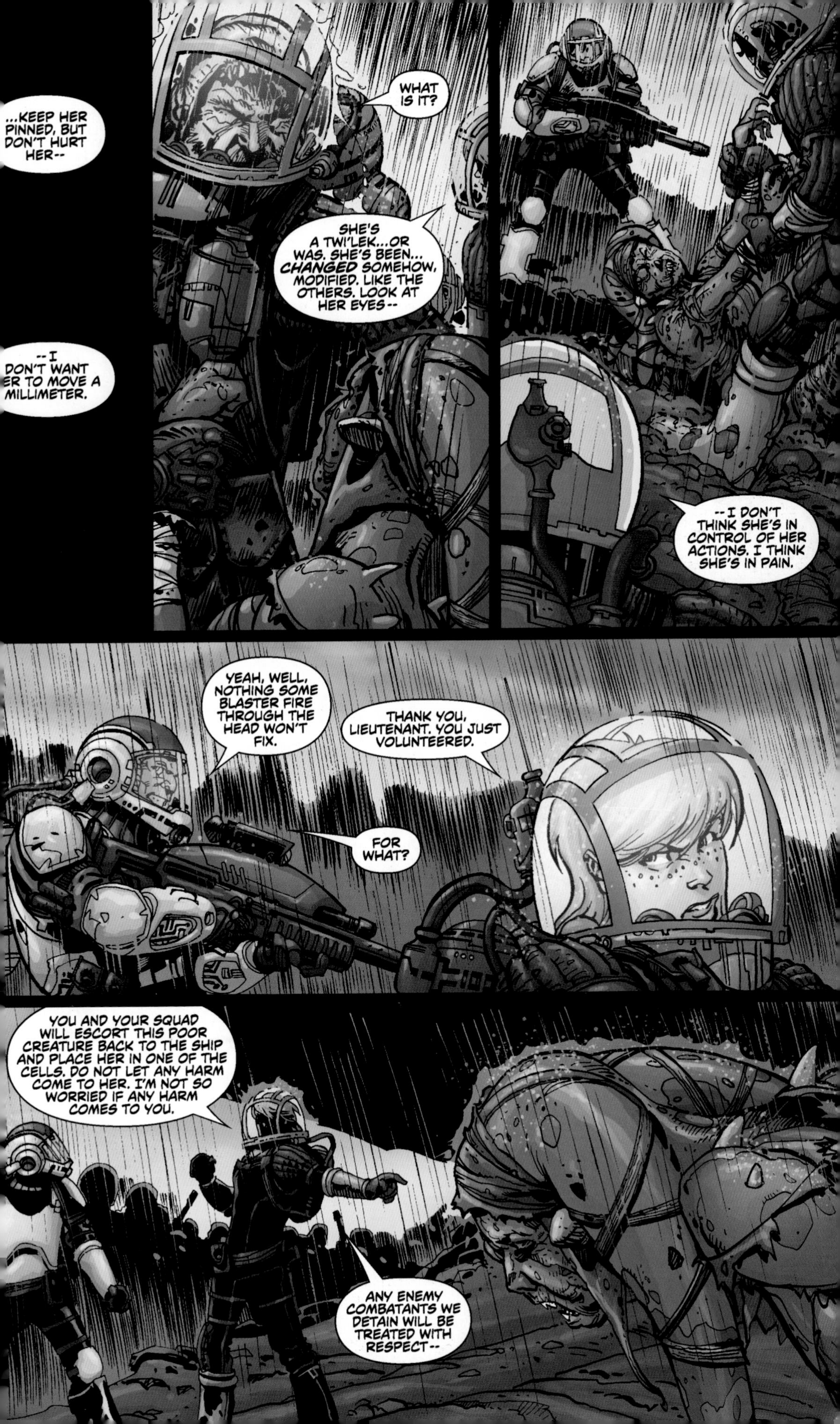
...KEEP HER PINNED, BUT DON'T HURT HER--
--I DON'T WANT ER TO MOVE A MILLIMETER.
WHAT IS IT?
SHE'S A TWI'LEK...OR WAS. SHE'S BEEN... CHANGED SOMEHOW, MODIFIED. LIKE THE OTHERS. LOOK AT HER EYES--
--I DON'T THINK SHE'S IN CONTROL OF HER ACTIONS. I THINK SHE'S IN PAIN.
YEAH, WELL, NOTHING SOME BLASTER FIRE THROUGH THE HEAD WON'T FIX.
THANK YOU, LIEUTENANT. YOU JUST VOLUNTEERED.
FOR WHAT?
YOU AND YOUR SQUAD WILL ESCORT THIS POOR CREATURE BACK TO THE SHIP AND PLACE HER IN ONE OF THE CELLS. DO NOT LET ANY HARM COME TO HER. I'M NOT SO WORRIED IF ANY HARM COMES TO YOU.
ANY ENEMY COMBATANTS WE DETAIN WILL BE TREATED WITH RESPECT--

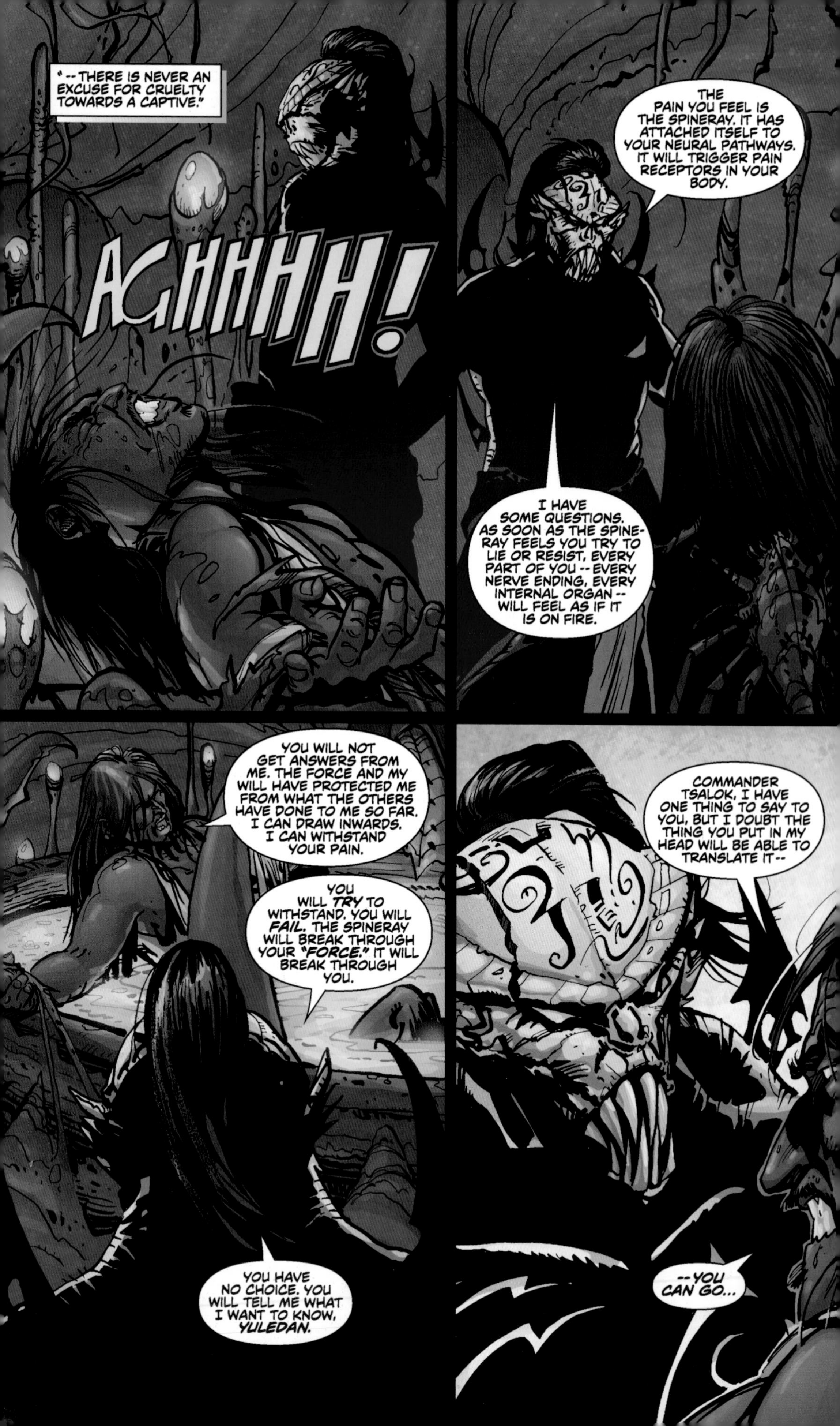
"--THERE IS NEVER AN EXCUSE FOR CRUELTY TOWARDS A CAPTIVE."
AGHHHH!
THE PAIN YOU FEEL IS THE SPINERAY. IT HAS ATTACHED ITSELF TO YOUR NEURAL PATHWAYS. IT WILL TRIGGER PAIN RECEPTORS IN YOUR BODY.
I HAVE SOME QUESTIONS. AS SOON AS THE SPINE-RAY FEELS YOU TRY TO LIE OR RESIST, EVERY PART OF YOU -- EVERY NERVE ENDING, EVERY INTERNAL ORGAN -- WILL FEEL AS IF IT IS ON FIRE.
YOU WILL NOT GET ANSWERS FROM ME. THE FORCE AND MY WILL HAVE PROTECTED ME FROM WHAT THE OTHERS HAVE DONE TO ME SO FAR. I CAN DRAW INWARDS. I CAN WITHSTAND YOUR PAIN.
YOU WILL *TRY* TO WITHSTAND. YOU WILL *FAIL.* THE SPINERAY WILL BREAK THROUGH YOUR *"FORCE."* IT WILL BREAK THROUGH YOU.
YOU HAVE NO CHOICE. YOU WILL TELL ME WHAT I WANT TO KNOW, *YULEDAN.*
COMMANDER TSALOK, I HAVE ONE THING TO SAY TO YOU, BUT I DOUBT THE THING YOU PUT IN MY HEAD WILL BE ABLE TO TRANSLATE IT --
--YOU CAN GO...

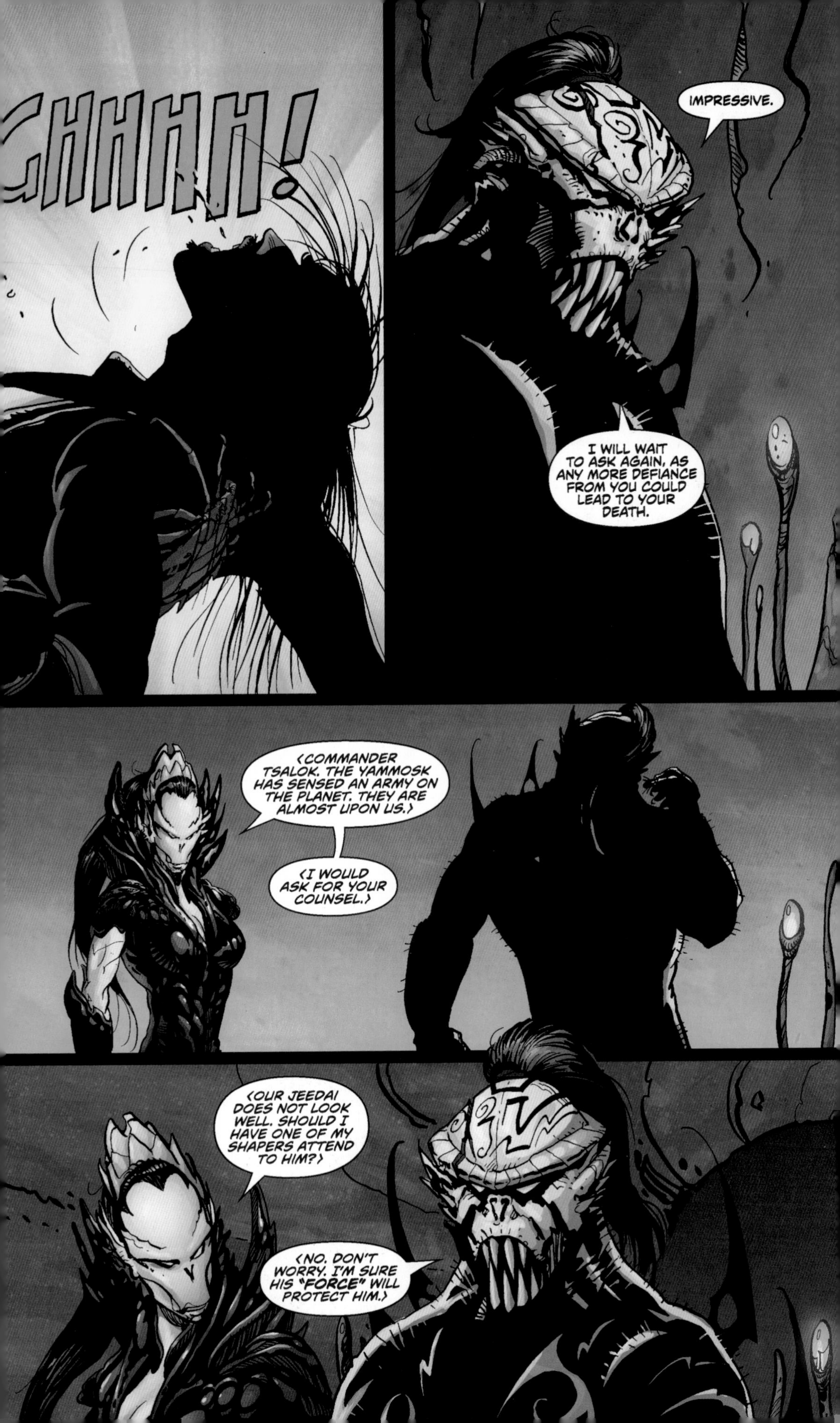

HHHH!
IMPRESSIVE.
I WILL WAIT TO ASK AGAIN, AS ANY MORE DEFIANCE FROM YOU COULD LEAD TO YOUR DEATH.
‹COMMANDER TSALOK. THE YAMMOSK HAS SENSED AN ARMY ON THE PLANET. THEY ARE ALMOST UPON US.›
‹I WOULD ASK FOR YOUR COUNSEL.›
‹OUR JEEDAI DOES NOT LOOK WELL. SHOULD I HAVE ONE OF MY SHAPERS ATTEND TO HIM?›
‹NO. DON'T WORRY. I'M SURE HIS "FORCE" WILL PROTECT HIM.›

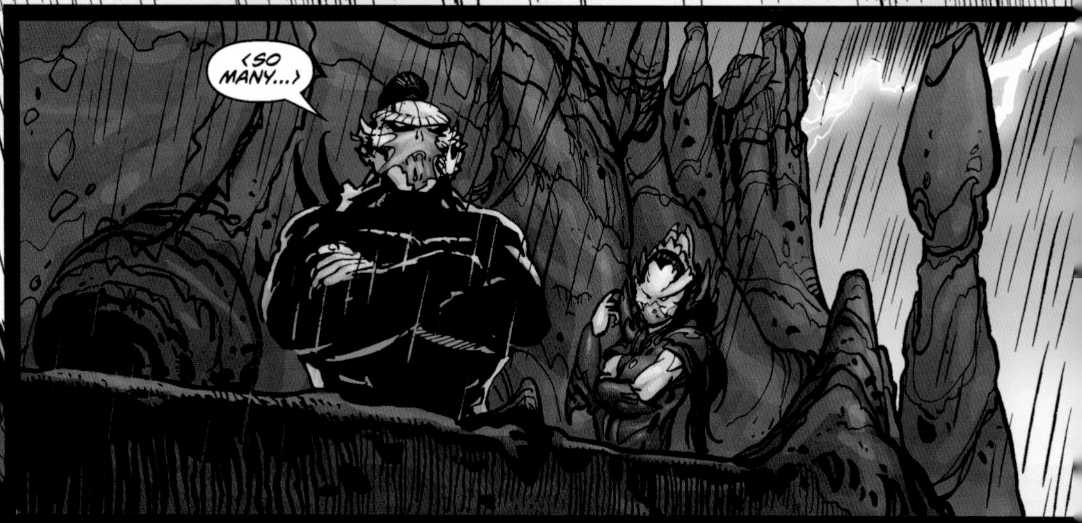
‹SO MANY...›
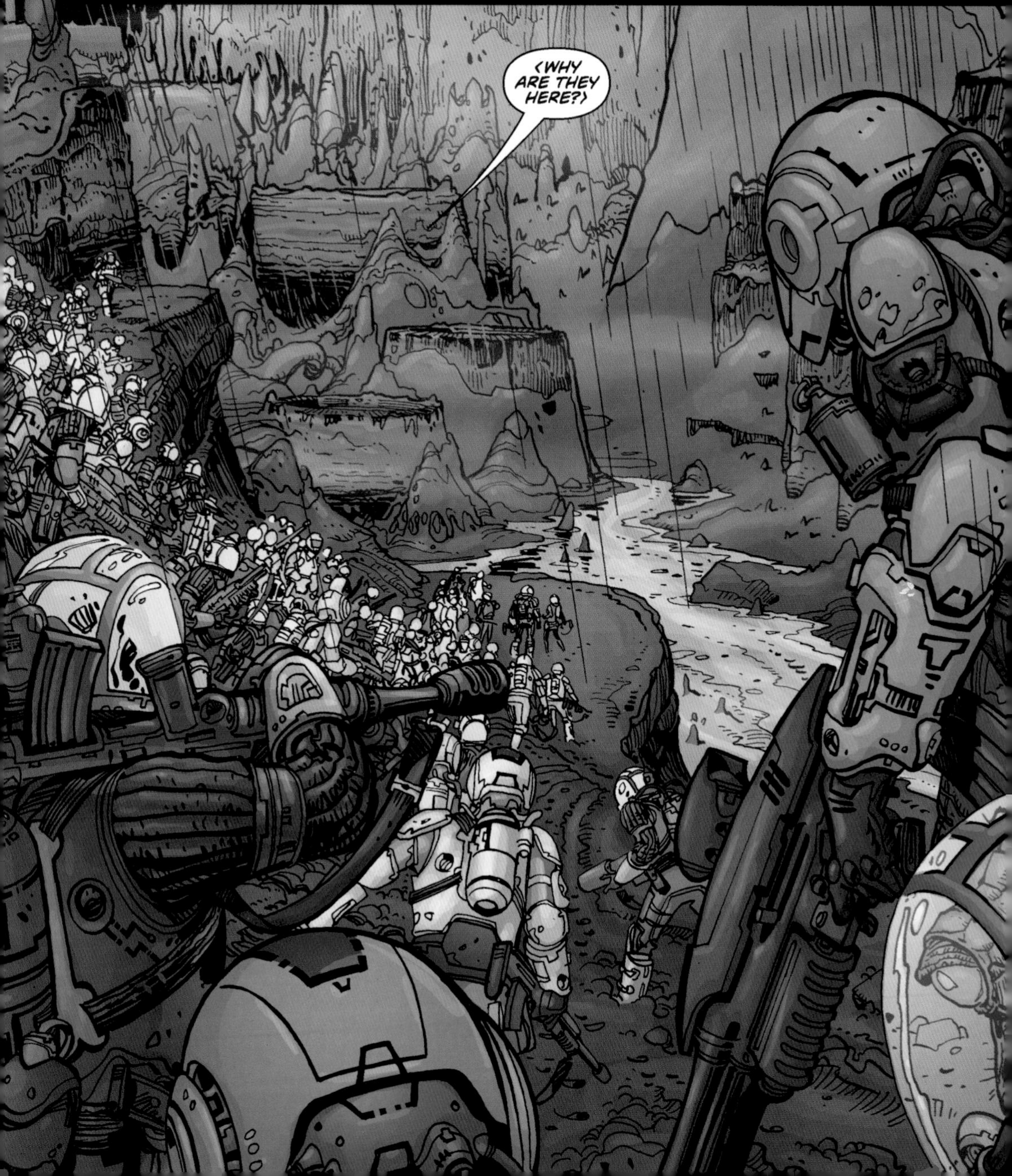
‹WHY ARE THEY HERE?›

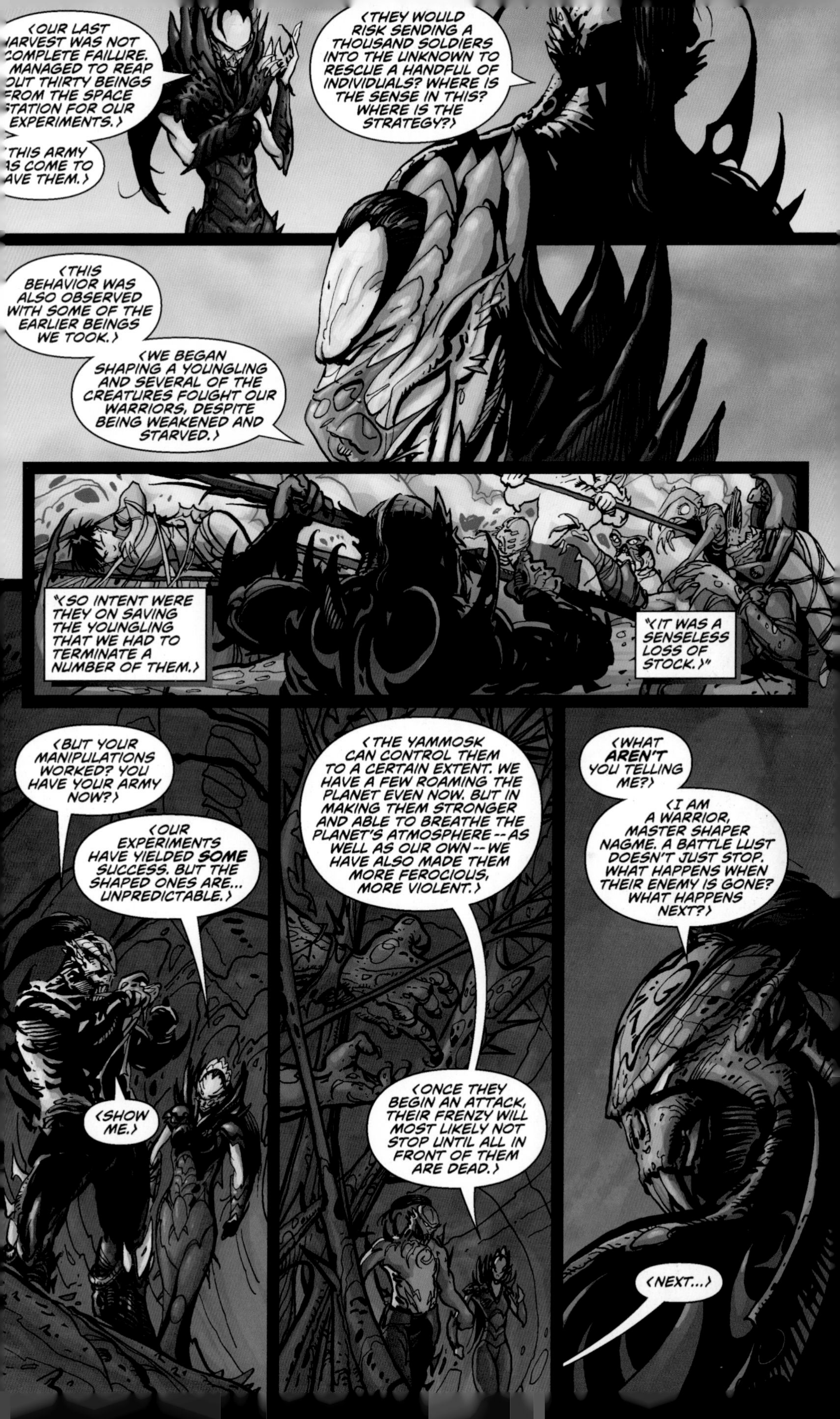
‹OUR LAST HARVEST WAS NOT COMPLETE FAILURE. MANAGED TO REAP OUT THIRTY BEINGS FROM THE SPACE STATION FOR OUR EXPERIMENTS.›
‹THIS ARMY AS COME TO AVE THEM.›
‹THEY WOULD RISK SENDING A THOUSAND SOLDIERS INTO THE UNKNOWN TO RESCUE A HANDFUL OF INDIVIDUALS? WHERE IS THE SENSE IN THIS? WHERE IS THE STRATEGY?›
‹THIS BEHAVIOR WAS ALSO OBSERVED WITH SOME OF THE EARLIER BEINGS WE TOOK.›
‹WE BEGAN SHAPING A YOUNGLING AND SEVERAL OF THE CREATURES FOUGHT OUR WARRIORS, DESPITE BEING WEAKENED AND STARVED.›
"‹SO INTENT WERE THEY ON SAVING THE YOUNGLING THAT WE HAD TO TERMINATE A NUMBER OF THEM.›
"‹IT WAS A SENSELESS LOSS OF STOCK.›"
‹BUT YOUR MANIPULATIONS WORKED? YOU HAVE YOUR ARMY NOW?›
‹OUR EXPERIMENTS HAVE YIELDED SOME SUCCESS. BUT THE SHAPED ONES ARE... UNPREDICTABLE.›
‹SHOW ME.›
‹THE YAMMOSK CAN CONTROL THEM TO A CERTAIN EXTENT. WE HAVE A FEW ROAMING THE PLANET EVEN NOW. BUT IN MAKING THEM STRONGER AND ABLE TO BREATHE THE PLANET'S ATMOSPHERE -- AS WELL AS OUR OWN -- WE HAVE ALSO MADE THEM MORE FEROCIOUS, MORE VIOLENT.›
‹ONCE THEY BEGIN AN ATTACK, THEIR FRENZY WILL MOST LIKELY NOT STOP UNTIL ALL IN FRONT OF THEM ARE DEAD.›
‹WHAT AREN'T YOU TELLING ME?›
‹I AM A WARRIOR, MASTER SHAPER NAGME. A BATTLE LUST DOESN'T JUST STOP. WHAT HAPPENS WHEN THEIR ENEMY IS GONE? WHAT HAPPENS NEXT?›
‹NEXT...›

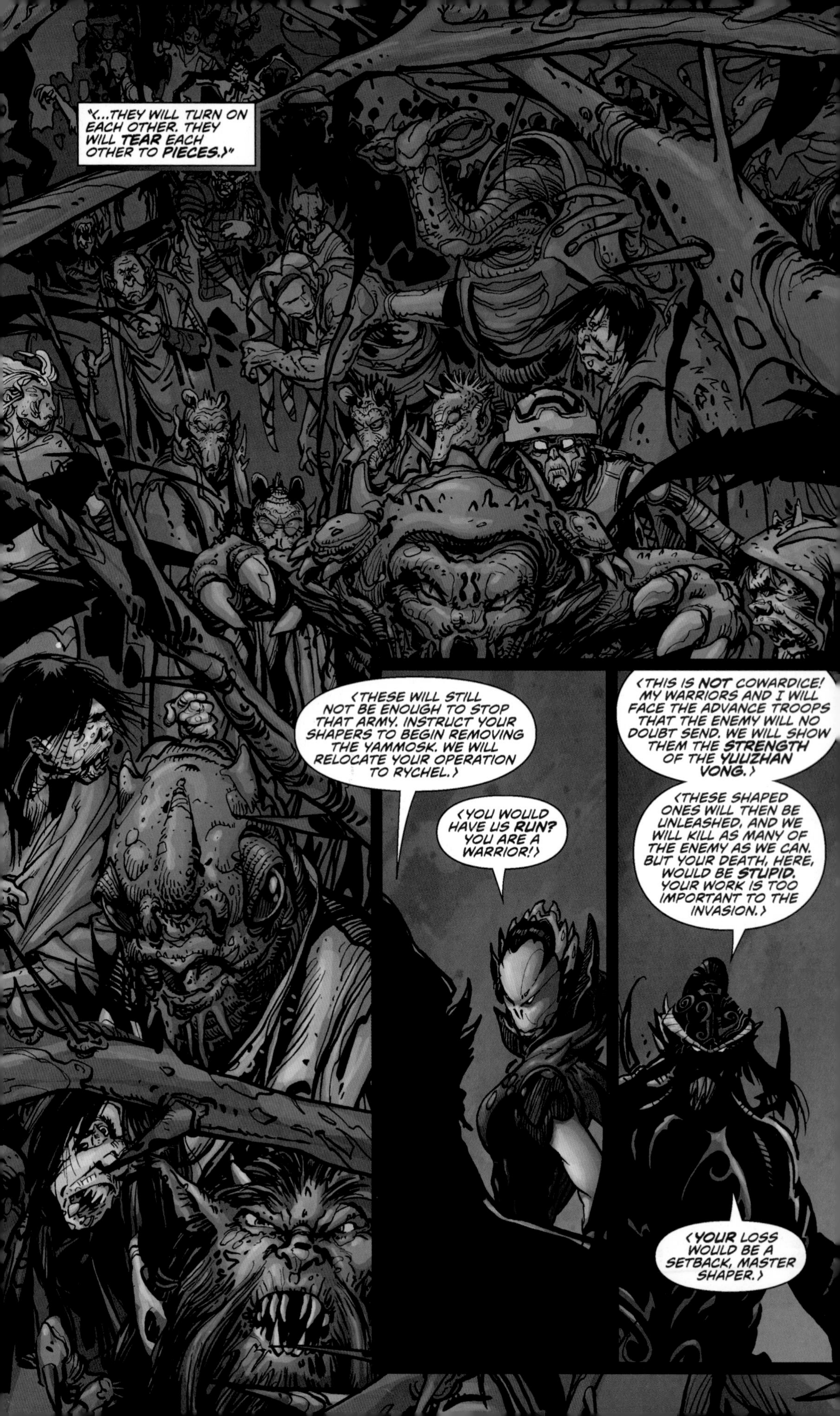
‹...THEY WILL TURN ON EACH OTHER. THEY WILL TEAR EACH OTHER TO PIECES.›"
‹THESE WILL STILL NOT BE ENOUGH TO STOP THAT ARMY. INSTRUCT YOUR SHAPERS TO BEGIN REMOVING THE YAMMOSK. WE WILL RELOCATE YOUR OPERATION TO RYCHEL.›
‹YOU WOULD HAVE US RUN? YOU ARE A WARRIOR!›
‹THIS IS NOT COWARDICE! MY WARRIORS AND I WILL FACE THE ADVANCE TROOPS THAT THE ENEMY WILL NO DOUBT SEND. WE WILL SHOW THEM THE STRENGTH OF THE YUUZHAN VONG.›
‹THESE SHAPED ONES WILL THEN BE UNLEASHED, AND WE WILL KILL AS MANY OF THE ENEMY AS WE CAN. BUT YOUR DEATH, HERE, WOULD BE STUPID. YOUR WORK IS TOO IMPORTANT TO THE INVASION.›
‹YOUR LOSS WOULD BE A SETBACK, MASTER SHAPER.›

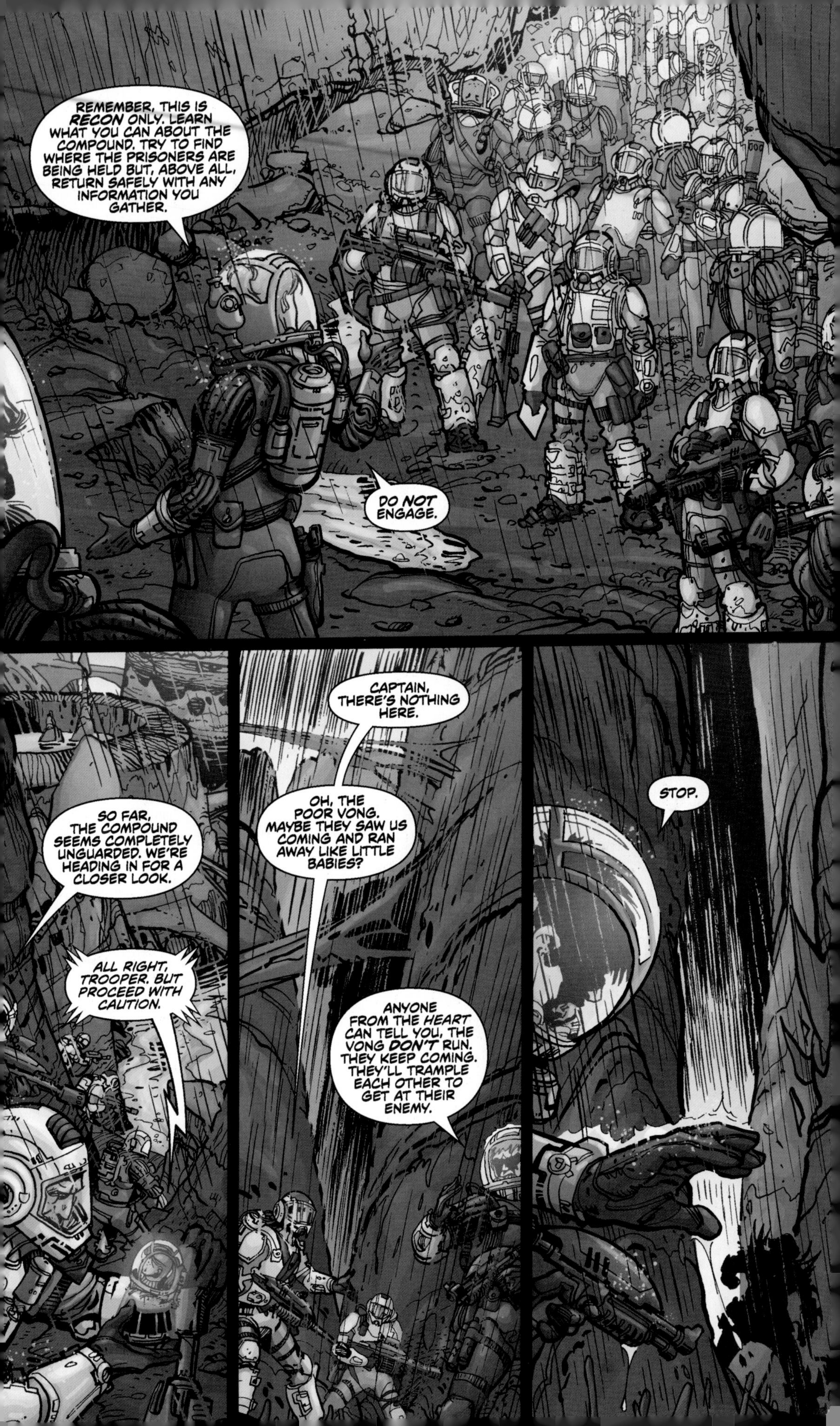
REMEMBER, THIS IS RECON ONLY. LEARN WHAT YOU CAN ABOUT THE COMPOUND. TRY TO FIND WHERE THE PRISONERS ARE BEING HELD BUT, ABOVE ALL, RETURN SAFELY WITH ANY INFORMATION YOU GATHER.
DO NOT ENGAGE.
SO FAR, THE COMPOUND SEEMS COMPLETELY UNGUARDED. WE'RE HEADING IN FOR A CLOSER LOOK.
ALL RIGHT, TROOPER. BUT PROCEED WITH CAUTION.
CAPTAIN, THERE'S NOTHING HERE.
OH, THE POOR VONG. MAYBE THEY SAW US COMING AND RAN AWAY LIKE LITTLE BABIES?
ANYONE FROM THE HEART CAN TELL YOU, THE VONG DON'T RUN. THEY KEEP COMING. THEY'LL TRAMPLE EACH OTHER TO GET AT THEIR ENEMY.
STOP.

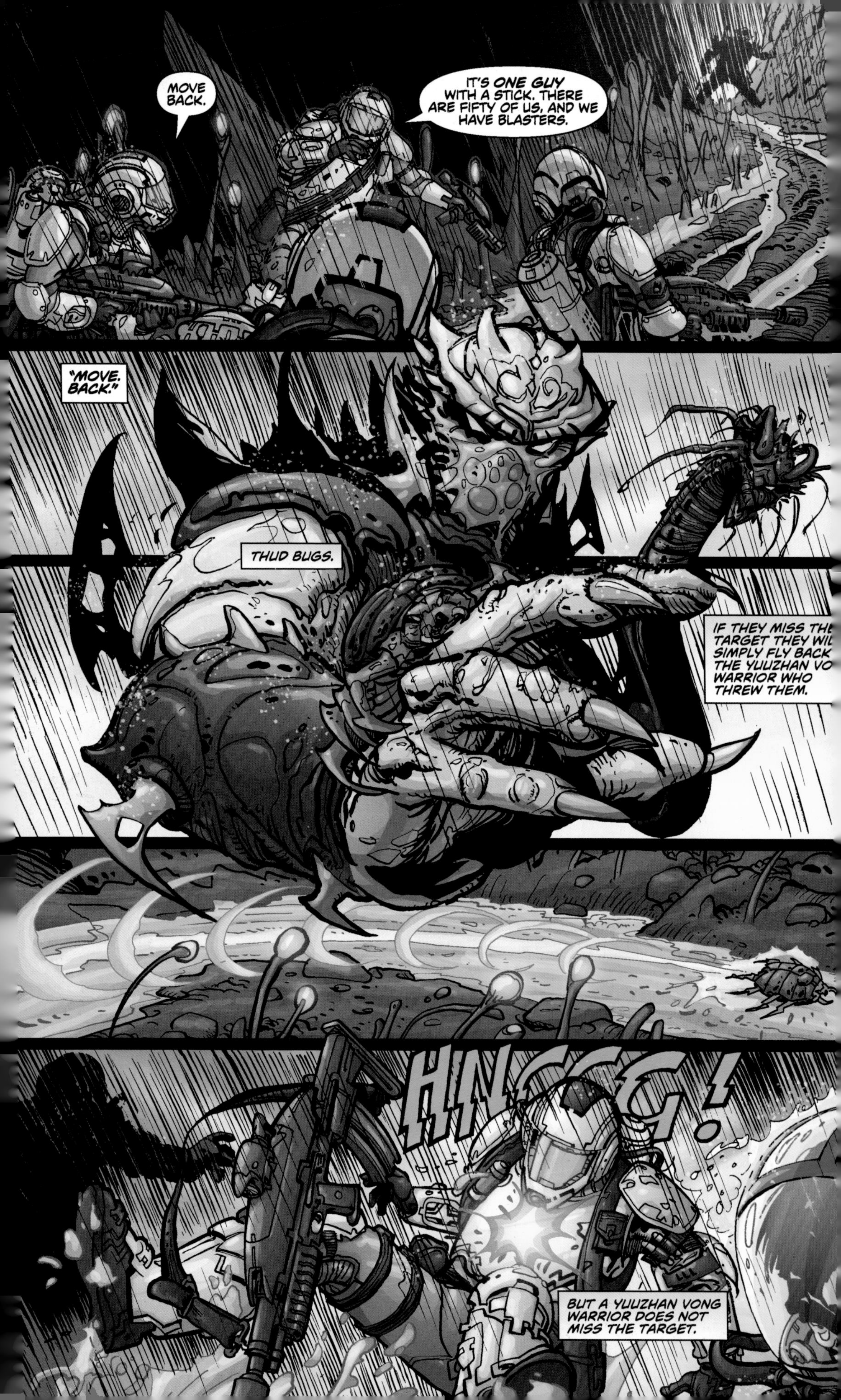
MOVE BACK.
IT'S ONE GUY WITH A STICK. THERE ARE FIFTY OF US, AND WE HAVE BLASTERS.
"MOVE. BACK."
THUD BUGS.
IF THEY MISS THE TARGET THEY WIL SIMPLY FLY BACK THE YUUZHAN VO WARRIOR WHO THREW THEM.
HNGGG!
BUT A YUUZHAN VONG WARRIOR DOES NOT MISS THE TARGET.

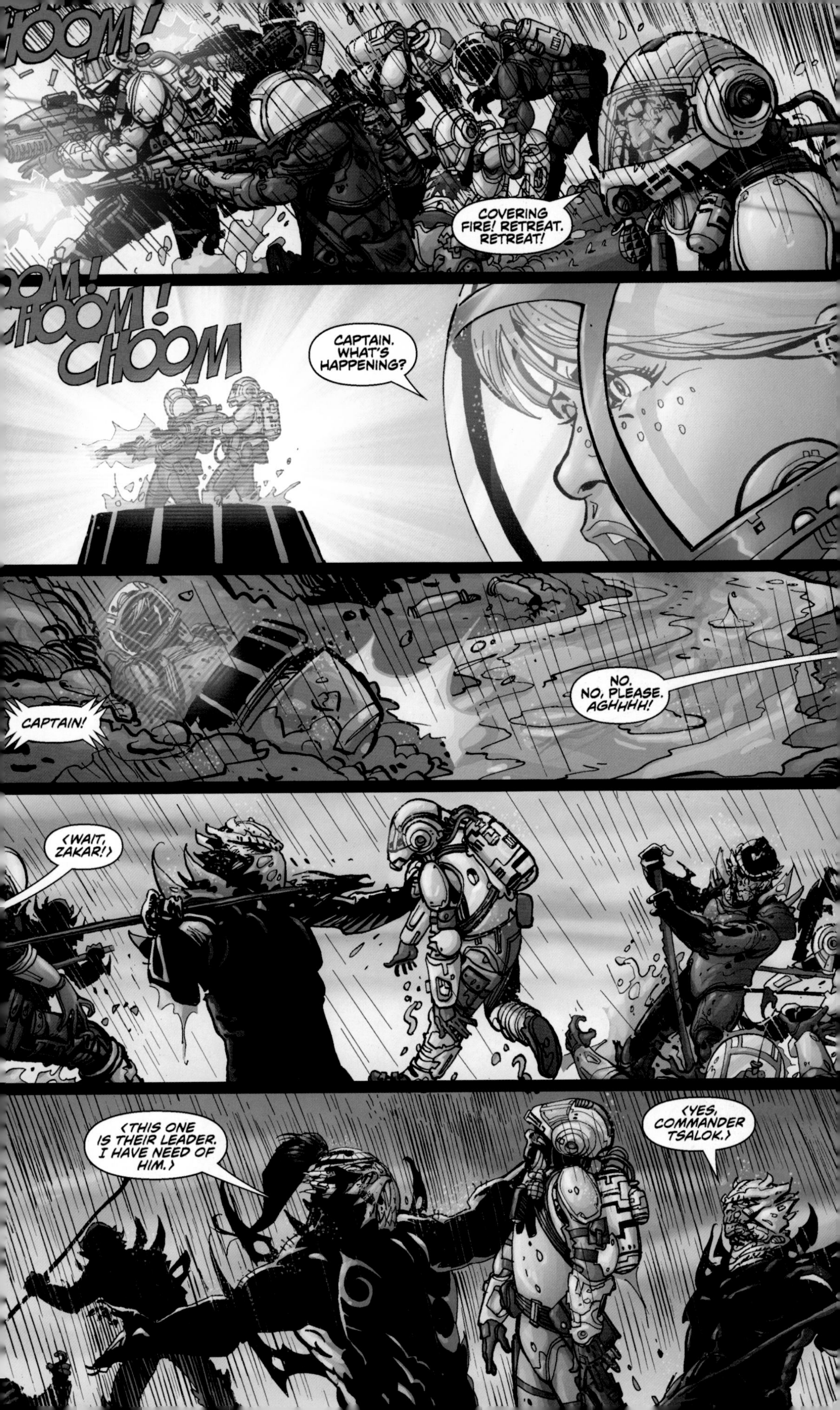
CHOOM!
COVERING FIRE! RETREAT. RETREAT!
CHOOM! CHOOM! CHOOM
CAPTAIN. WHAT'S HAPPENING?
CAPTAIN!
NO. NO, PLEASE. AGHHHH!
<WAIT, ZAKAR!>
<THIS ONE IS THEIR LEADER. I HAVE NEED OF HIM.>
<YES, COMMANDER TSALOK.>

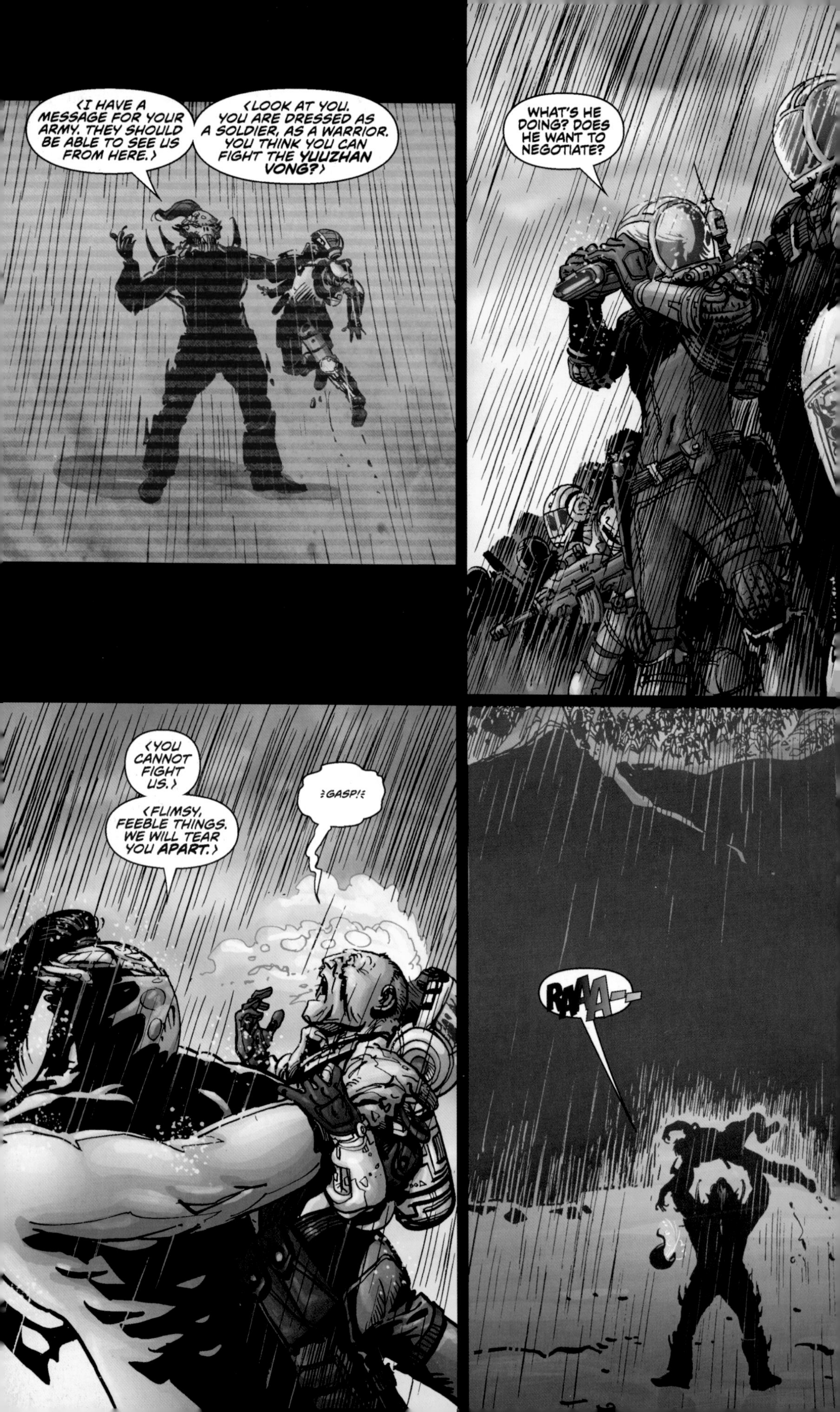
‹I HAVE A MESSAGE FOR YOUR ARMY. THEY SHOULD BE ABLE TO SEE US FROM HERE.›
‹LOOK AT YOU. YOU ARE DRESSED AS A SOLDIER, AS A WARRIOR. YOU THINK YOU CAN FIGHT THE YUUZHAN VONG?›
WHAT'S HE DOING? DOES HE WANT TO NEGOTIATE?
‹YOU CANNOT FIGHT US.›
‹FLIMSY, FEEBLE THINGS. WE WILL TEAR YOU APART.›
GASP!
RAAA--

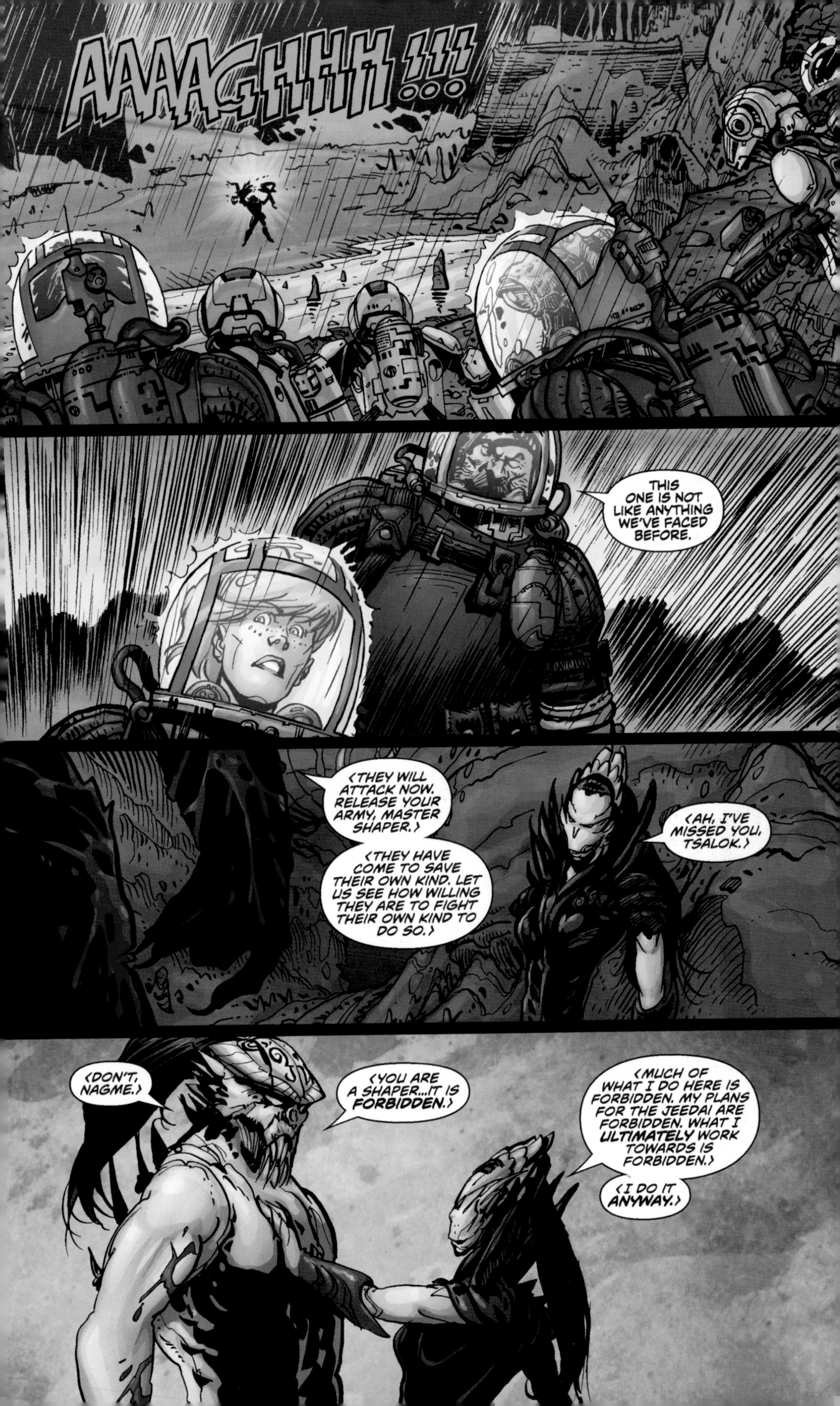
AAAAGHHHH!!!...
THIS ONE IS NOT LIKE ANYTHING WE'VE FACED BEFORE.
‹THEY WILL ATTACK NOW. RELEASE YOUR ARMY, MASTER SHAPER.›
‹THEY HAVE COME TO SAVE THEIR OWN KIND. LET US SEE HOW WILLING THEY ARE TO FIGHT THEIR OWN KIND TO DO SO.›
‹AH, I'VE MISSED YOU, TSALOK.›
‹DON'T, NAGME.›
‹YOU ARE A SHAPER...IT IS **FORBIDDEN**.›
‹MUCH OF WHAT I DO HERE IS FORBIDDEN. MY PLANS FOR THE JEEDAI ARE FORBIDDEN. WHAT I **ULTIMATELY** WORK TOWARDS IS FORBIDDEN.›
‹I DO IT **ANYWAY**.›

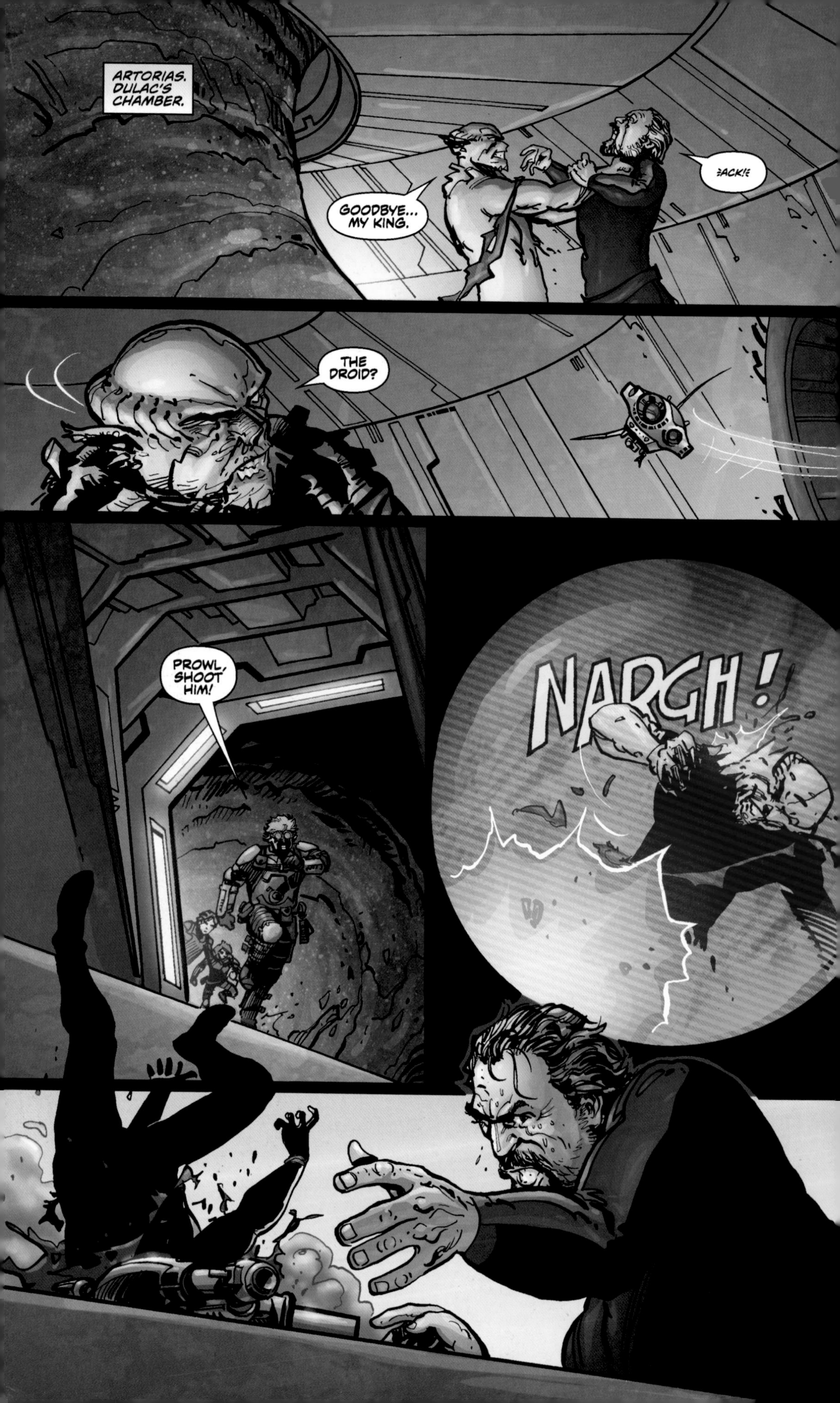
ARTORIAS. DULAC'S CHAMBER.
GOODBYE... MY KING.
ACK!
THE DROID?
PROWL, SHOOT HIM!
NARGH!

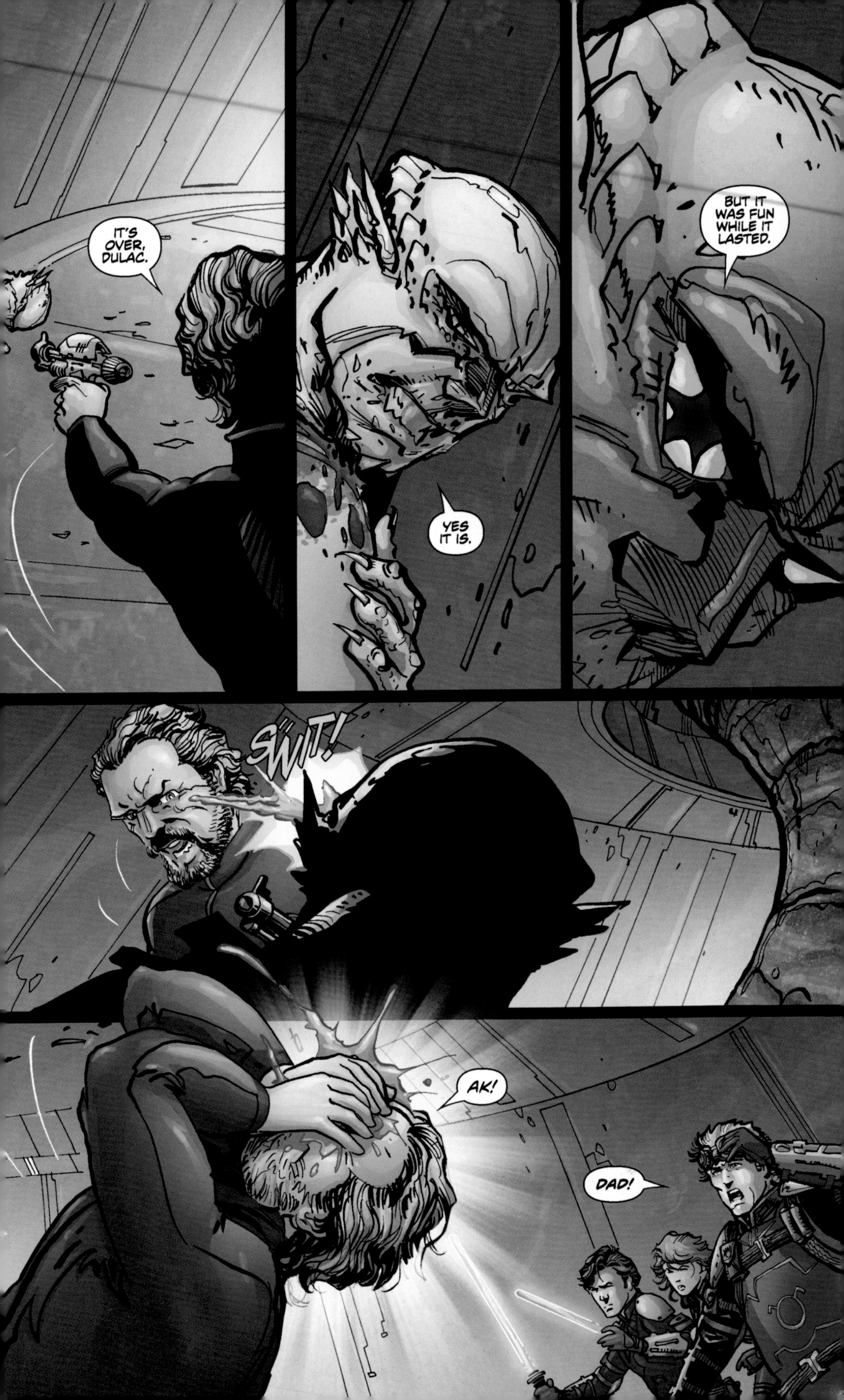
IT'S OVER, DULAC.
YES IT IS.
BUT IT WAS FUN WHILE IT LASTED.
SWIT!
AK!
DAD!

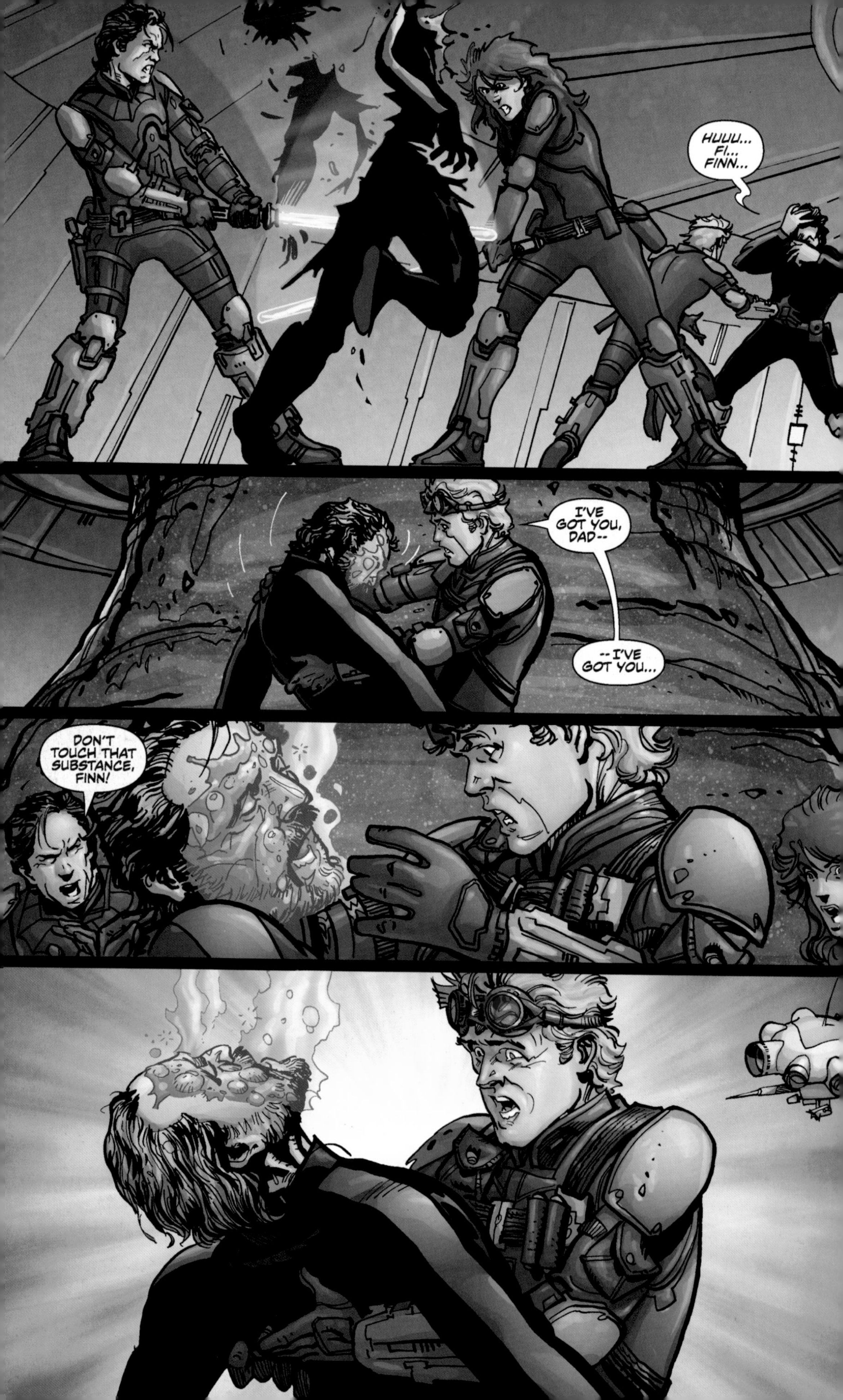
HUUU... FI... FINN...
I'VE GOT YOU, DAD--
--I'VE GOT YOU...
DON'T TOUCH THAT SUBSTANCE, FINN!

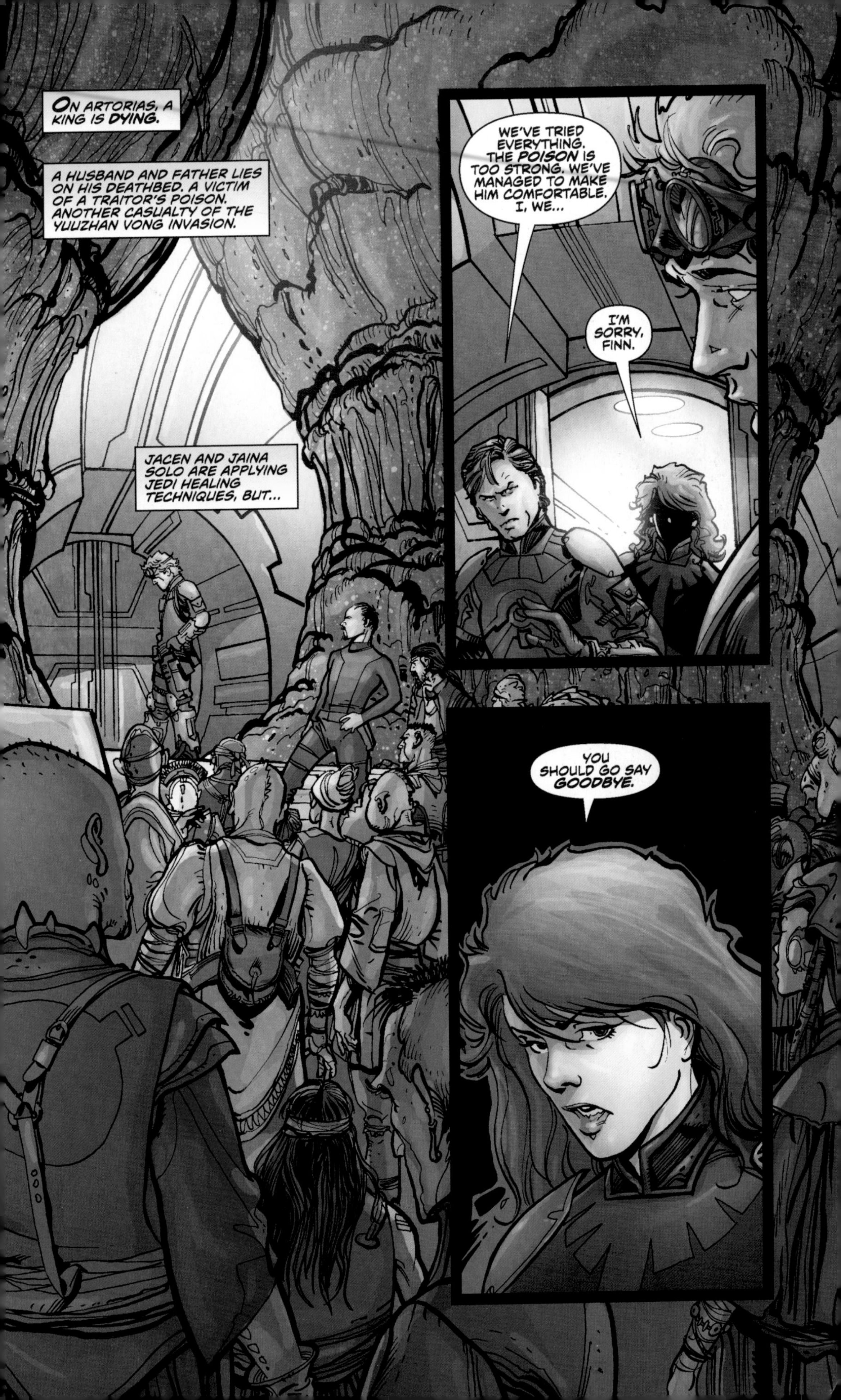
ON ARTORIAS, A KING IS DYING.
A HUSBAND AND FATHER LIES ON HIS DEATHBED. A VICTIM OF A TRAITOR'S POISON. ANOTHER CASUALTY OF THE YUUZHAN VONG INVASION.
JACEN AND JAINA SOLO ARE APPLYING JEDI HEALING TECHNIQUES, BUT...
WE'VE TRIED EVERYTHING. THE POISON IS TOO STRONG. WE'VE MANAGED TO MAKE HIM COMFORTABLE. I, WE...
I'M SORRY, FINN.
YOU SHOULD GO SAY GOODBYE.

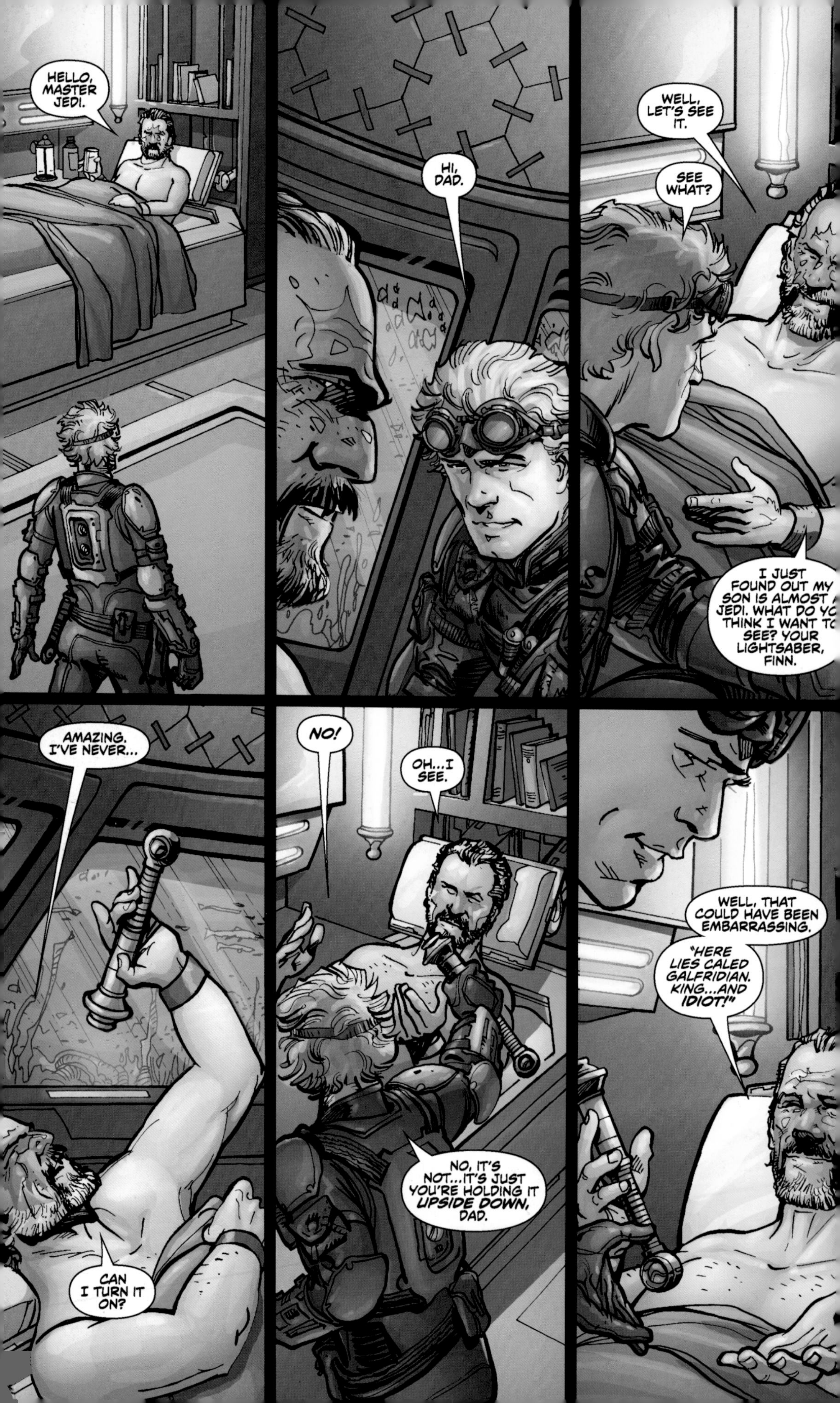
HELLO, MASTER JEDI.
HI, DAD.
WELL, LET'S SEE IT.
SEE WHAT?
I JUST FOUND OUT MY SON IS ALMOST A JEDI. WHAT DO YOU THINK I WANT TO SEE? YOUR LIGHTSABER, FINN.
AMAZING. I'VE NEVER...
CAN I TURN IT ON?
NO!
OH...I SEE.
NO, IT'S NOT...IT'S JUST YOU'RE HOLDING IT UPSIDE DOWN, DAD.
WELL, THAT COULD HAVE BEEN EMBARRASSING.
"HERE LIES CALED GALFRIDIAN. KING...AND IDIOT!"

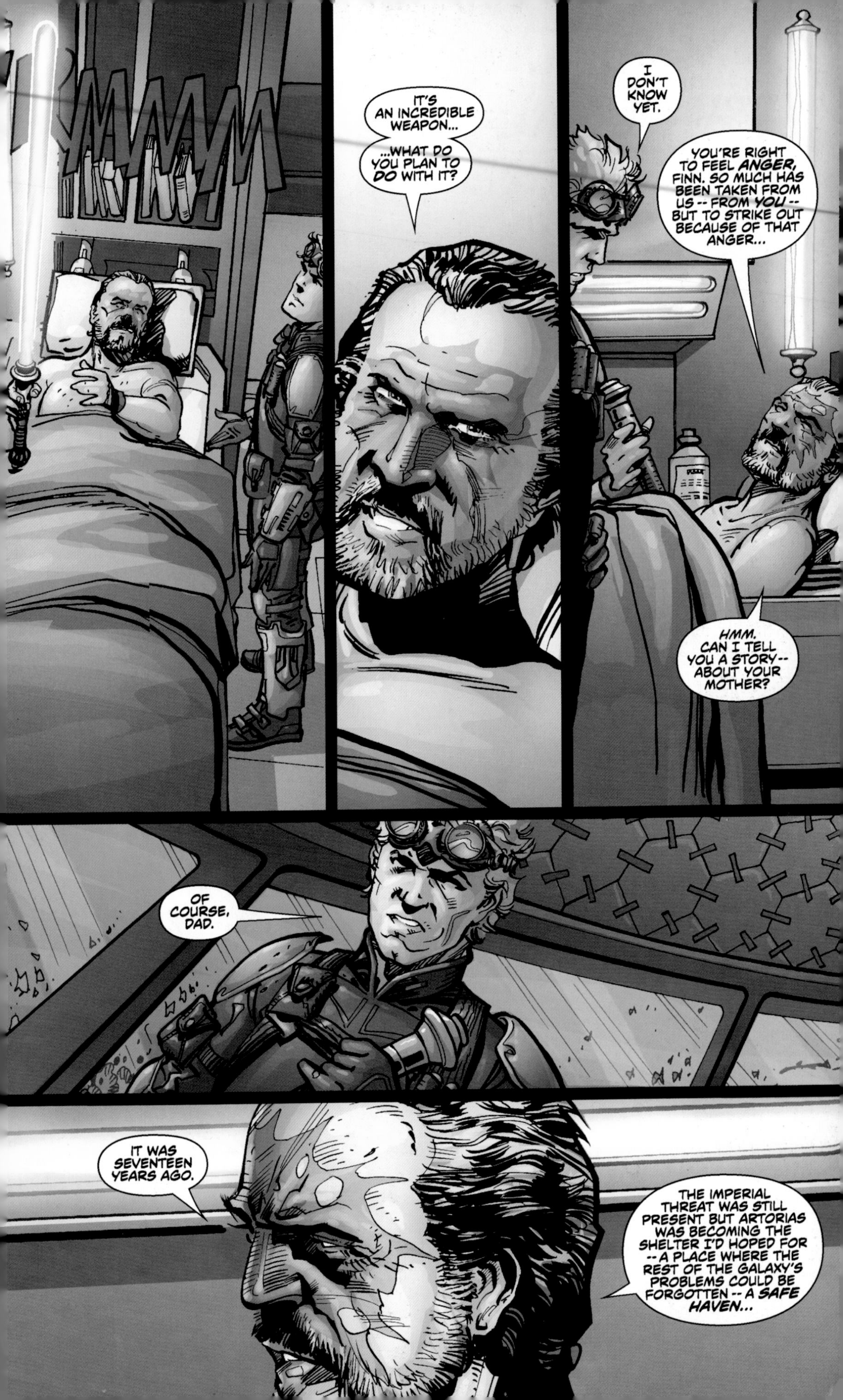

VMMMMM
IT'S AN INCREDIBLE WEAPON...
...WHAT DO YOU PLAN TO *DO* WITH IT?
I DON'T KNOW YET.
YOU'RE RIGHT TO FEEL *ANGER*, FINN. SO MUCH HAS BEEN TAKEN FROM US -- FROM *YOU* -- BUT TO STRIKE OUT BECAUSE OF THAT ANGER...
HMM. CAN I TELL YOU A STORY-- ABOUT YOUR MOTHER?
OF COURSE, DAD.
IT WAS SEVENTEEN YEARS AGO.
THE IMPERIAL THREAT WAS STILL PRESENT BUT ARTORIAS WAS BECOMING THE SHELTER I'D HOPED FOR -- A PLACE WHERE THE REST OF THE GALAXY'S PROBLEMS COULD BE FORGOTTEN -- A *SAFE HAVEN*...

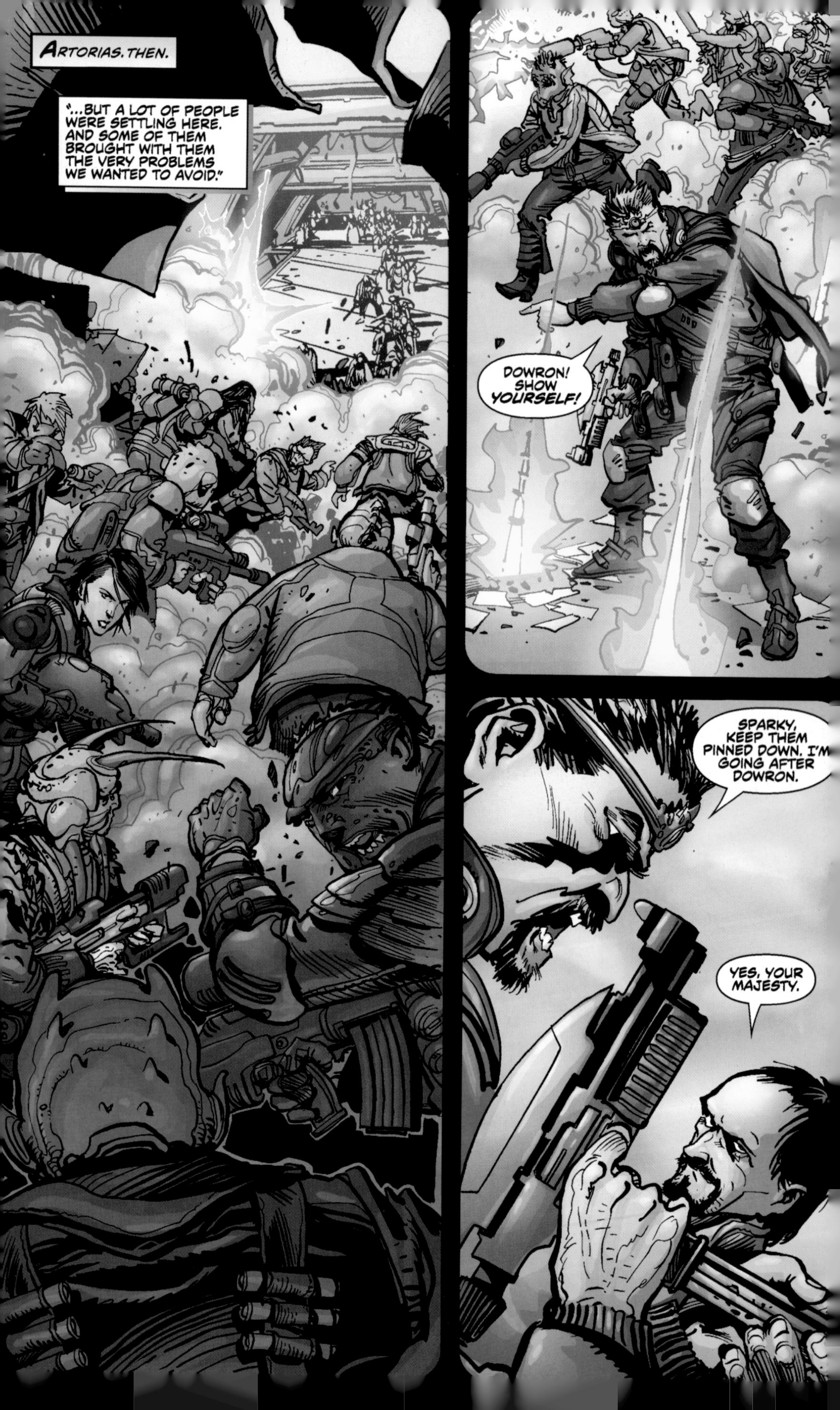
ARTORIAS. THEN.
"...BUT A LOT OF PEOPLE WERE SETTLING HERE. AND SOME OF THEM BROUGHT WITH THEM THE VERY PROBLEMS WE WANTED TO AVOID."
DOWRON! SHOW YOURSELF!
SPARKY, KEEP THEM PINNED DOWN. I'M GOING AFTER DOWRON.
YES, YOUR MAJESTY.

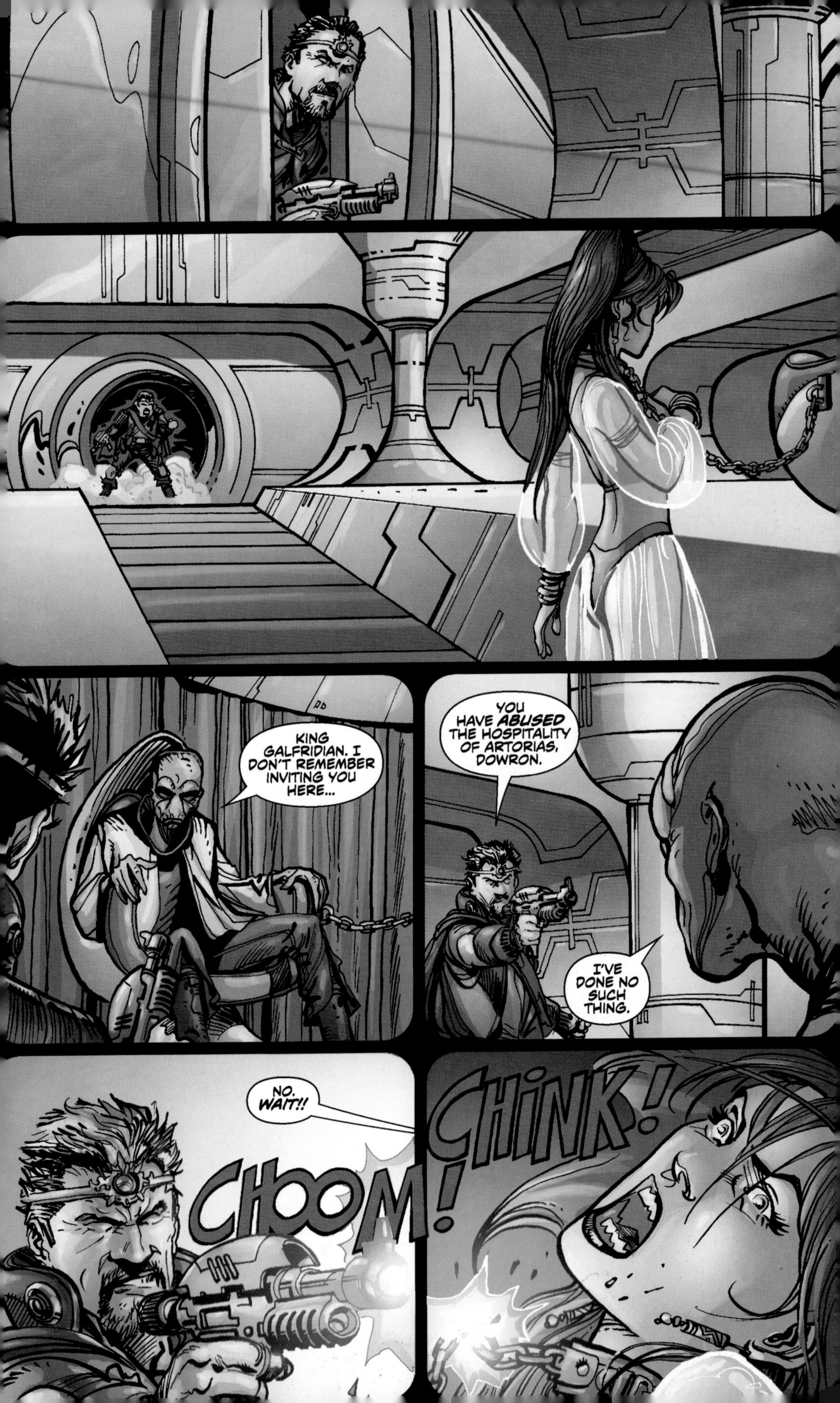
KING GALFRIDIAN. I DON'T REMEMBER INVITING YOU HERE...
YOU HAVE ABUSED THE HOSPITALITY OF ARTORIAS, DOWRON.
I'VE DONE NO SUCH THING.
NO. WAIT!!
CHOOM!
CHINK!

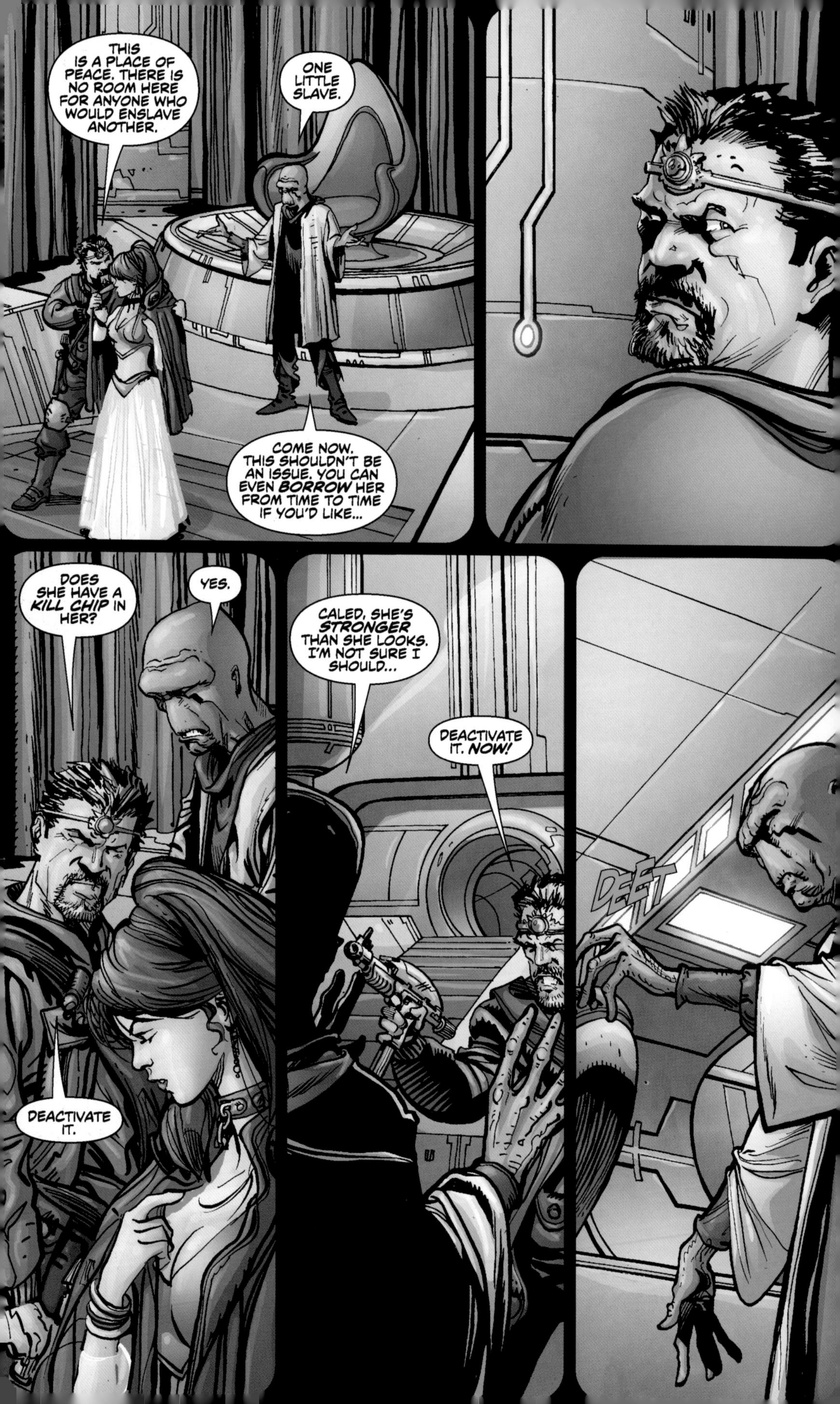

THIS IS A PLACE OF PEACE. THERE IS NO ROOM HERE FOR ANYONE WHO WOULD ENSLAVE ANOTHER.
ONE LITTLE SLAVE.
COME NOW. THIS SHOULDN'T BE AN ISSUE. YOU CAN EVEN BORROW HER FROM TIME TO TIME IF YOU'D LIKE...
DOES SHE HAVE A KILL CHIP IN HER?
YES.
DEACTIVATE IT.
CALED, SHE'S STRONGER THAN SHE LOOKS. I'M NOT SURE I SHOULD...
DEACTIVATE IT. NOW!
DEET

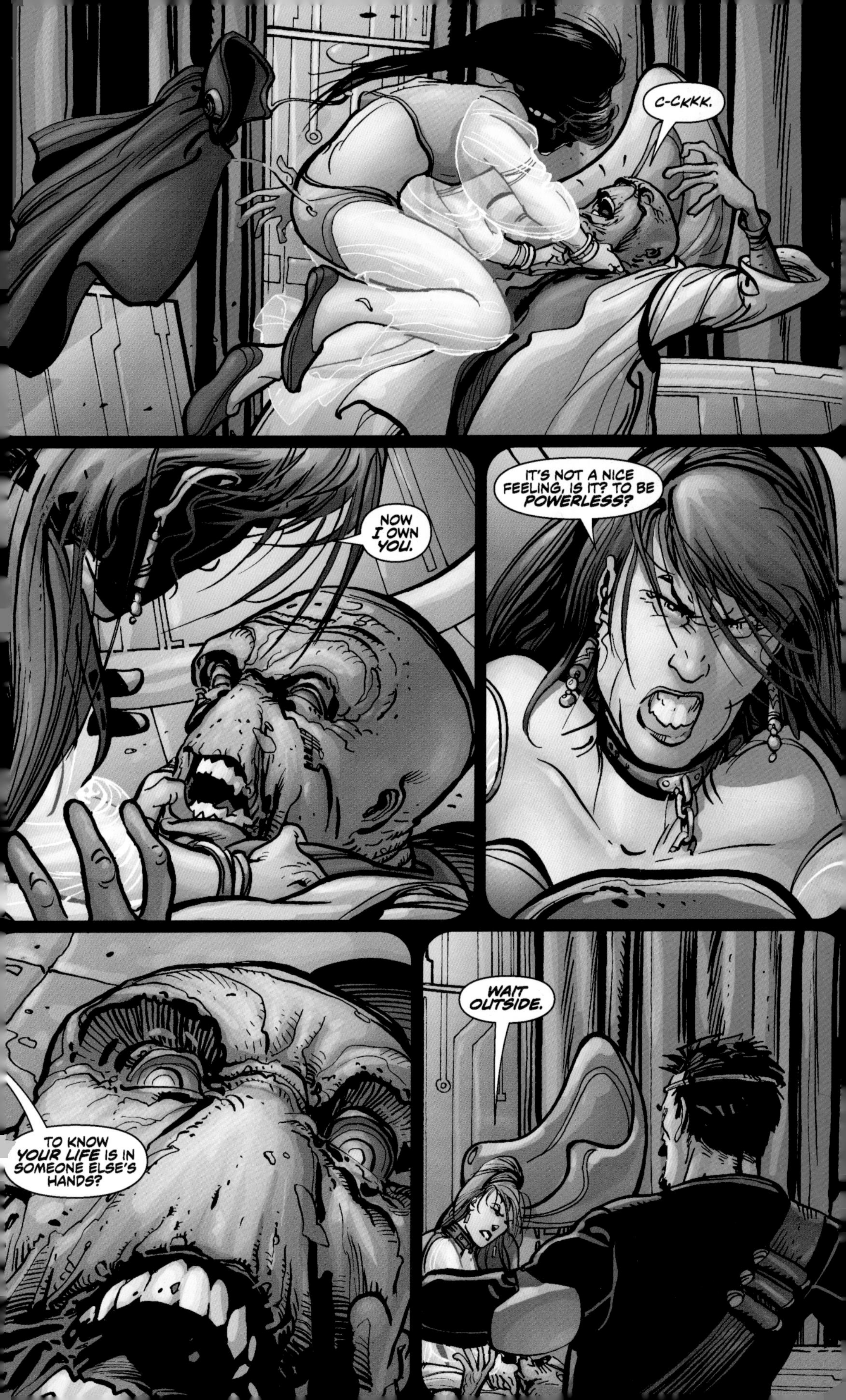
C-CKKK.
NOW I OWN YOU.
IT'S NOT A NICE FEELING, IS IT? TO BE POWERLESS?
TO KNOW YOUR LIFE IS IN SOMEONE ELSE'S HANDS?
WAIT OUTSIDE.

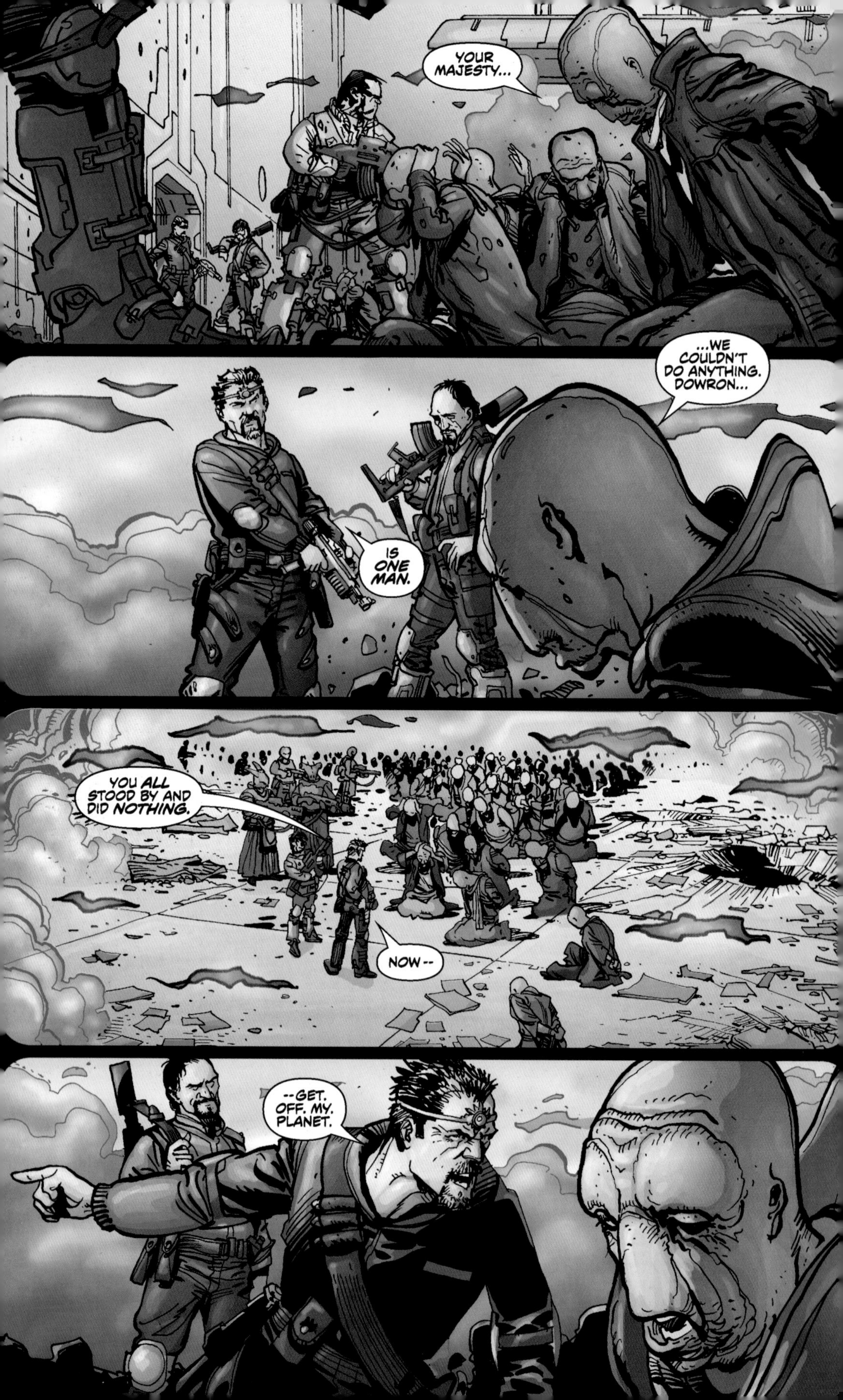
YOUR MAJESTY...
...WE COULDN'T DO ANYTHING. DOWRON...
IS ONE MAN.
YOU ALL STOOD BY AND DID NOTHING.
NOW--
--GET. OFF. MY. PLANET.

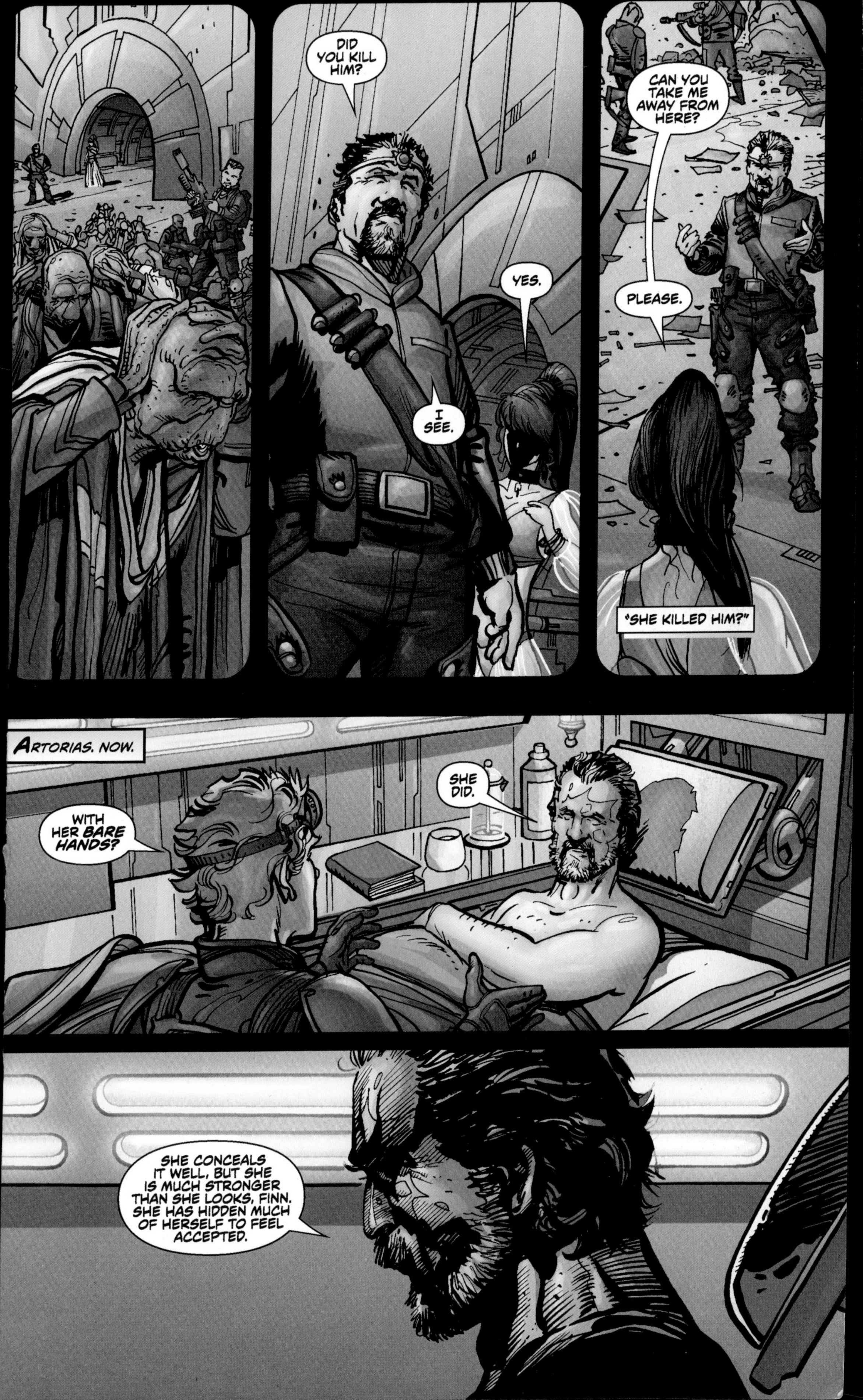
DID YOU KILL HIM?
YES.
I SEE.
CAN YOU TAKE ME AWAY FROM HERE?
PLEASE.
"SHE KILLED HIM?"
ARTORIAS. NOW.
SHE DID.
WITH HER *BARE HANDS?*
SHE CONCEALS IT WELL, BUT SHE IS MUCH STRONGER THAN SHE LOOKS, FINN. SHE HAS HIDDEN MUCH OF HERSELF TO FEEL ACCEPTED.

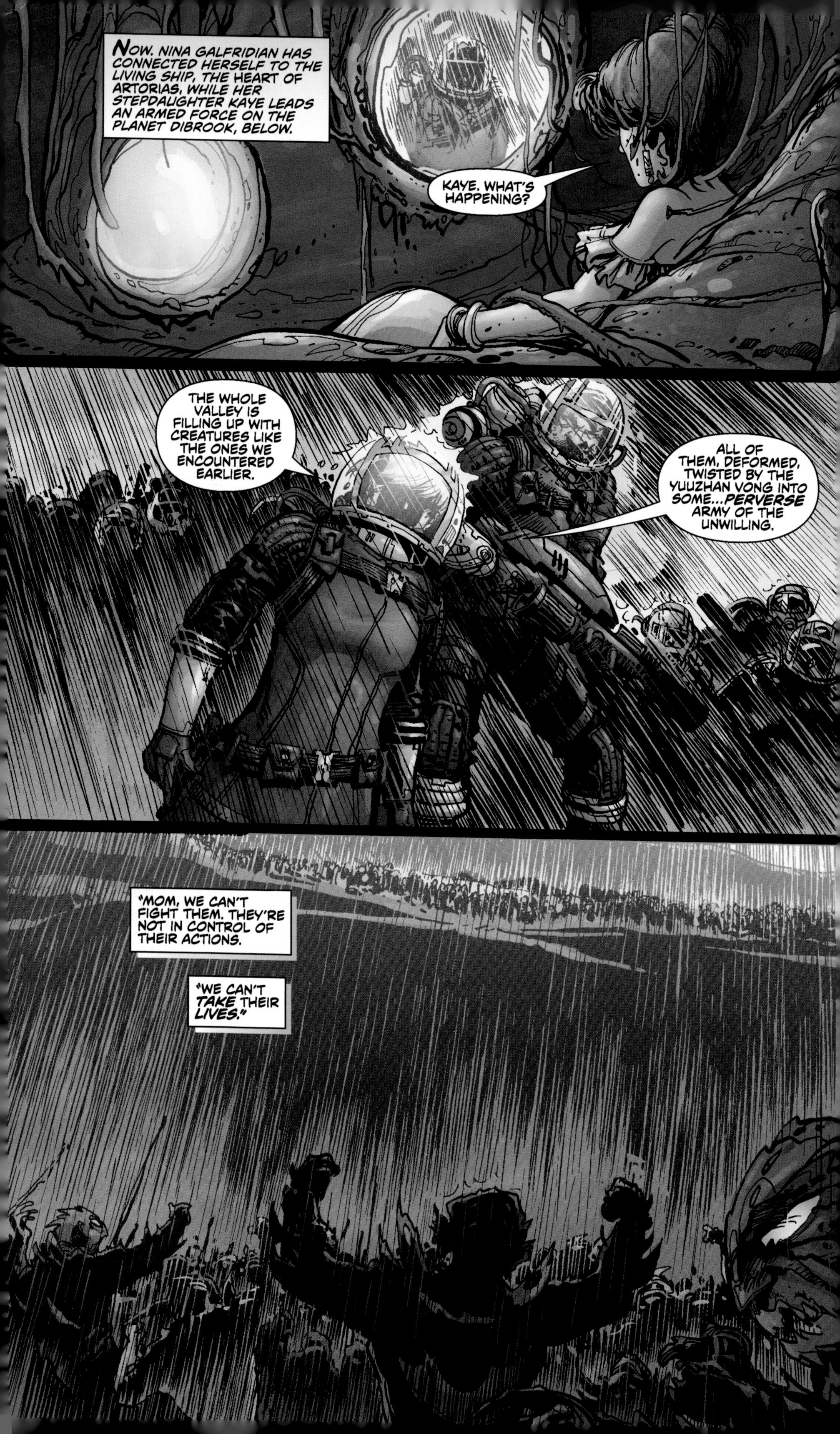
NOW. NINA GALFRIDIAN HAS CONNECTED HERSELF TO THE LIVING SHIP, THE HEART OF ARTORIAS, WHILE HER STEPDAUGHTER KAYE LEADS AN ARMED FORCE ON THE PLANET DIBROOK, BELOW.
KAYE. WHAT'S HAPPENING?
THE WHOLE VALLEY IS FILLING UP WITH CREATURES LIKE THE ONES WE ENCOUNTERED EARLIER.
ALL OF THEM, DEFORMED, TWISTED BY THE YUUZHAN VONG INTO SOME... PERVERSE ARMY OF THE UNWILLING.
"MOM, WE CAN'T FIGHT THEM. THEY'RE NOT IN CONTROL OF THEIR ACTIONS.
"WE CAN'T TAKE THEIR LIVES."

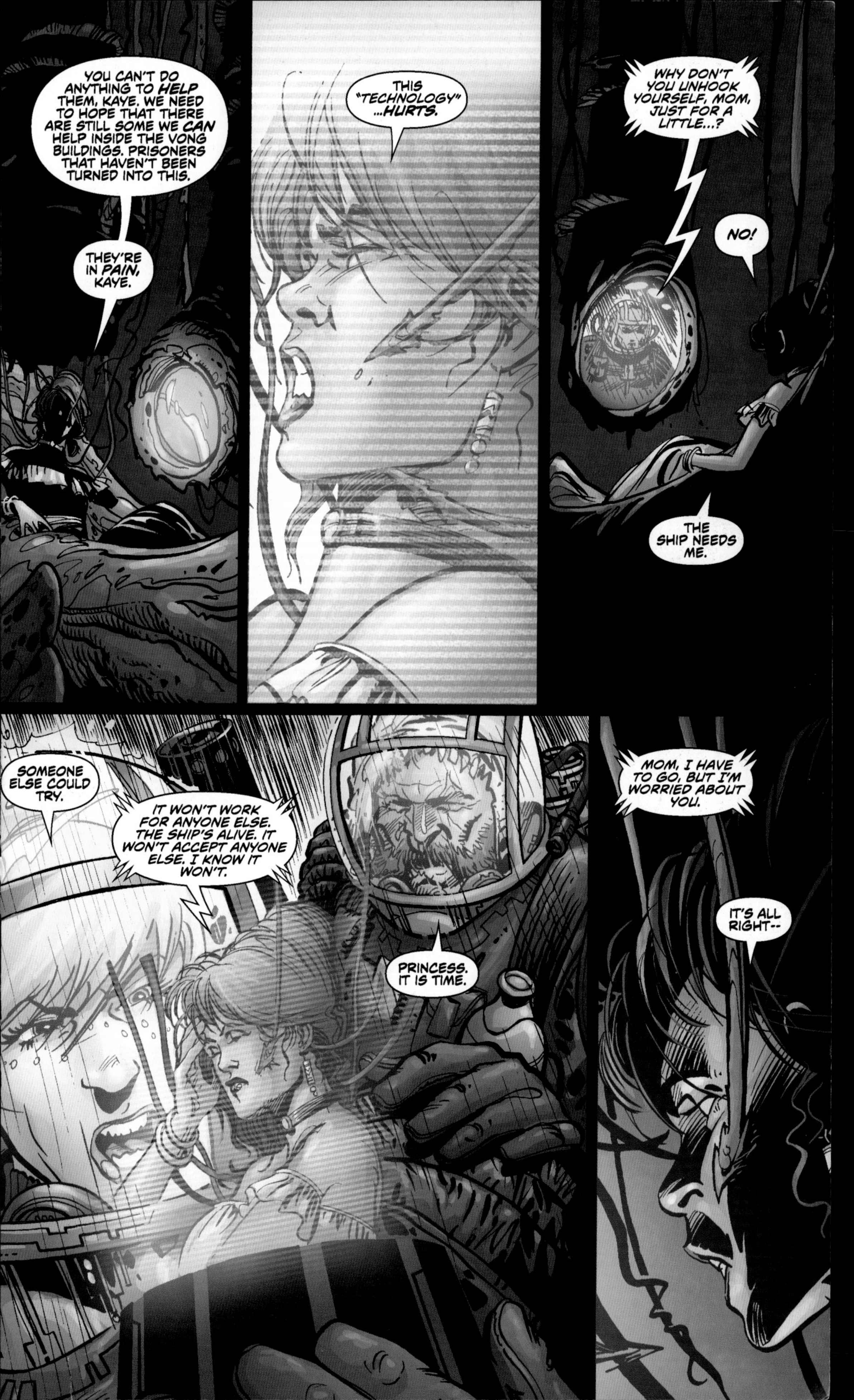

YOU CAN'T DO ANYTHING TO HELP THEM, KAYE. WE NEED TO HOPE THAT THERE ARE STILL SOME WE CAN HELP INSIDE THE VONG BUILDINGS. PRISONERS THAT HAVEN'T BEEN TURNED INTO THIS.
THEY'RE IN PAIN, KAYE.
THIS "TECHNOLOGY" ...HURTS.
WHY DON'T YOU UNHOOK YOURSELF, MOM, JUST FOR A LITTLE...?
NO!
THE SHIP NEEDS ME.
SOMEONE ELSE COULD TRY.
IT WON'T WORK FOR ANYONE ELSE. THE SHIP'S ALIVE. IT WON'T ACCEPT ANYONE ELSE. I KNOW IT WON'T.
PRINCESS. IT IS TIME.
MOM, I HAVE TO GO, BUT I'M WORRIED ABOUT YOU.
IT'S ALL RIGHT--

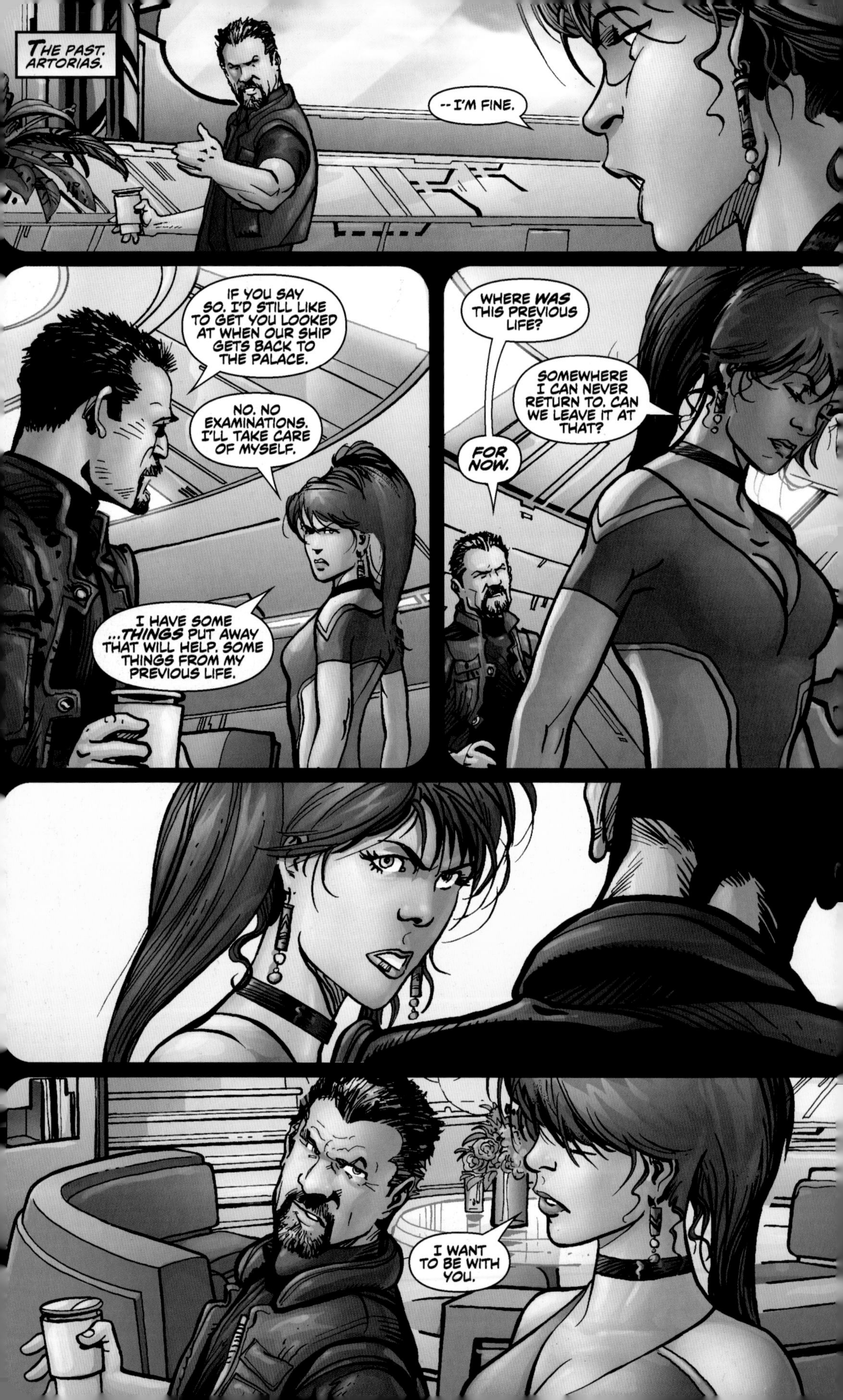
THE PAST. ARTORIAS.
-- I'M FINE.
IF YOU SAY SO. I'D STILL LIKE TO GET YOU LOOKED AT WHEN OUR SHIP GETS BACK TO THE PALACE.
NO. NO EXAMINATIONS. I'LL TAKE CARE OF MYSELF.
I HAVE SOME ...THINGS PUT AWAY THAT WILL HELP. SOME THINGS FROM MY PREVIOUS LIFE.
WHERE WAS THIS PREVIOUS LIFE?
SOMEWHERE I CAN NEVER RETURN TO. CAN WE LEAVE IT AT THAT?
FOR NOW.
I WANT TO BE WITH YOU.

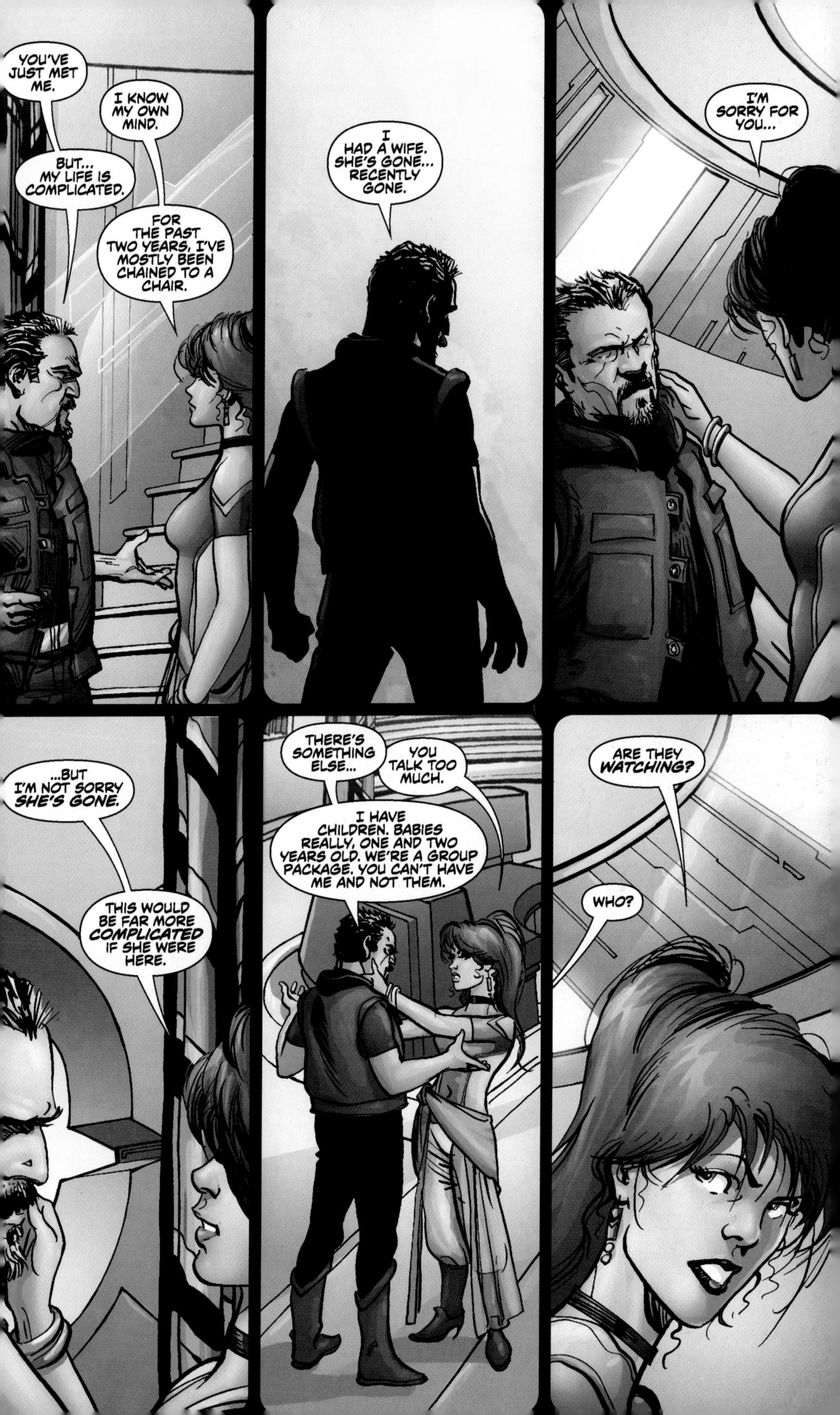
YOU'VE JUST MET ME.
I KNOW MY OWN MIND.
BUT... MY LIFE IS COMPLICATED.
FOR THE PAST TWO YEARS, I'VE MOSTLY BEEN CHAINED TO A CHAIR.
I HAD A WIFE. SHE'S GONE... RECENTLY GONE.
I'M SORRY FOR YOU...
...BUT I'M NOT SORRY *SHE'S GONE.*
THIS WOULD BE FAR MORE *COMPLICATED* IF SHE WERE HERE.
THERE'S SOMETHING ELSE...
YOU TALK TOO MUCH.
I HAVE CHILDREN. BABIES REALLY, ONE AND TWO YEARS OLD. WE'RE A GROUP PACKAGE. YOU CAN'T HAVE ME AND NOT THEM.
ARE THEY *WATCHING?*
WHO?

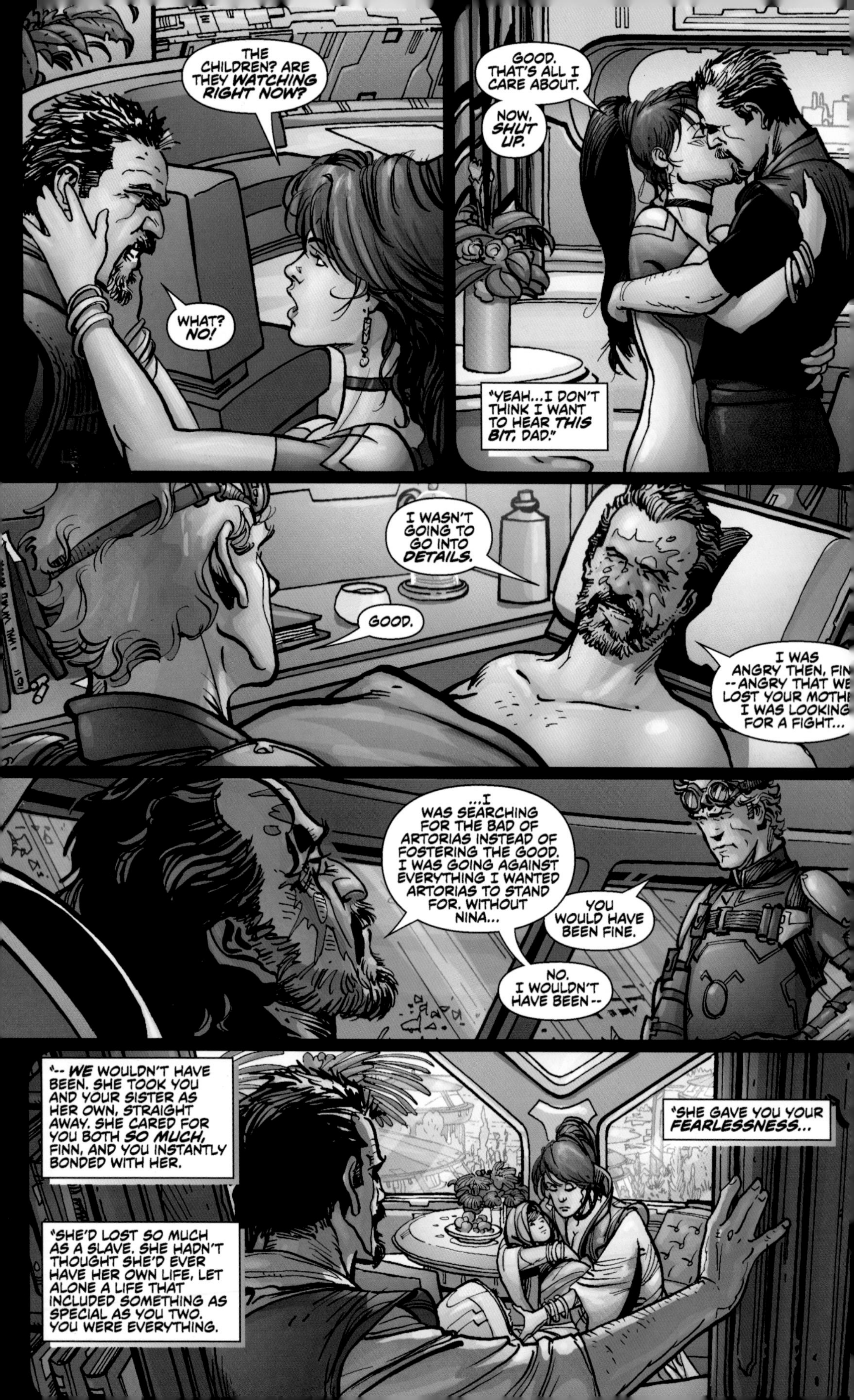

THE CHILDREN? ARE THEY WATCHING RIGHT NOW?
WHAT? NO!
GOOD. THAT'S ALL I CARE ABOUT.
NOW, SHUT UP.
"YEAH...I DON'T THINK I WANT TO HEAR THIS BIT, DAD."
I WASN'T GOING TO GO INTO DETAILS.
GOOD.
I WAS ANGRY THEN, FIN --ANGRY THAT WE LOST YOUR MOTH I WAS LOOKING FOR A FIGHT...
...I WAS SEARCHING FOR THE BAD OF ARTORIAS INSTEAD OF FOSTERING THE GOOD. I WAS GOING AGAINST EVERYTHING I WANTED ARTORIAS TO STAND FOR. WITHOUT NINA...
YOU WOULD HAVE BEEN FINE.
NO. I WOULDN'T HAVE BEEN--
"--WE WOULDN'T HAVE BEEN. SHE TOOK YOU AND YOUR SISTER AS HER OWN, STRAIGHT AWAY. SHE CARED FOR YOU BOTH SO MUCH, FINN, AND YOU INSTANTLY BONDED WITH HER.
"SHE'D LOST SO MUCH AS A SLAVE. SHE HADN'T THOUGHT SHE'D EVER HAVE HER OWN LIFE, LET ALONE A LIFE THAT INCLUDED SOMETHING AS SPECIAL AS YOU TWO. YOU WERE EVERYTHING.
"SHE GAVE YOU YOUR FEARLESSNESS...

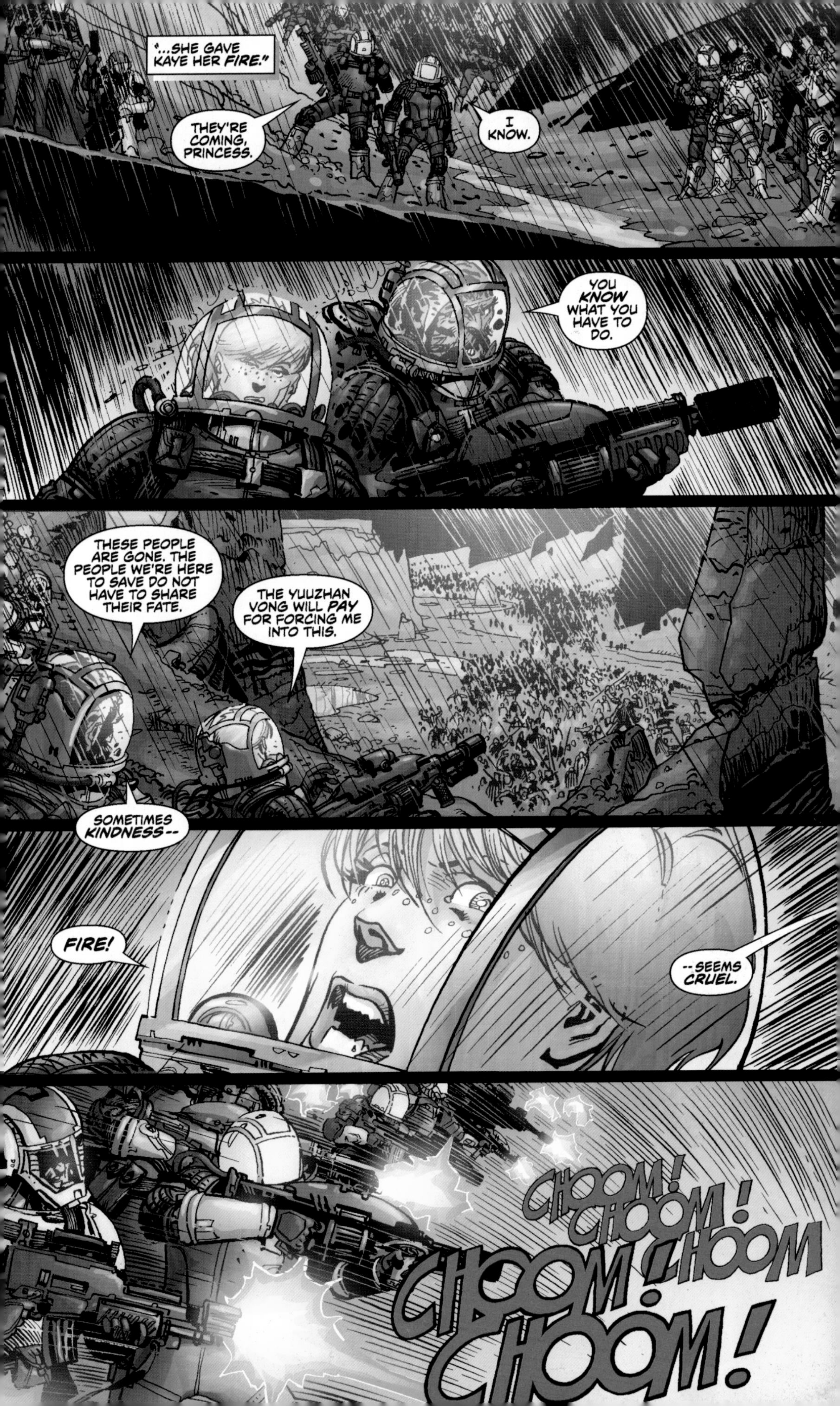
"...SHE GAVE KAYE HER FIRE."
THEY'RE COMING, PRINCESS.
I KNOW.
YOU KNOW WHAT YOU HAVE TO DO.
THESE PEOPLE ARE GONE. THE PEOPLE WE'RE HERE TO SAVE DO NOT HAVE TO SHARE THEIR FATE.
THE YUUZHAN VONG WILL PAY FOR FORCING ME INTO THIS.
SOMETIMES KINDNESS--
FIRE!
--SEEMS CRUEL.
CHOOM! CHOOM! CHOOM! CHOOM CHOOM!

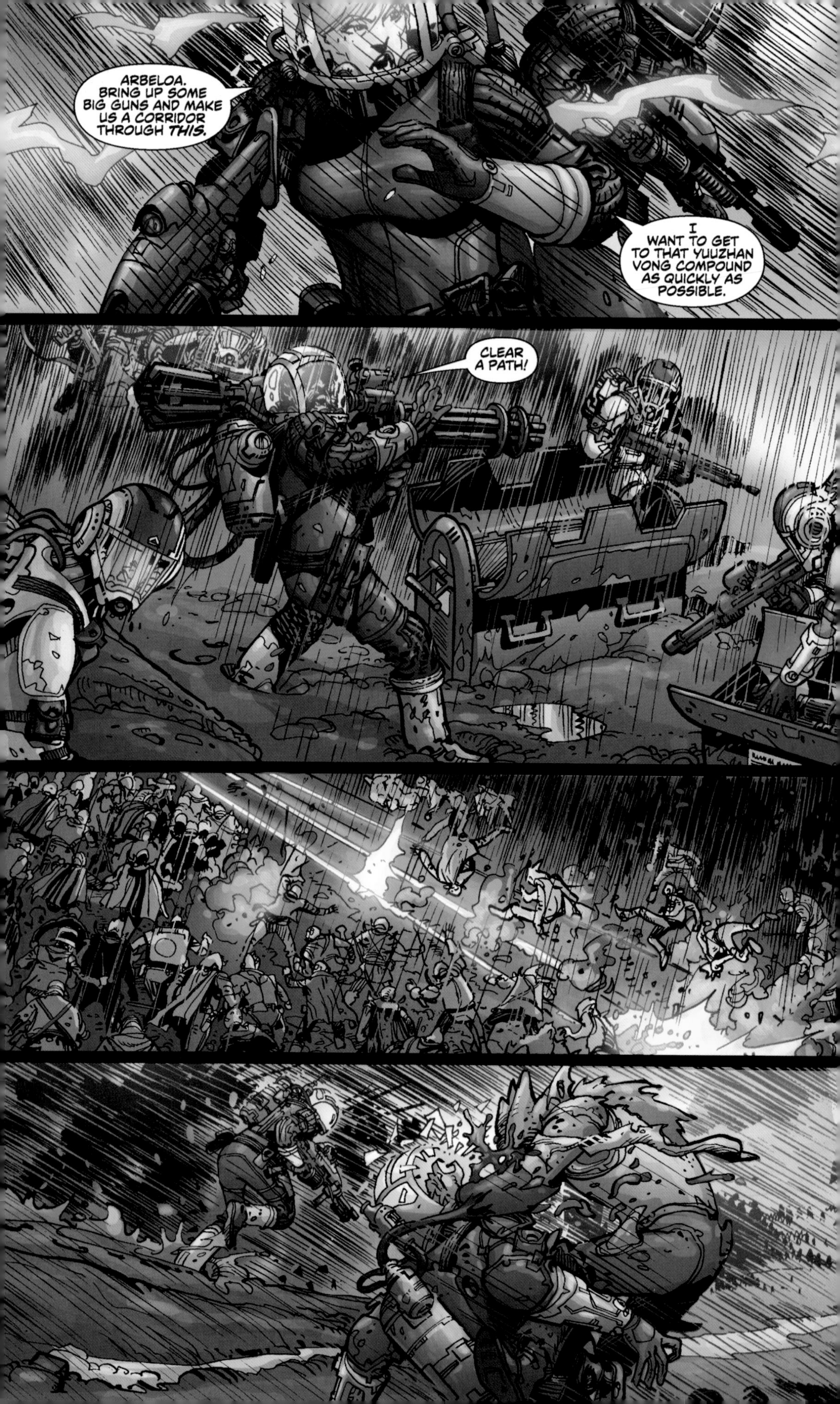
ARBELOA. BRING UP SOME BIG GUNS AND MAKE US A CORRIDOR THROUGH *THIS*.
I WANT TO GET TO THAT YUUZHAN VONG COMPOUND AS QUICKLY AS POSSIBLE.
CLEAR A PATH!

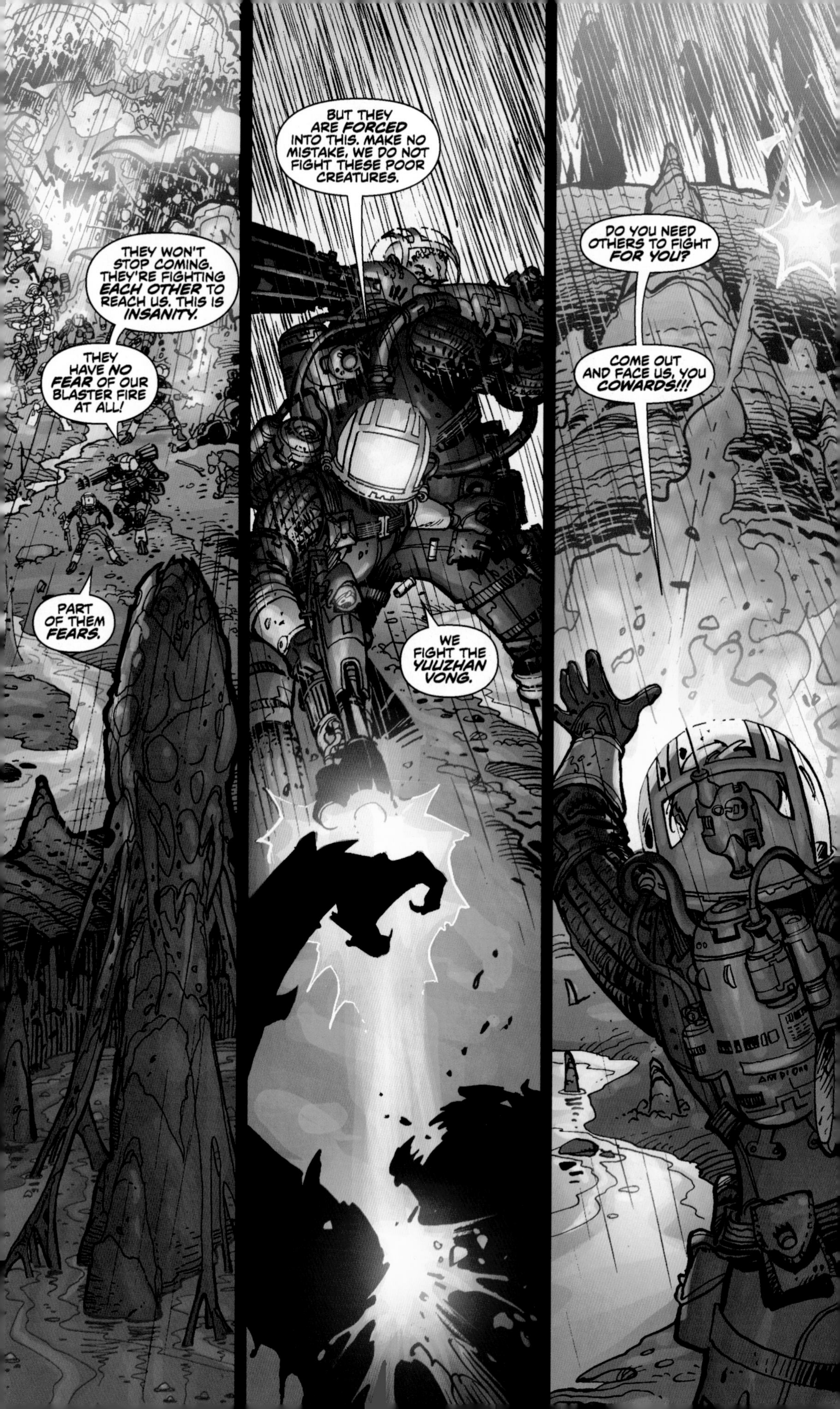
THEY WON'T STOP COMING. THEY'RE FIGHTING EACH OTHER TO REACH US. THIS IS INSANITY.
THEY HAVE NO FEAR OF OUR BLASTER FIRE AT ALL!
PART OF THEM FEARS.
BUT THEY ARE FORCED INTO THIS. MAKE NO MISTAKE, WE DO NOT FIGHT THESE POOR CREATURES.
WE FIGHT THE YUUZHAN VONG.
DO YOU NEED OTHERS TO FIGHT FOR YOU?
COME OUT AND FACE US, YOU COWARDS!!!

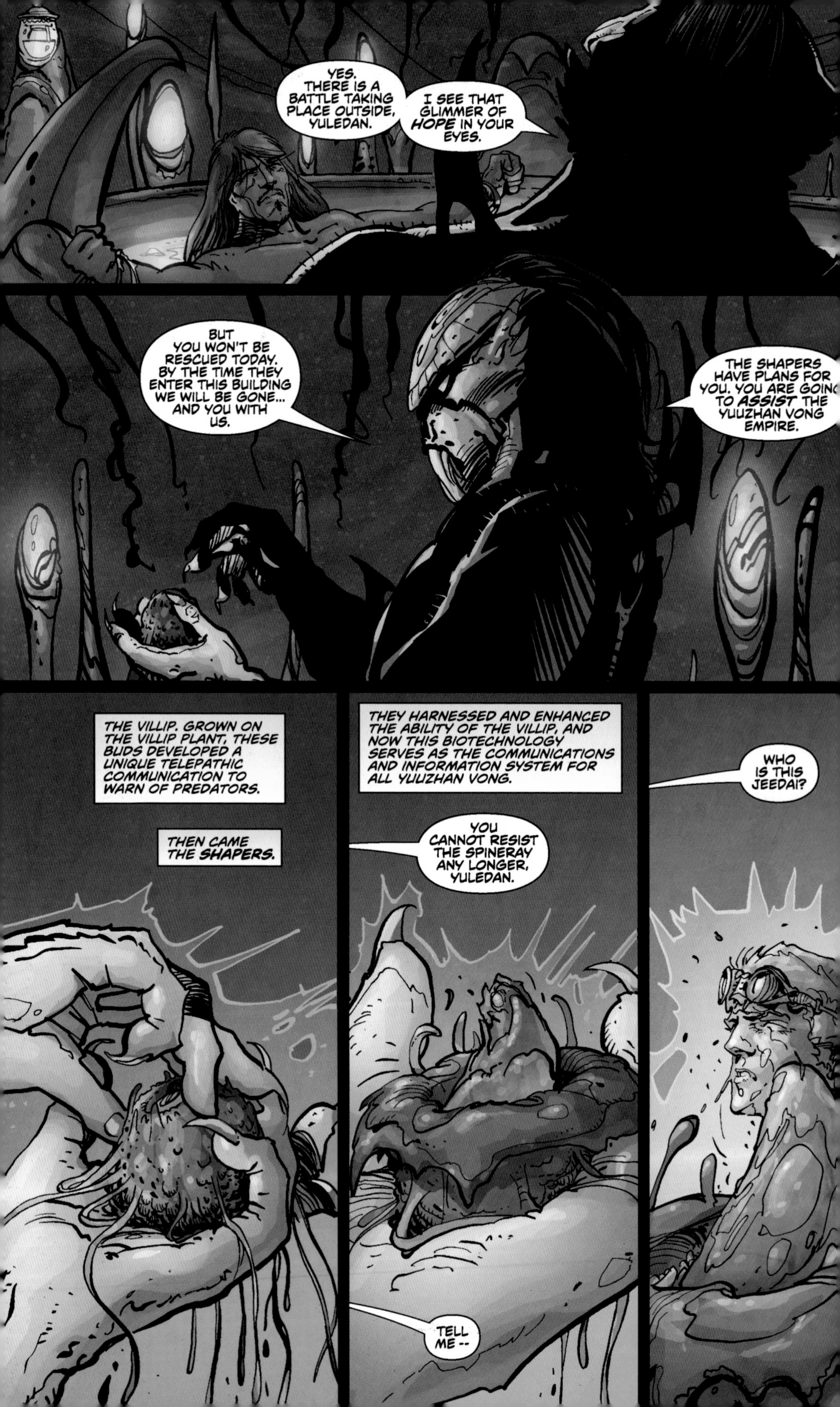
YES. THERE IS A BATTLE TAKING PLACE OUTSIDE, YULEDAN.
I SEE THAT GLIMMER OF HOPE IN YOUR EYES.
BUT YOU WON'T BE RESCUED TODAY. BY THE TIME THEY ENTER THIS BUILDING WE WILL BE GONE... AND YOU WITH US.
THE SHAPERS HAVE PLANS FOR YOU. YOU ARE GOING TO ASSIST THE YUUZHAN VONG EMPIRE.
THE VILLIP. GROWN ON THE VILLIP PLANT, THESE BUDS DEVELOPED A UNIQUE TELEPATHIC COMMUNICATION TO WARN OF PREDATORS.
THEN CAME THE SHAPERS.
THEY HARNESSED AND ENHANCED THE ABILITY OF THE VILLIP, AND NOW THIS BIOTECHNOLOGY SERVES AS THE COMMUNICATIONS AND INFORMATION SYSTEM FOR ALL YUUZHAN VONG.
YOU CANNOT RESIST THE SPINERAY ANY LONGER, YULEDAN.
TELL ME --
WHO IS THIS JEEDAI?

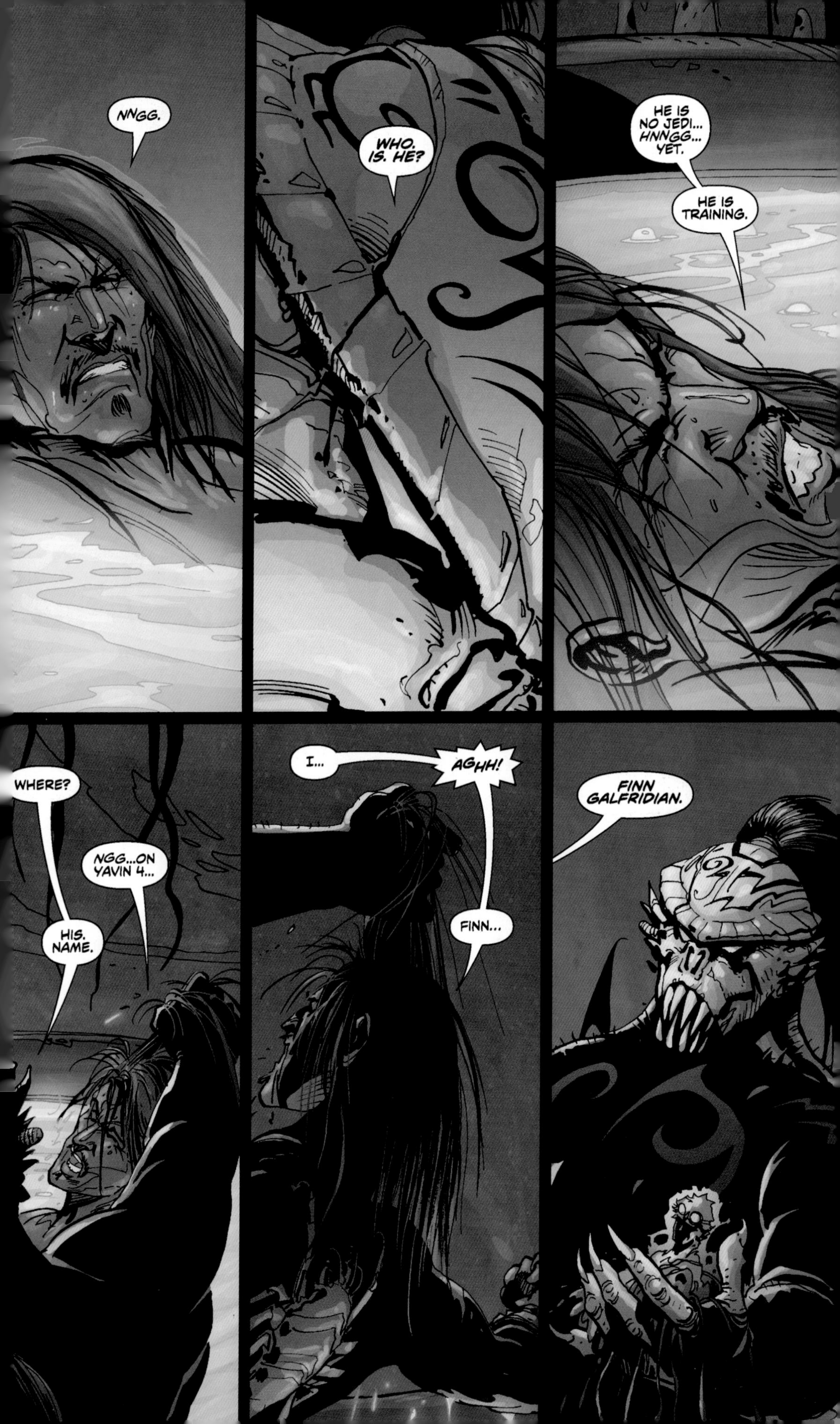
NNGG.
WHO. IS. HE?
HE IS NO JEDI... HNNGG... YET.
HE IS TRAINING.
WHERE?
NGG...ON YAVIN 4...
HIS. NAME.
I...
AGHH!
FINN...
FINN GALFRIDIAN.

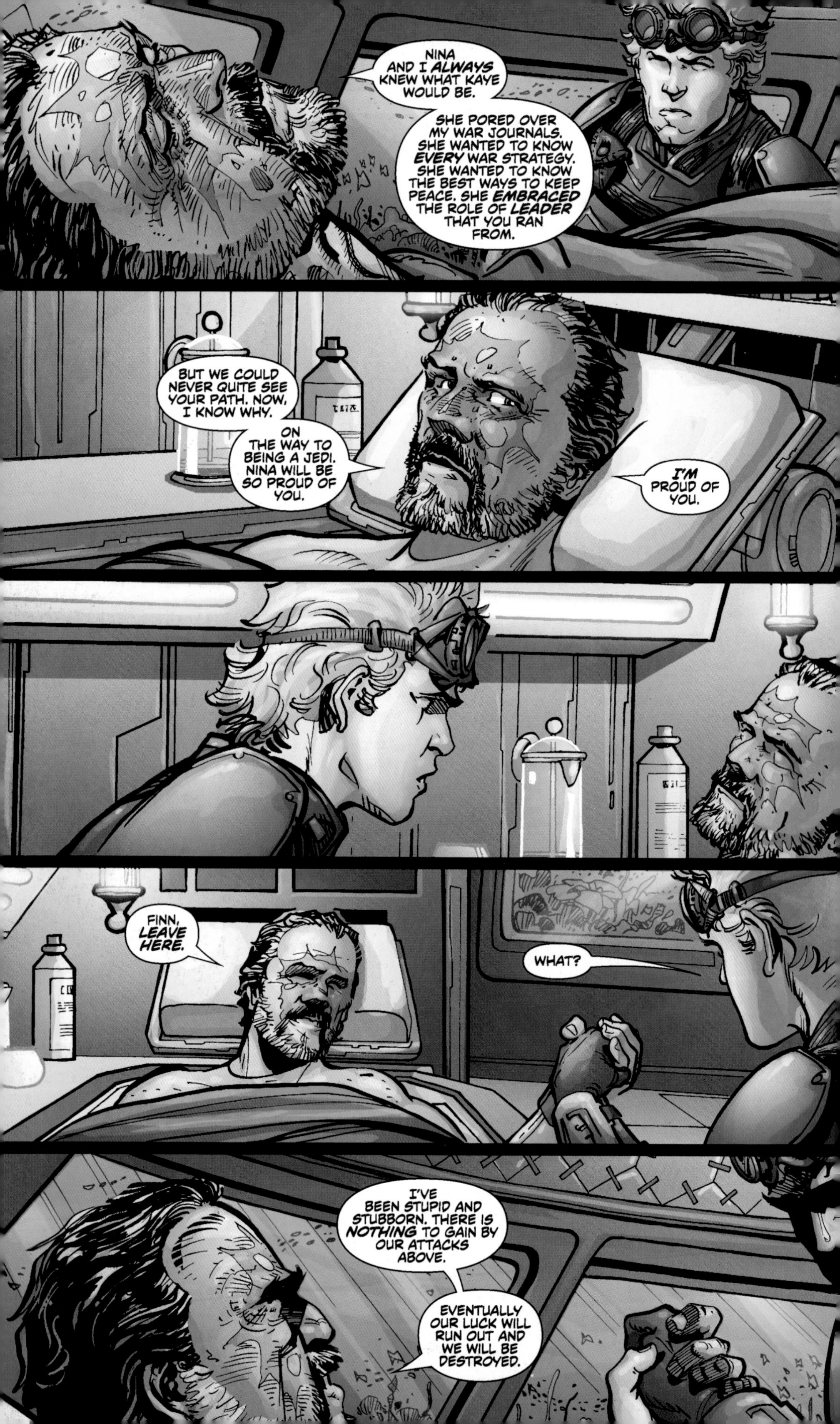
NINA AND I ALWAYS KNEW WHAT KAYE WOULD BE.
SHE PORED OVER MY WAR JOURNALS. SHE WANTED TO KNOW EVERY WAR STRATEGY. SHE WANTED TO KNOW THE BEST WAYS TO KEEP PEACE. SHE EMBRACED THE ROLE OF LEADER THAT YOU RAN FROM.
BUT WE COULD NEVER QUITE SEE YOUR PATH. NOW, I KNOW WHY.
ON THE WAY TO BEING A JEDI. NINA WILL BE SO PROUD OF YOU.
I'M PROUD OF YOU.
FINN, LEAVE HERE.
WHAT?
I'VE BEEN STUPID AND STUBBORN. THERE IS NOTHING TO GAIN BY OUR ATTACKS ABOVE.
EVENTUALLY OUR LUCK WILL RUN OUT AND WE WILL BE DESTROYED.

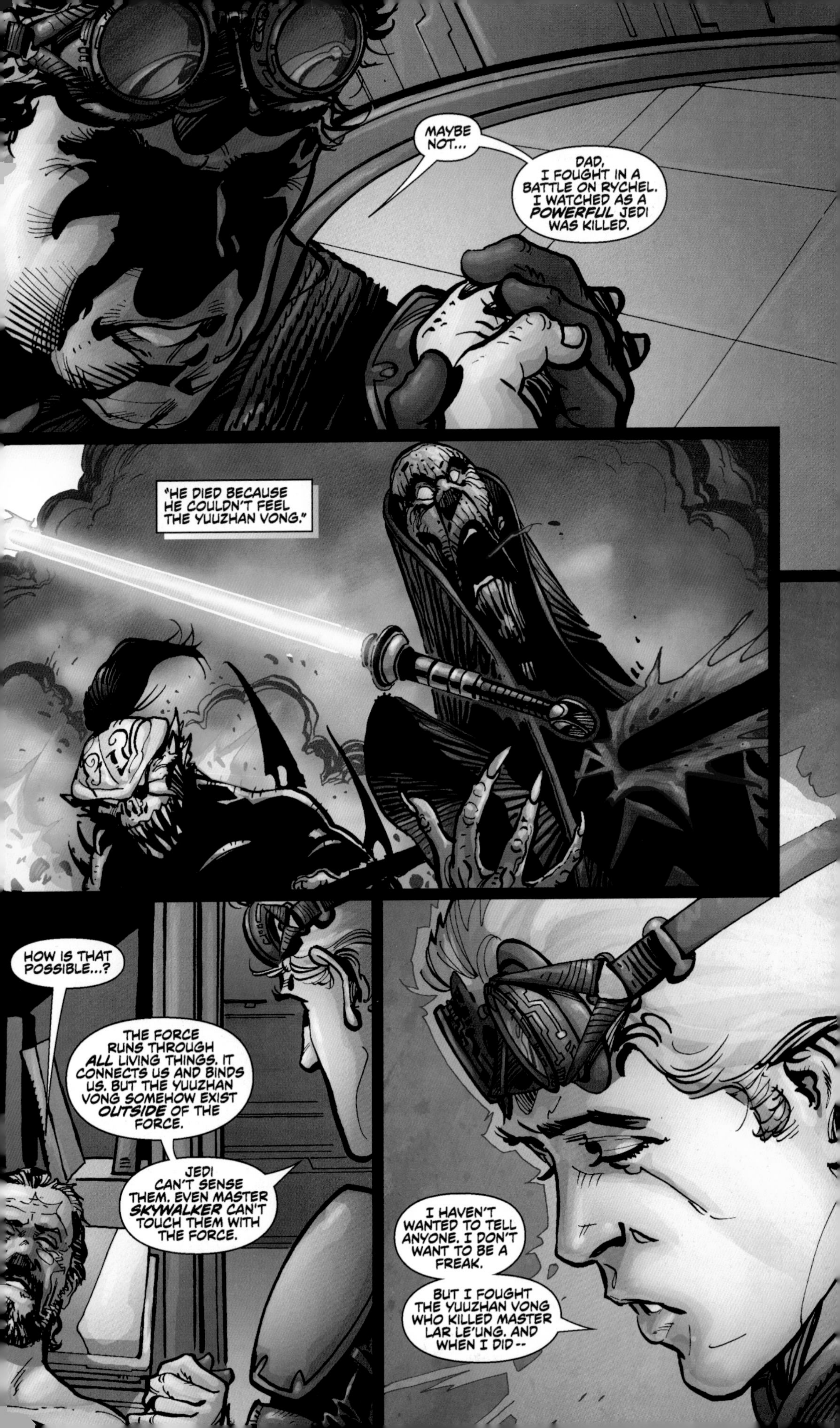
MAYBE NOT...
DAD, I FOUGHT IN A BATTLE ON RYCHEL. I WATCHED AS A *POWERFUL* JEDI WAS KILLED.
"HE DIED BECAUSE HE COULDN'T FEEL THE YUUZHAN VONG."
HOW IS THAT POSSIBLE...?
THE FORCE RUNS THROUGH *ALL* LIVING THINGS. IT CONNECTS US AND BINDS US. BUT THE YUUZHAN VONG SOMEHOW EXIST *OUTSIDE* OF THE FORCE.
JEDI CAN'T SENSE THEM. EVEN MASTER *SKYWALKER* CAN'T TOUCH THEM WITH THE FORCE.
I HAVEN'T WANTED TO TELL ANYONE. I DON'T WANT TO BE A FREAK.
BUT I FOUGHT THE YUUZHAN VONG WHO KILLED MASTER LAR LE'UNG. AND WHEN I DID --

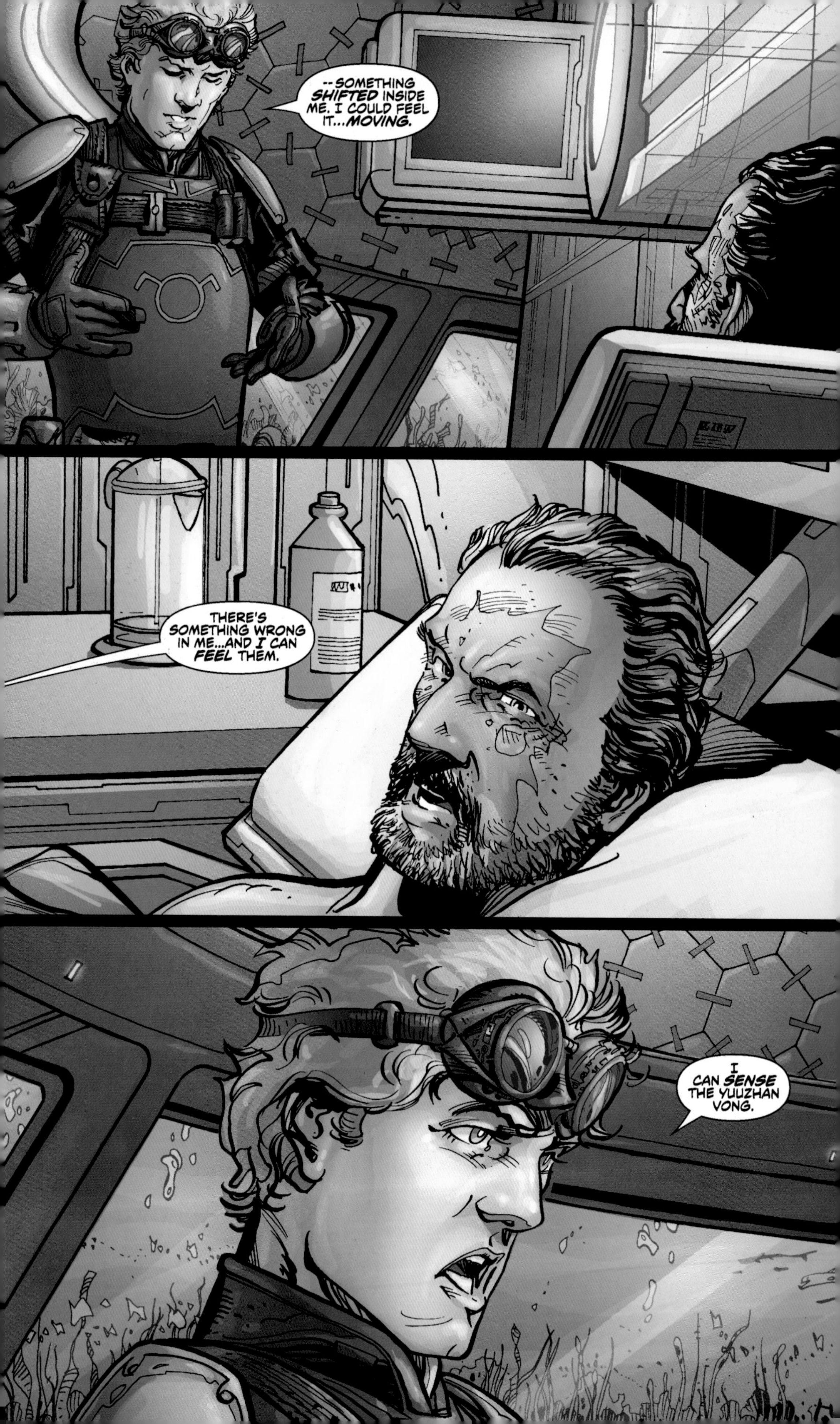
--SOMETHING SHIFTED INSIDE ME. I COULD FEEL IT...MOVING.
THERE'S SOMETHING WRONG IN ME...AND I CAN FEEL THEM.
I CAN SENSE THE YUUZHAN VONG.

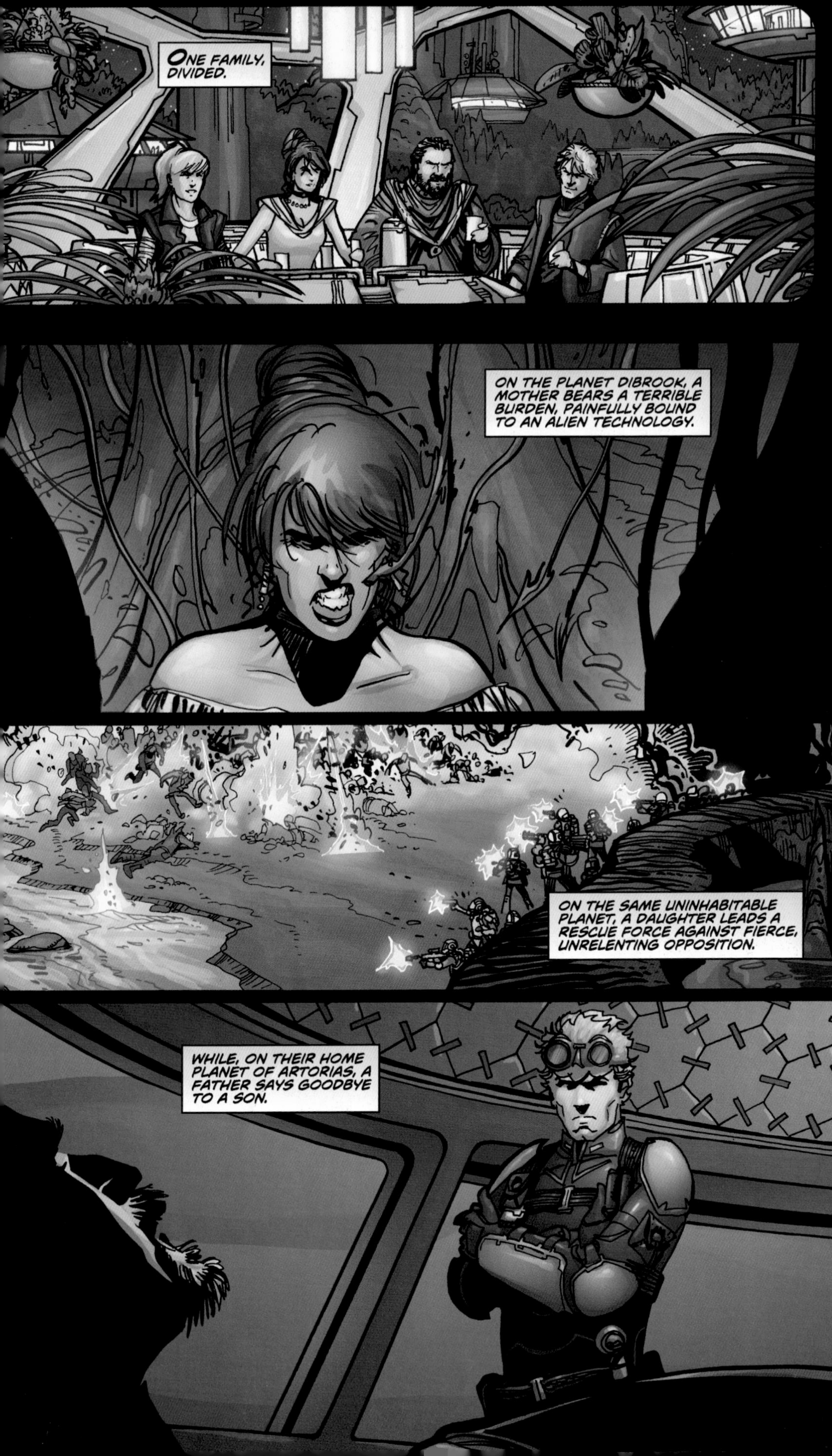
ONE FAMILY, DIVIDED.
ON THE PLANET DIBROOK, A MOTHER BEARS A TERRIBLE BURDEN, PAINFULLY BOUND TO AN ALIEN TECHNOLOGY.
ON THE SAME UNINHABITABLE PLANET, A DAUGHTER LEADS A RESCUE FORCE AGAINST FIERCE, UNRELENTING OPPOSITION.
WHILE, ON THEIR HOME PLANET OF ARTORIAS, A FATHER SAYS GOODBYE TO A SON.

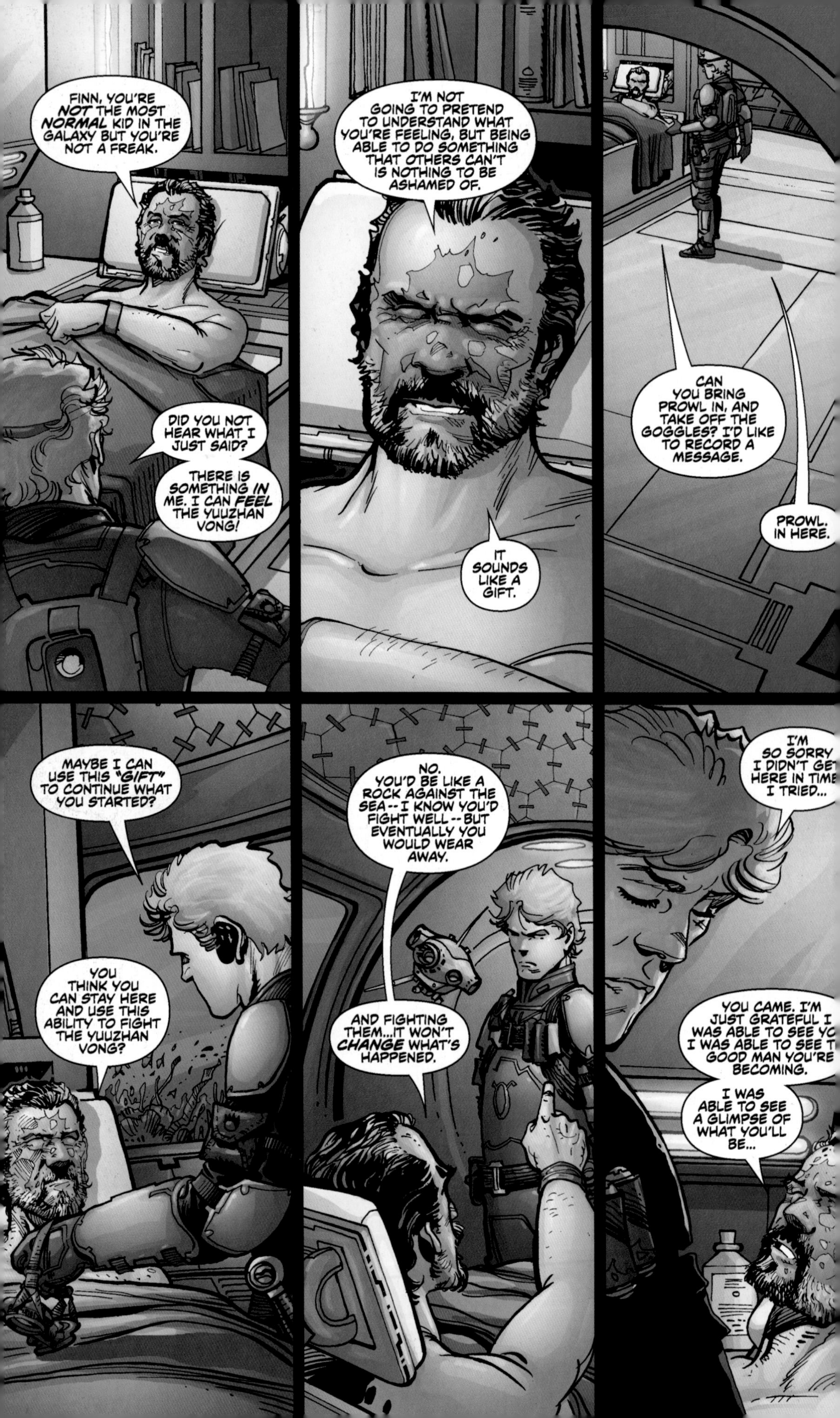
FINN, YOU'RE NOT THE MOST NORMAL KID IN THE GALAXY BUT YOU'RE NOT A FREAK.
DID YOU NOT HEAR WHAT I JUST SAID?
THERE IS SOMETHING IN ME. I CAN FEEL THE YUUZHAN VONG!
I'M NOT GOING TO PRETEND TO UNDERSTAND WHAT YOU'RE FEELING, BUT BEING ABLE TO DO SOMETHING THAT OTHERS CAN'T IS NOTHING TO BE ASHAMED OF.
IT SOUNDS LIKE A GIFT.
CAN YOU BRING PROWL IN, AND TAKE OFF THE GOGGLES? I'D LIKE TO RECORD A MESSAGE.
PROWL. IN HERE.
MAYBE I CAN USE THIS "GIFT" TO CONTINUE WHAT YOU STARTED?
YOU THINK YOU CAN STAY HERE AND USE THIS ABILITY TO FIGHT THE YUUZHAN VONG?
NO. YOU'D BE LIKE A ROCK AGAINST THE SEA -- I KNOW YOU'D FIGHT WELL -- BUT EVENTUALLY YOU WOULD WEAR AWAY.
AND FIGHTING THEM...IT WON'T CHANGE WHAT'S HAPPENED.
I'M SO SORRY I DIDN'T GET HERE IN TIME I TRIED...
YOU CAME. I'M JUST GRATEFUL I WAS ABLE TO SEE YO I WAS ABLE TO SEE T GOOD MAN YOU'RE BECOMING.
I WAS ABLE TO SEE A GLIMPSE OF WHAT YOU'LL BE...

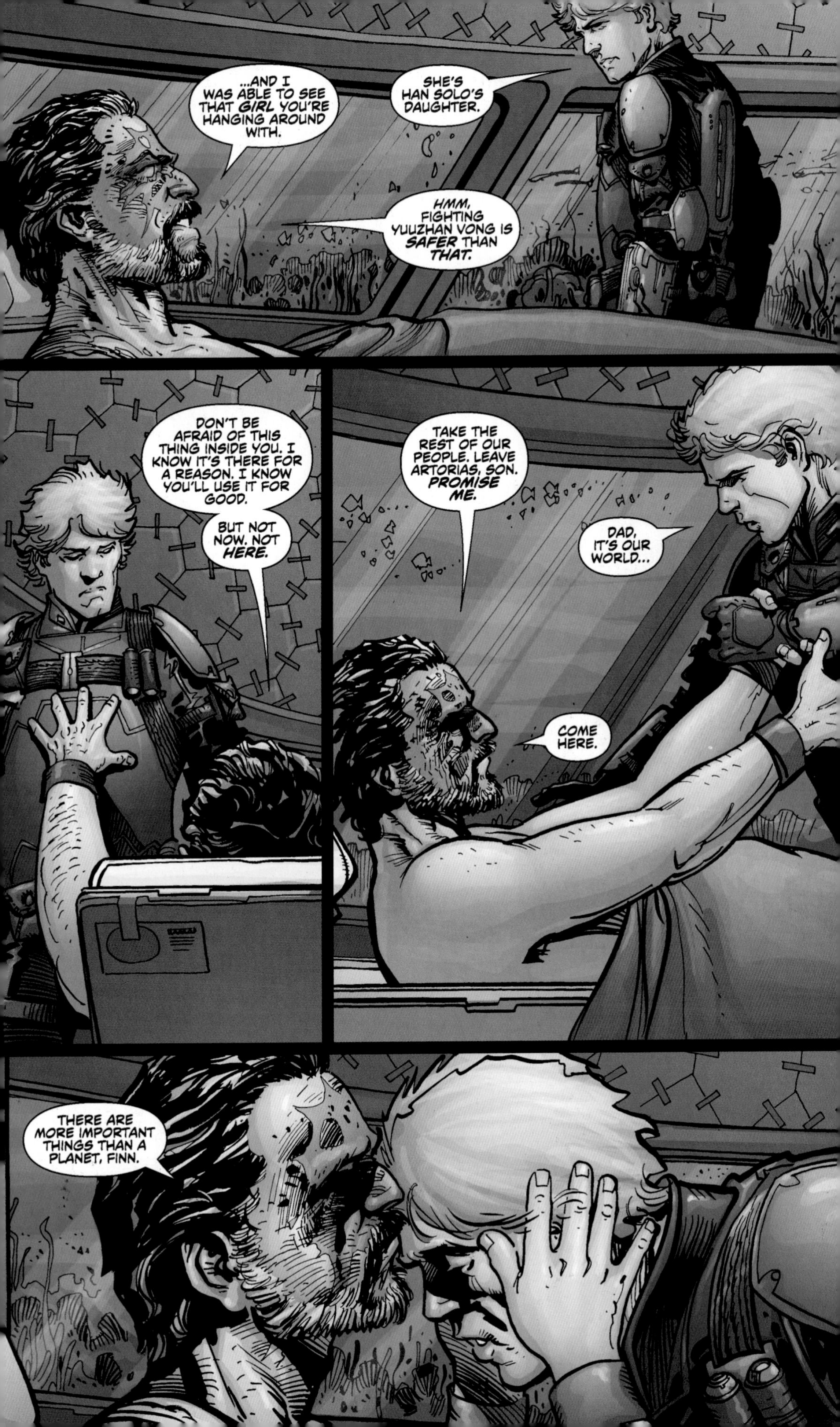
...AND I WAS ABLE TO SEE THAT GIRL YOU'RE HANGING AROUND WITH.
SHE'S HAN SOLO'S DAUGHTER.
HMM, FIGHTING YUUZHAN VONG IS SAFER THAN THAT.
DON'T BE AFRAID OF THIS THING INSIDE YOU. I KNOW IT'S THERE FOR A REASON. I KNOW YOU'LL USE IT FOR GOOD.
BUT NOT NOW. NOT HERE.
TAKE THE REST OF OUR PEOPLE. LEAVE ARTORIAS, SON. PROMISE ME.
DAD, IT'S OUR WORLD...
COME HERE.
THERE ARE MORE IMPORTANT THINGS THAN A PLANET, FINN.

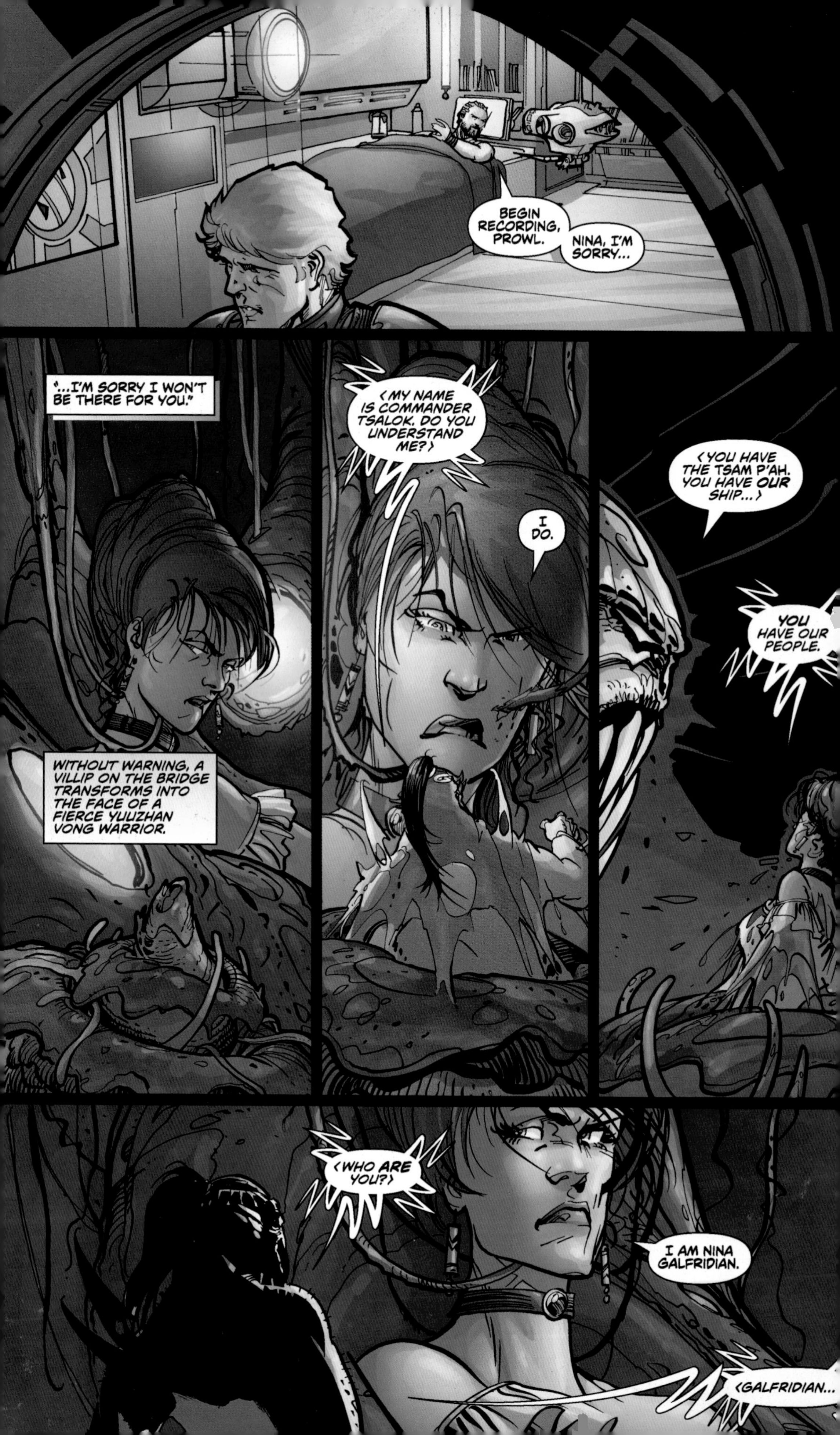
BEGIN RECORDING, PROWL.
NINA, I'M SORRY...
"...I'M SORRY I WON'T BE THERE FOR YOU."
WITHOUT WARNING, A VILLIP ON THE BRIDGE TRANSFORMS INTO THE FACE OF A FIERCE YUUZHAN VONG WARRIOR.
‹MY NAME IS COMMANDER TSALOK. DO YOU UNDERSTAND ME?›
I DO.
‹YOU HAVE THE TSAM P'AH. YOU HAVE OUR SHIP...›
YOU HAVE OUR PEOPLE.
‹WHO ARE YOU?›
I AM NINA GALFRIDIAN.
‹GALFRIDIAN...

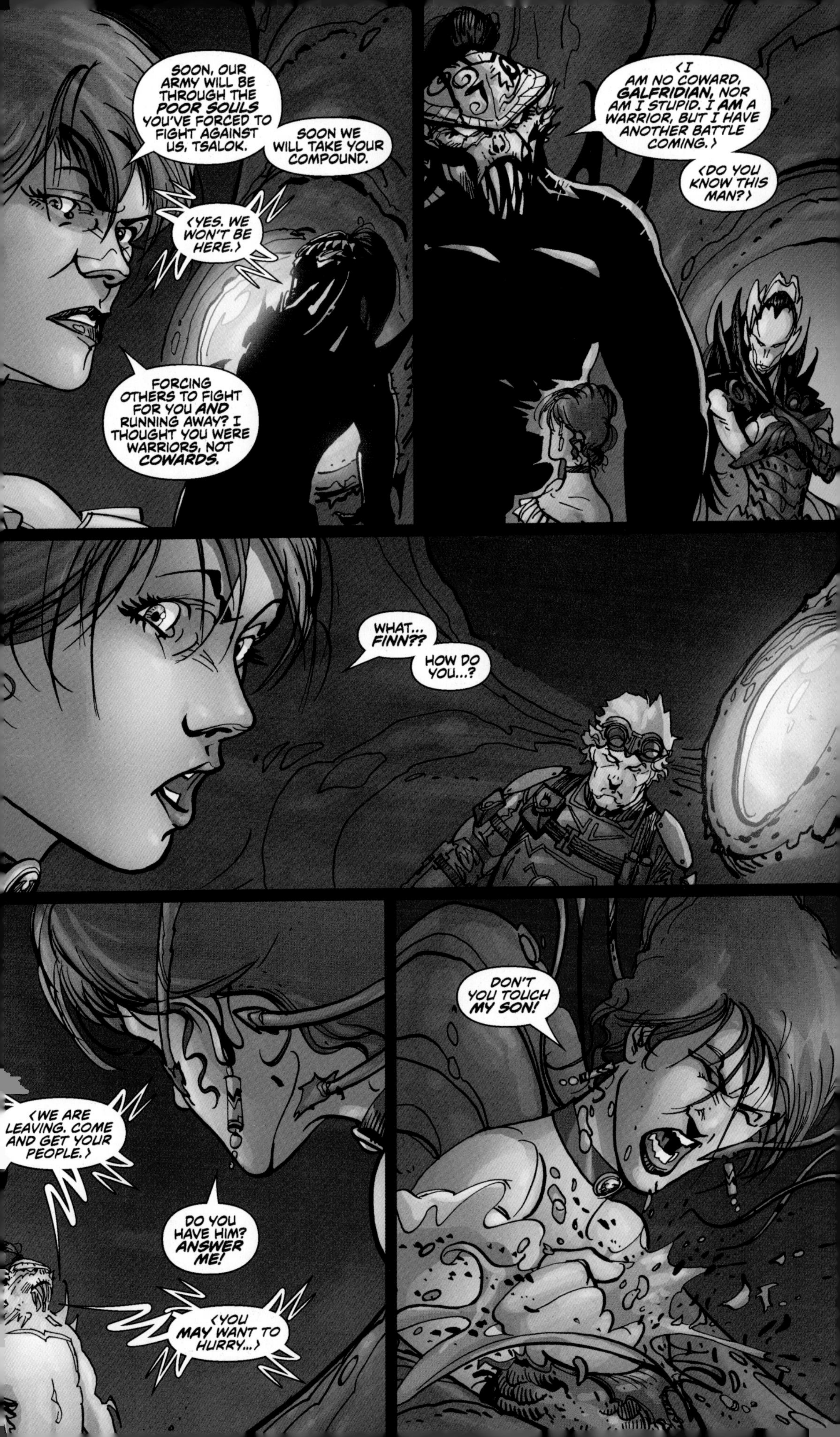
SOON, OUR ARMY WILL BE THROUGH THE POOR SOULS YOU'VE FORCED TO FIGHT AGAINST US, TSALOK.
SOON WE WILL TAKE YOUR COMPOUND.
‹YES. WE WON'T BE HERE.›
FORCING OTHERS TO FIGHT FOR YOU AND RUNNING AWAY? I THOUGHT YOU WERE WARRIORS, NOT COWARDS.
‹I AM NO COWARD, GALFRIDIAN, NOR AM I STUPID. I AM A WARRIOR, BUT I HAVE ANOTHER BATTLE COMING.›
‹DO YOU KNOW THIS MAN?›
WHAT... FINN??
HOW DO YOU...?
‹WE ARE LEAVING. COME AND GET YOUR PEOPLE.›
DO YOU HAVE HIM? ANSWER ME!
‹YOU MAY WANT TO HURRY...›
DON'T YOU TOUCH MY SON!

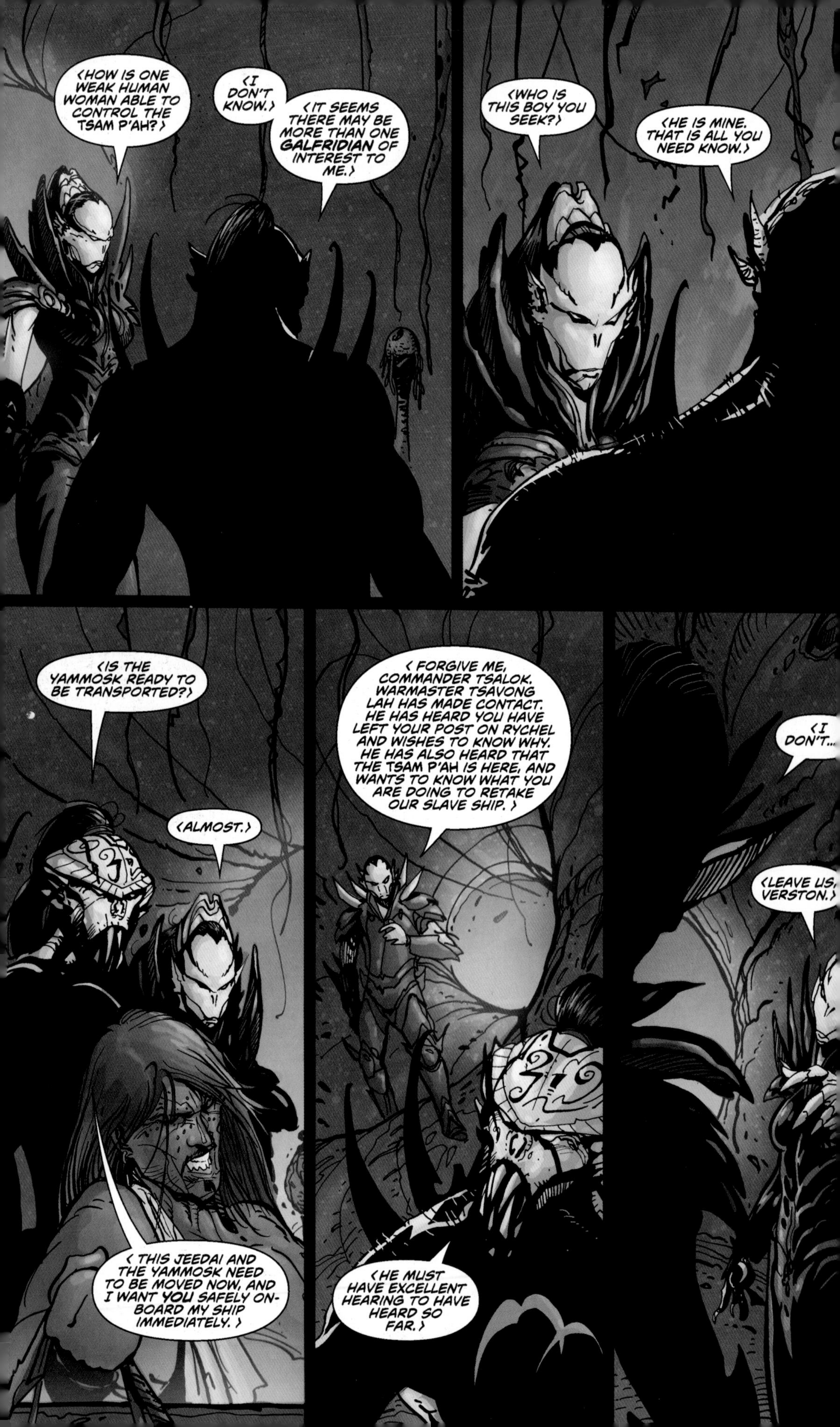
‹HOW IS ONE WEAK HUMAN WOMAN ABLE TO CONTROL THE TSAM P'AH?›
‹I DON'T KNOW.›
‹IT SEEMS THERE MAY BE MORE THAN ONE GALFRIDIAN OF INTEREST TO ME.›
‹WHO IS THIS BOY YOU SEEK?›
‹HE IS MINE. THAT IS ALL YOU NEED KNOW.›
‹IS THE YAMMOSK READY TO BE TRANSPORTED?›
‹ALMOST.›
‹THIS JEEDAI AND THE YAMMOSK NEED TO BE MOVED NOW, AND I WANT YOU SAFELY ON-BOARD MY SHIP IMMEDIATELY.›
‹FORGIVE ME, COMMANDER TSALOK. WARMASTER TSAVONG LAH HAS MADE CONTACT. HE HAS HEARD YOU HAVE LEFT YOUR POST ON RYCHEL AND WISHES TO KNOW WHY. HE HAS ALSO HEARD THAT THE TSAM P'AH IS HERE, AND WANTS TO KNOW WHAT YOU ARE DOING TO RETAKE OUR SLAVE SHIP.›
‹HE MUST HAVE EXCELLENT HEARING TO HAVE HEARD SO FAR.›
‹I DON'T...
‹LEAVE US, VERSTON.

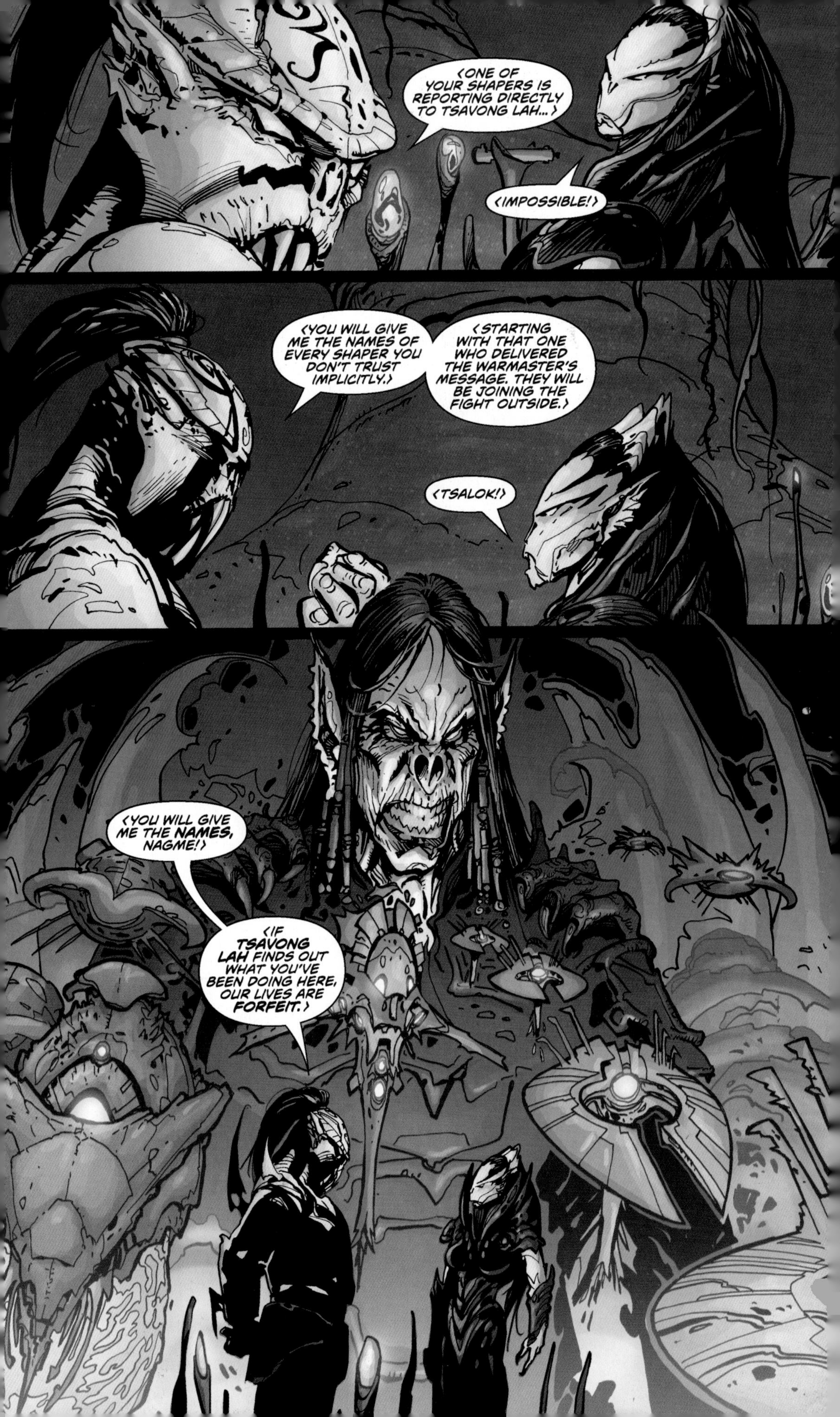
‹ONE OF YOUR SHAPERS IS REPORTING DIRECTLY TO TSAVONG LAH...›
‹IMPOSSIBLE!›
‹YOU WILL GIVE ME THE NAMES OF EVERY SHAPER YOU DON'T TRUST IMPLICITLY.›
‹STARTING WITH THAT ONE WHO DELIVERED THE WARMASTER'S MESSAGE. THEY WILL BE JOINING THE FIGHT OUTSIDE.›
‹TSALOK!›
‹YOU WILL GIVE ME THE **NAMES**, NAGME!›
‹IF **TSAVONG LAH** FINDS OUT WHAT YOU'VE BEEN DOING HERE, OUR LIVES ARE **FORFEIT**.›

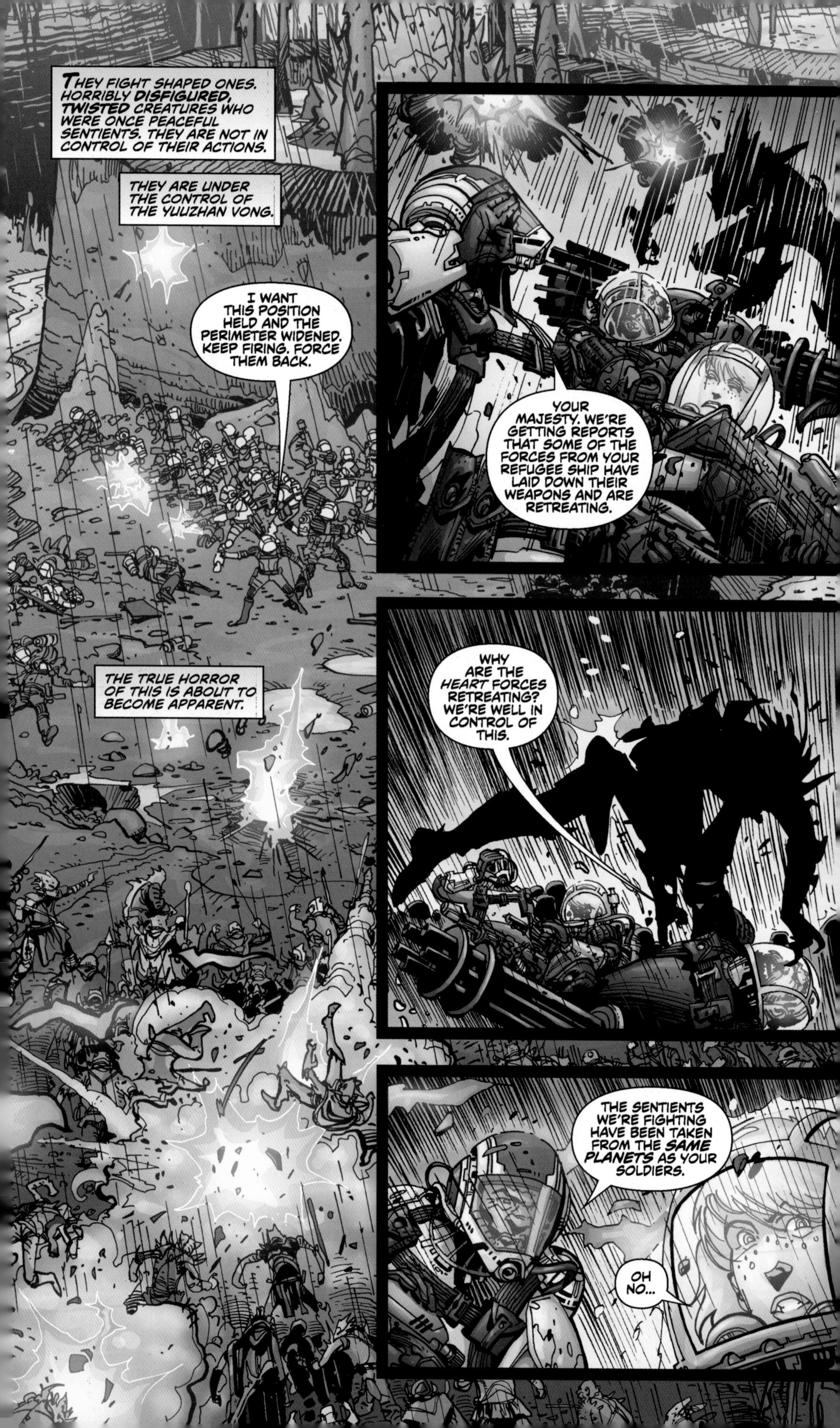
THEY FIGHT SHAPED ONES. HORRIBLY DISFIGURED, TWISTED CREATURES WHO WERE ONCE PEACEFUL SENTIENTS. THEY ARE NOT IN CONTROL OF THEIR ACTIONS.
THEY ARE UNDER THE CONTROL OF THE YUUZHAN VONG.
I WANT THIS POSITION HELD AND THE PERIMETER WIDENED. KEEP FIRING. FORCE THEM BACK.
YOUR MAJESTY. WE'RE GETTING REPORTS THAT SOME OF THE FORCES FROM YOUR REFUGEE SHIP HAVE LAID DOWN THEIR WEAPONS AND ARE RETREATING.
THE TRUE HORROR OF THIS IS ABOUT TO BECOME APPARENT.
WHY ARE THE HEART FORCES RETREATING? WE'RE WELL IN CONTROL OF THIS.
THE SENTIENTS WE'RE FIGHTING HAVE BEEN TAKEN FROM THE SAME PLANETS AS YOUR SOLDIERS.
OH NO...

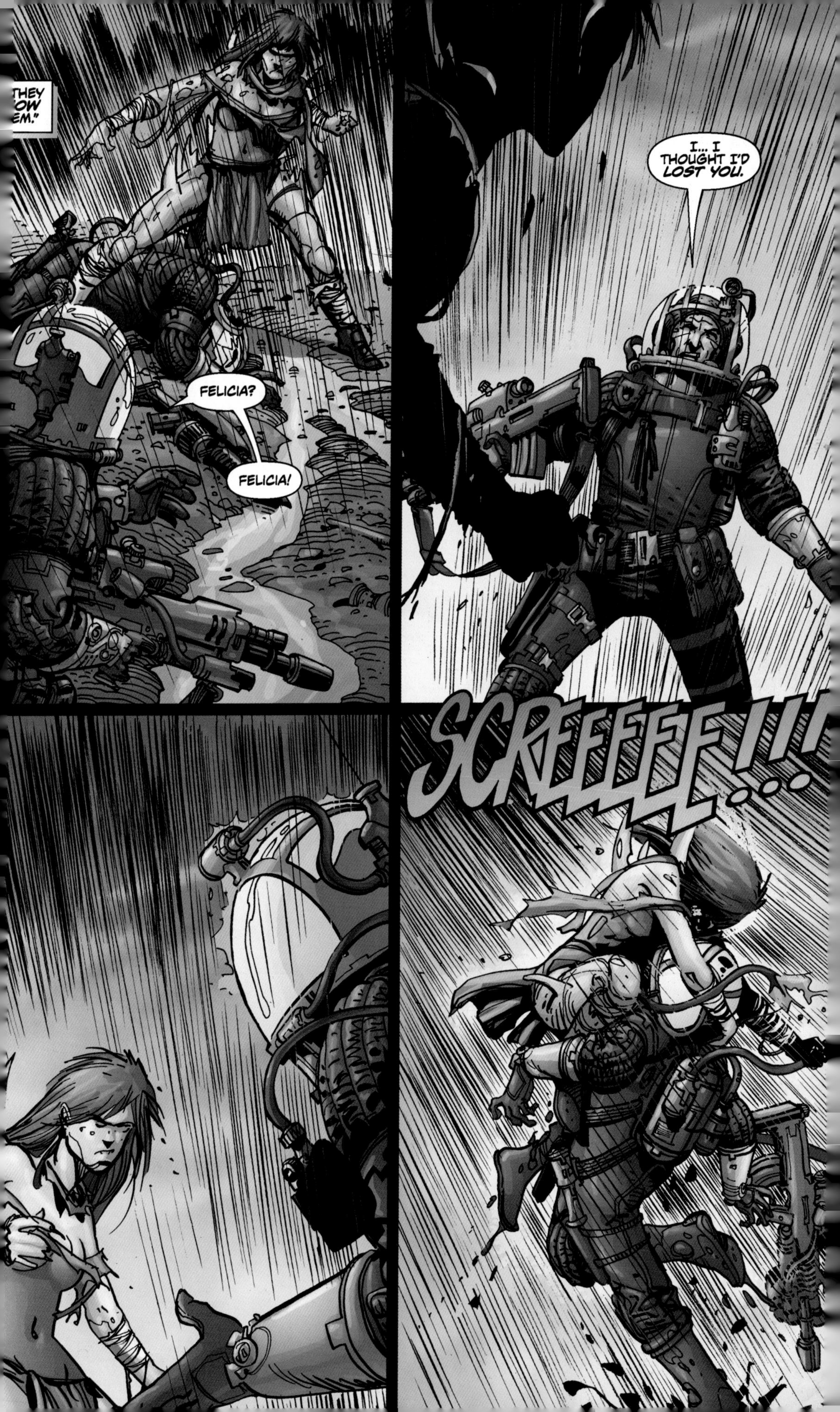
FELICIA?
FELICIA!
I... I THOUGHT I'D LOST YOU.
SCREEEEE!!!...

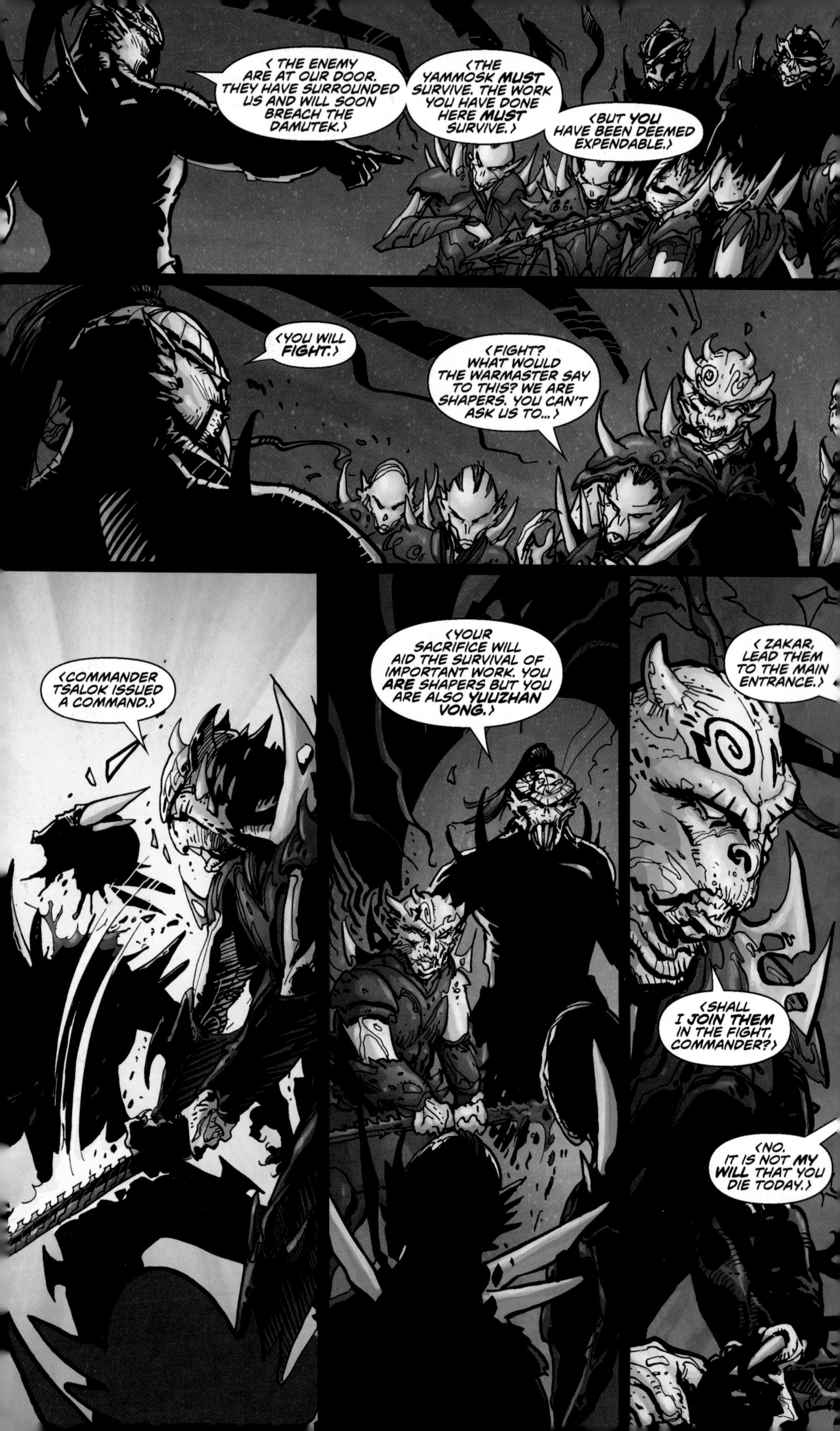

‹THE ENEMY ARE AT OUR DOOR. THEY HAVE SURROUNDED US AND WILL SOON BREACH THE DAMUTEK.›
‹THE YAMMOSK MUST SURVIVE. THE WORK YOU HAVE DONE HERE MUST SURVIVE.›
‹BUT YOU HAVE BEEN DEEMED EXPENDABLE.›
‹YOU WILL FIGHT.›
‹FIGHT? WHAT WOULD THE WARMASTER SAY TO THIS? WE ARE SHAPERS. YOU CAN'T ASK US TO...›
‹COMMANDER TSALOK ISSUED A COMMAND.›
‹YOUR SACRIFICE WILL AID THE SURVIVAL OF IMPORTANT WORK. YOU ARE SHAPERS BUT YOU ARE ALSO YUUZHAN VONG.›
‹ZAKAR, LEAD THEM TO THE MAIN ENTRANCE.›
‹SHALL I JOIN THEM IN THE FIGHT, COMMANDER?›
‹NO. IT IS NOT MY WILL THAT YOU DIE TODAY.›

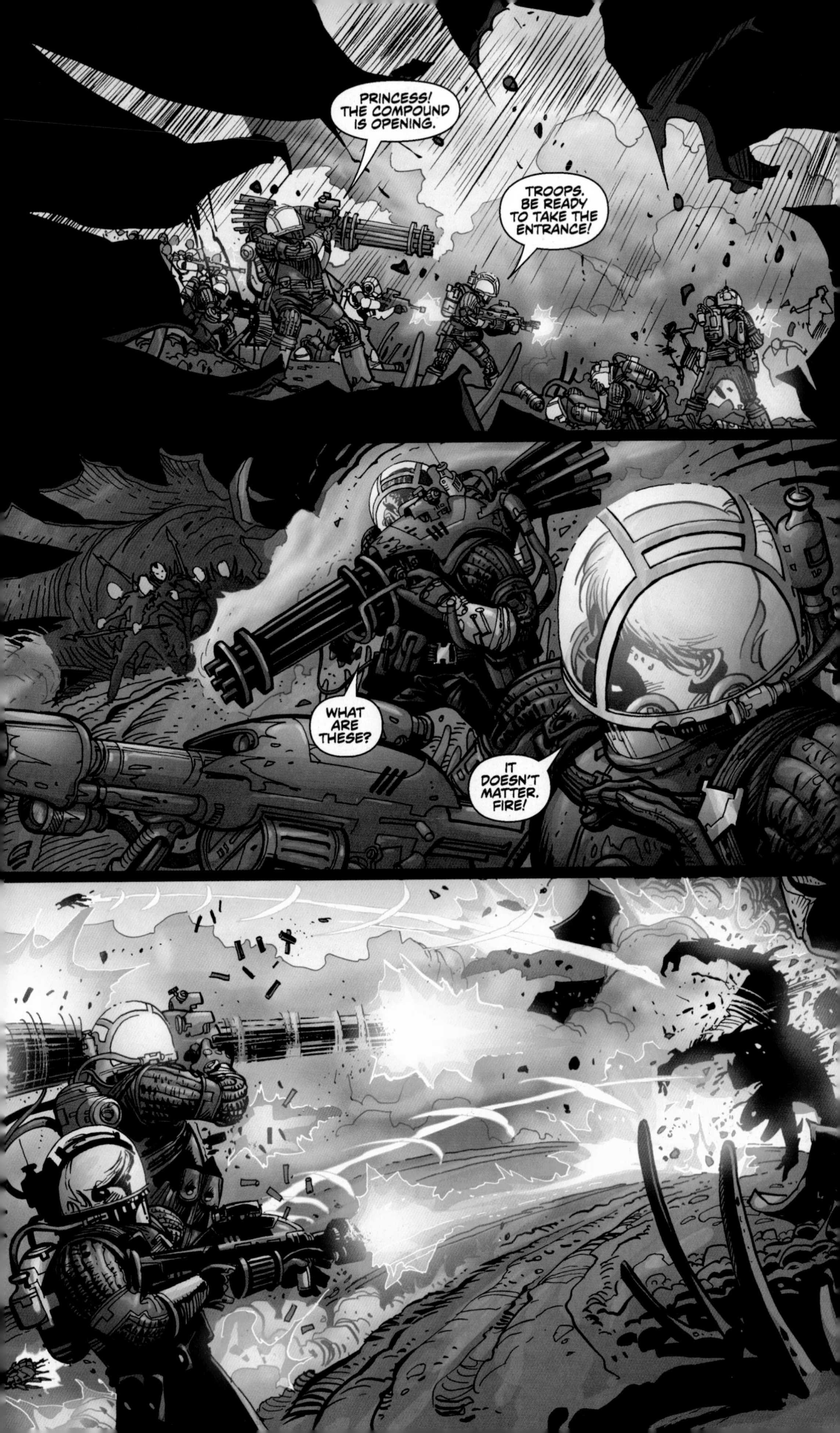
PRINCESS! THE COMPOUND IS OPENING.
TROOPS. BE READY TO TAKE THE ENTRANCE!
WHAT ARE THESE?
IT DOESN'T MATTER. FIRE!

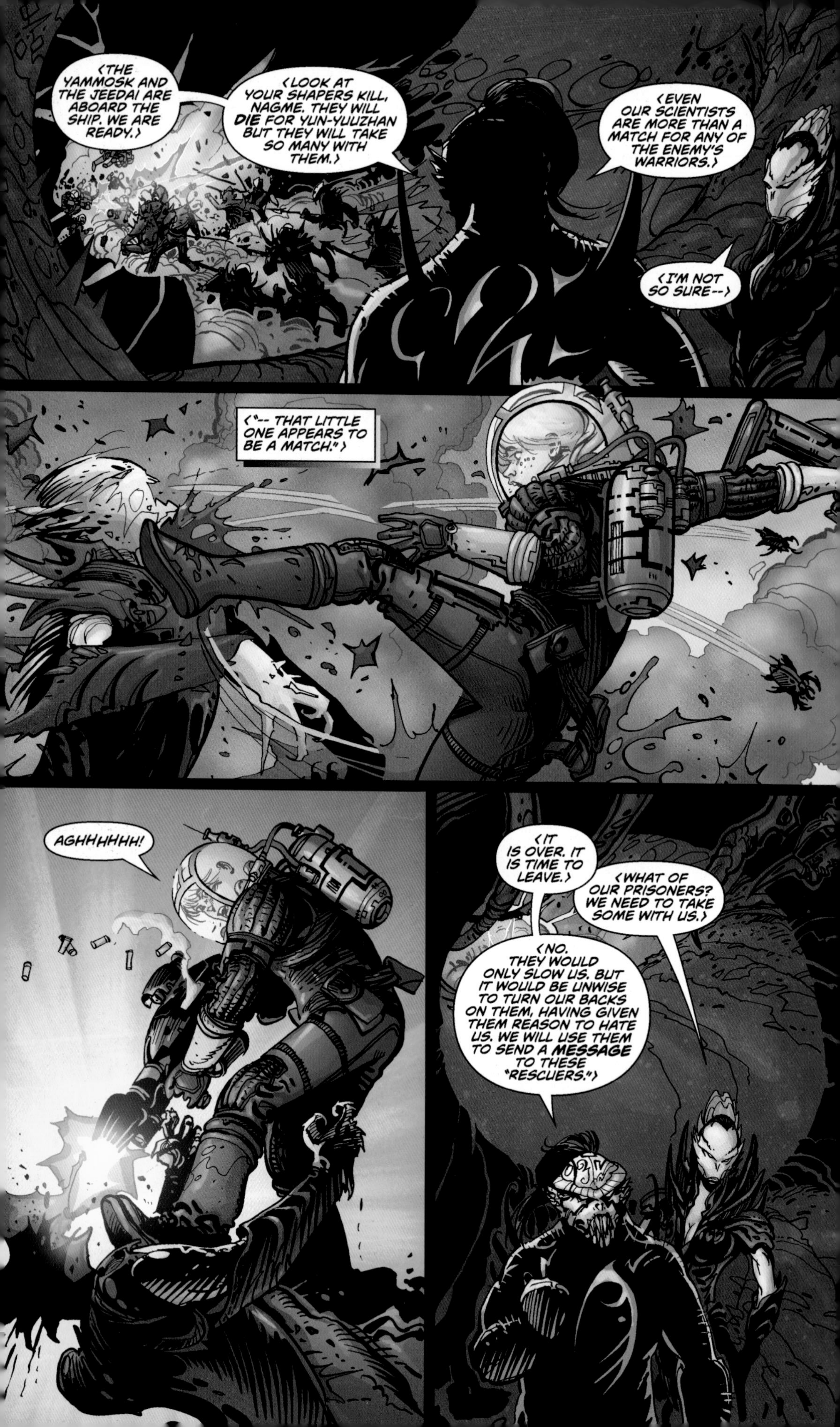

‹THE YAMMOSK AND THE JEEDAI ARE ABOARD THE SHIP. WE ARE READY.›
‹LOOK AT YOUR SHAPERS KILL, NAGME. THEY WILL **DIE** FOR YUN-YUUZHAN BUT THEY WILL TAKE SO MANY WITH THEM.›
‹EVEN OUR SCIENTISTS ARE MORE THAN A MATCH FOR ANY OF THE ENEMY'S WARRIORS.›
‹I'M NOT SO SURE--›
‹"-- THAT LITTLE ONE APPEARS TO BE A MATCH."›
AGHHHHHH!
‹IT IS OVER. IT IS TIME TO LEAVE.›
‹WHAT OF OUR PRISONERS? WE NEED TO TAKE SOME WITH US.›
‹NO. THEY WOULD ONLY SLOW US. BUT IT WOULD BE UNWISE TO TURN OUR BACKS ON THEM, HAVING GIVEN THEM REASON TO HATE US. WE WILL USE THEM TO SEND A **MESSAGE** TO THESE "RESCUERS."›

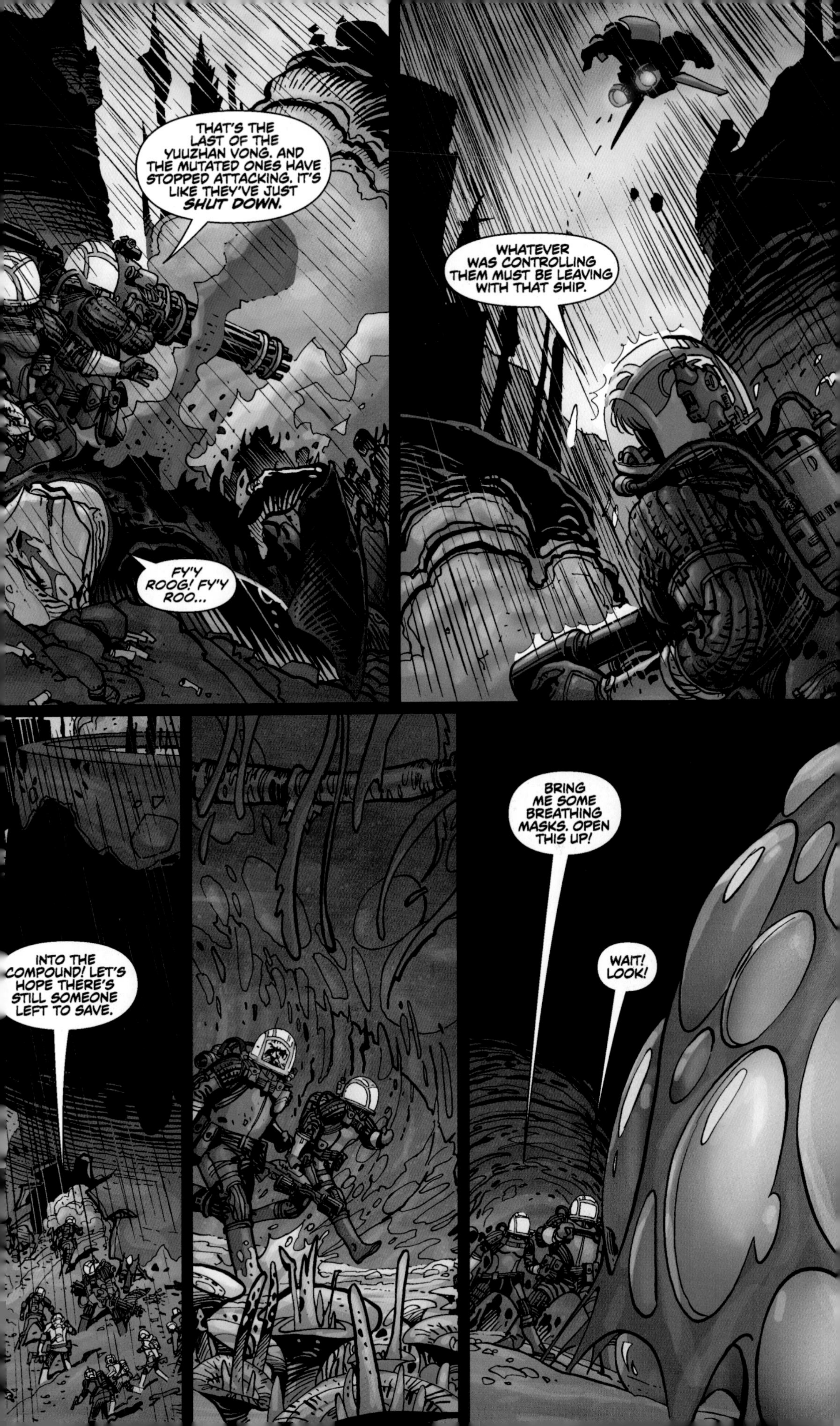
THAT'S THE LAST OF THE YUUZHAN VONG. AND THE MUTATED ONES HAVE STOPPED ATTACKING. IT'S LIKE THEY'VE JUST *SHUT DOWN.*
FY'Y ROOG! FY'Y ROO...
WHATEVER WAS CONTROLLING THEM MUST BE LEAVING WITH THAT SHIP.
INTO THE COMPOUND! LET'S HOPE THERE'S STILL SOMEONE LEFT TO SAVE.
BRING ME SOME BREATHING MASKS. OPEN THIS UP!
WAIT! LOOK!

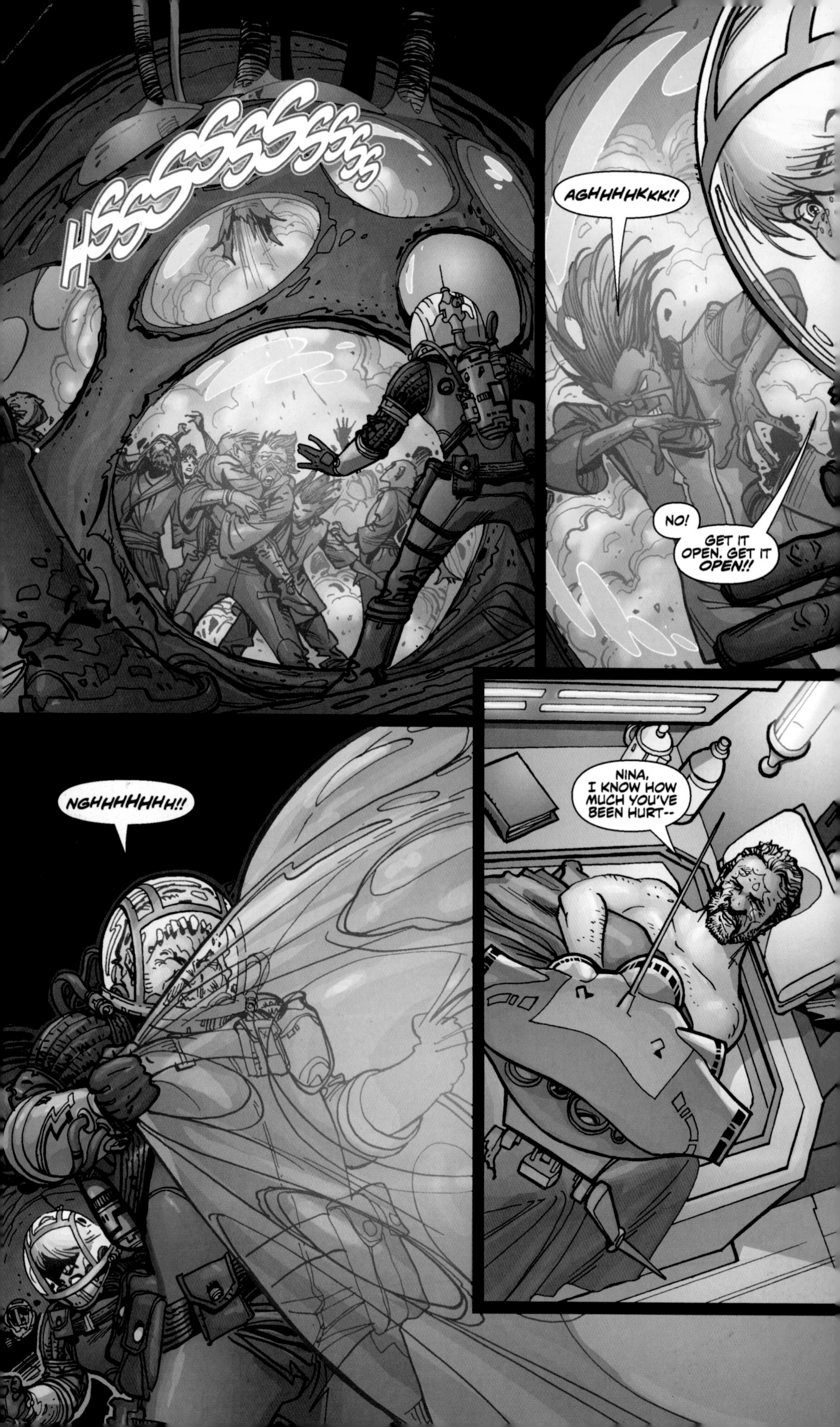
HSSSSSSSSSSS
AGHHHHKKK!!
NO!
GET IT OPEN. GET IT OPEN!!
NGHHHHHHH!!
NINA, I KNOW HOW MUCH YOU'VE BEEN HURT--

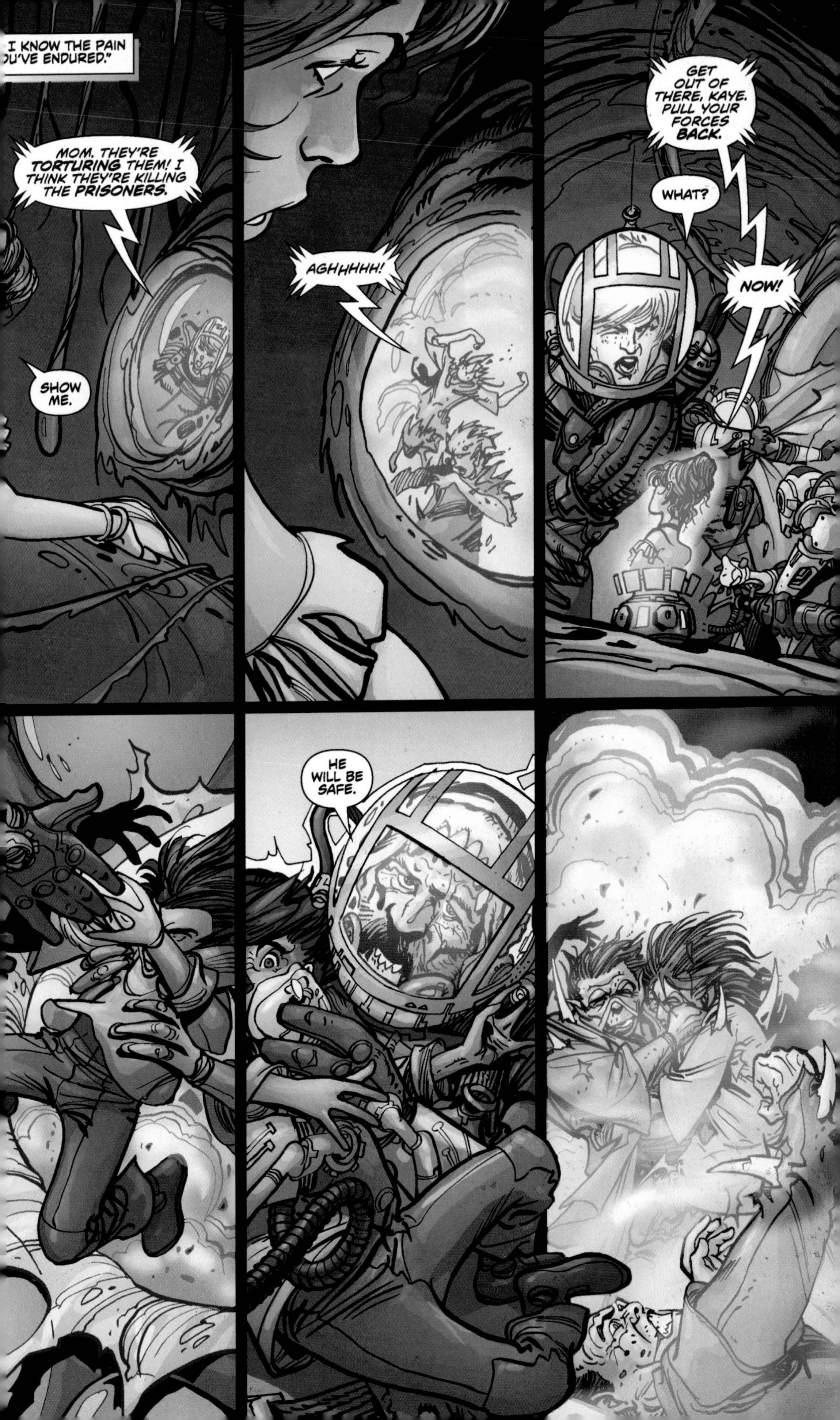

"I KNOW THE PAIN YOU'VE ENDURED."
MOM. THEY'RE TORTURING THEM! I THINK THEY'RE KILLING THE PRISONERS.
SHOW ME.
AGHHHHH!
GET OUT OF THERE, KAYE. PULL YOUR FORCES BACK.
WHAT?
NOW!
HE WILL BE SAFE.

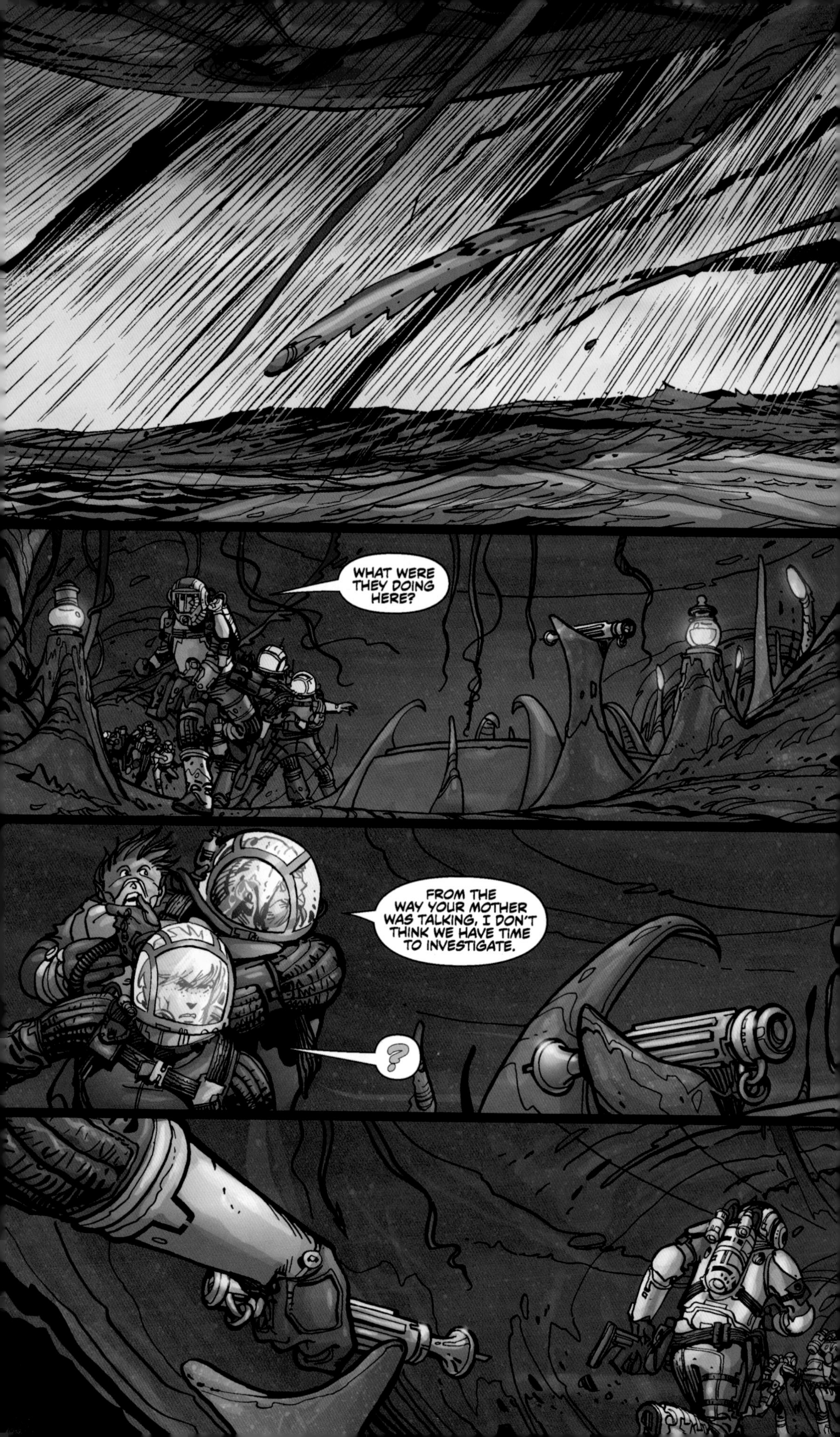
WHAT WERE THEY DOING HERE?
FROM THE WAY YOUR MOTHER WAS TALKING, I DON'T THINK WE HAVE TIME TO INVESTIGATE.
?

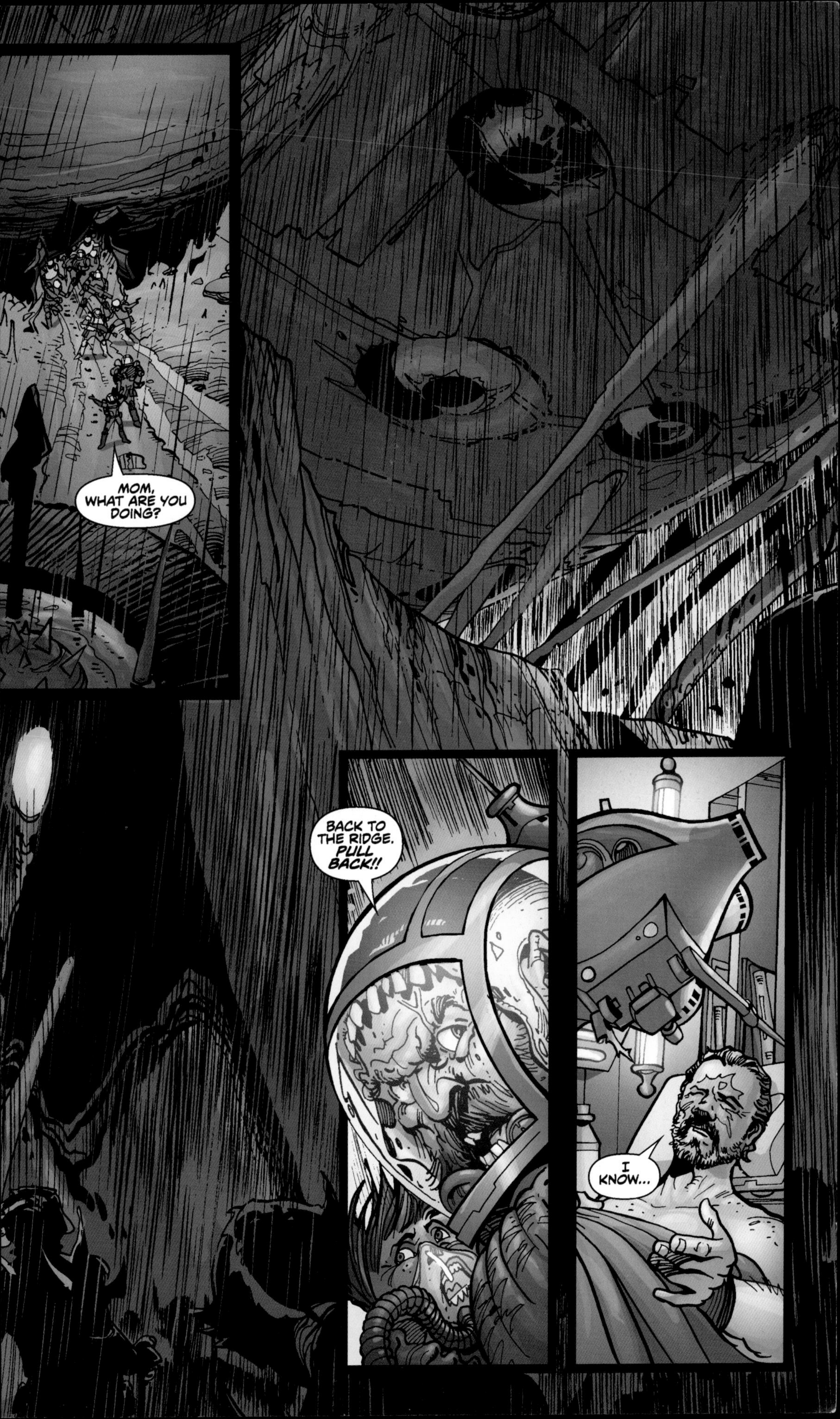
MOM, WHAT ARE YOU DOING?
BACK TO THE RIDGE. PULL BACK!!
I KNOW...

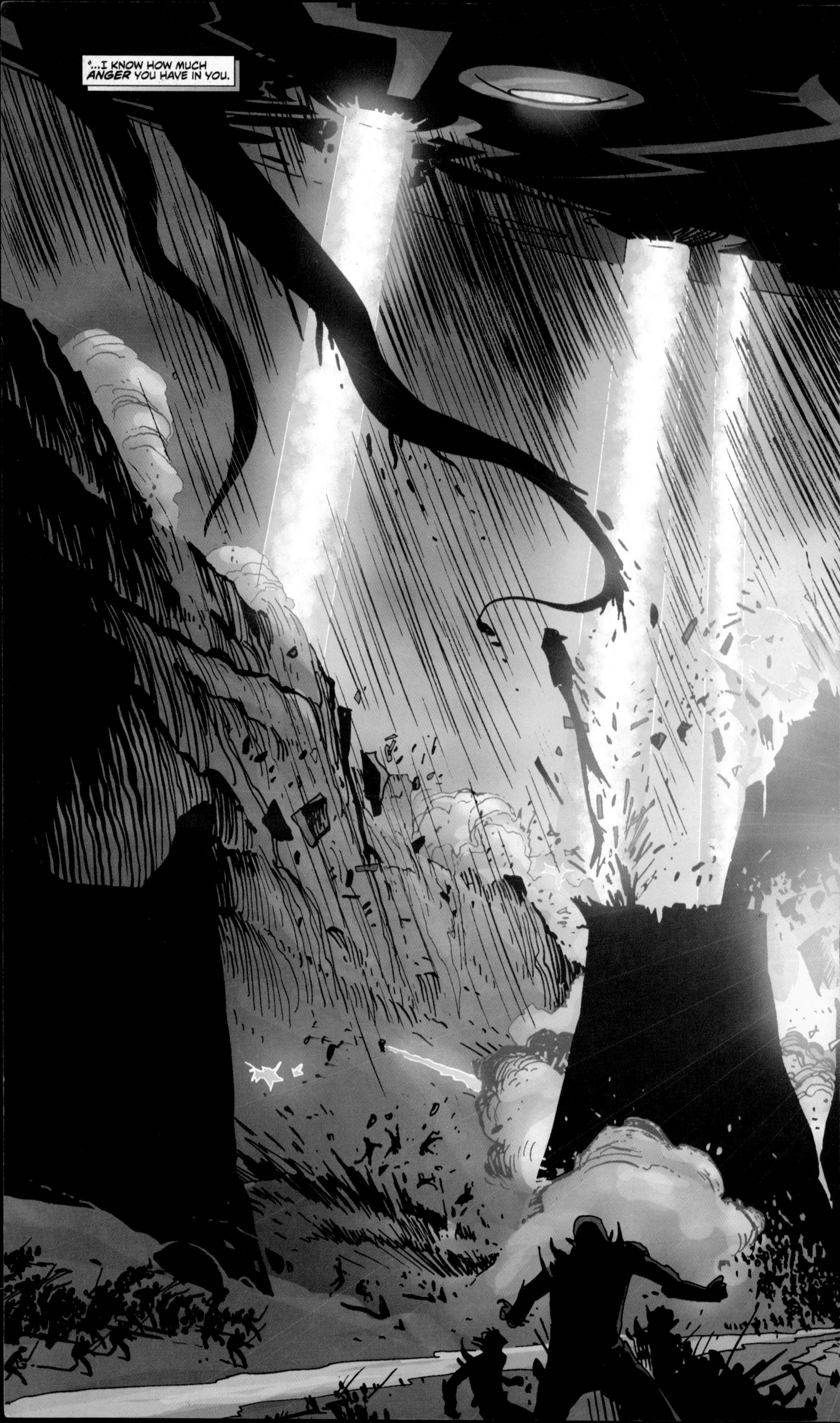
"...I KNOW HOW MUCH ANGER YOU HAVE IN YOU.

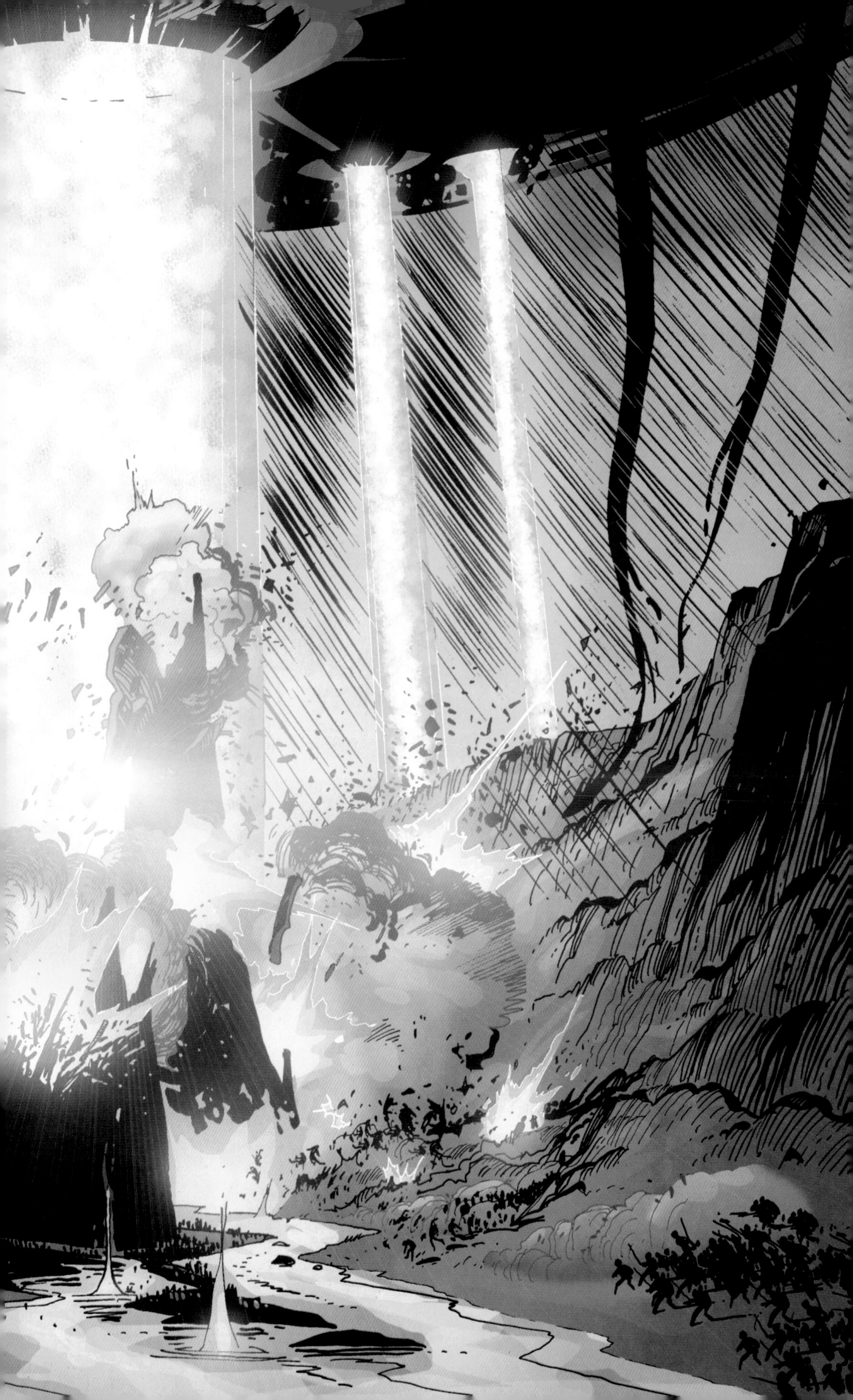

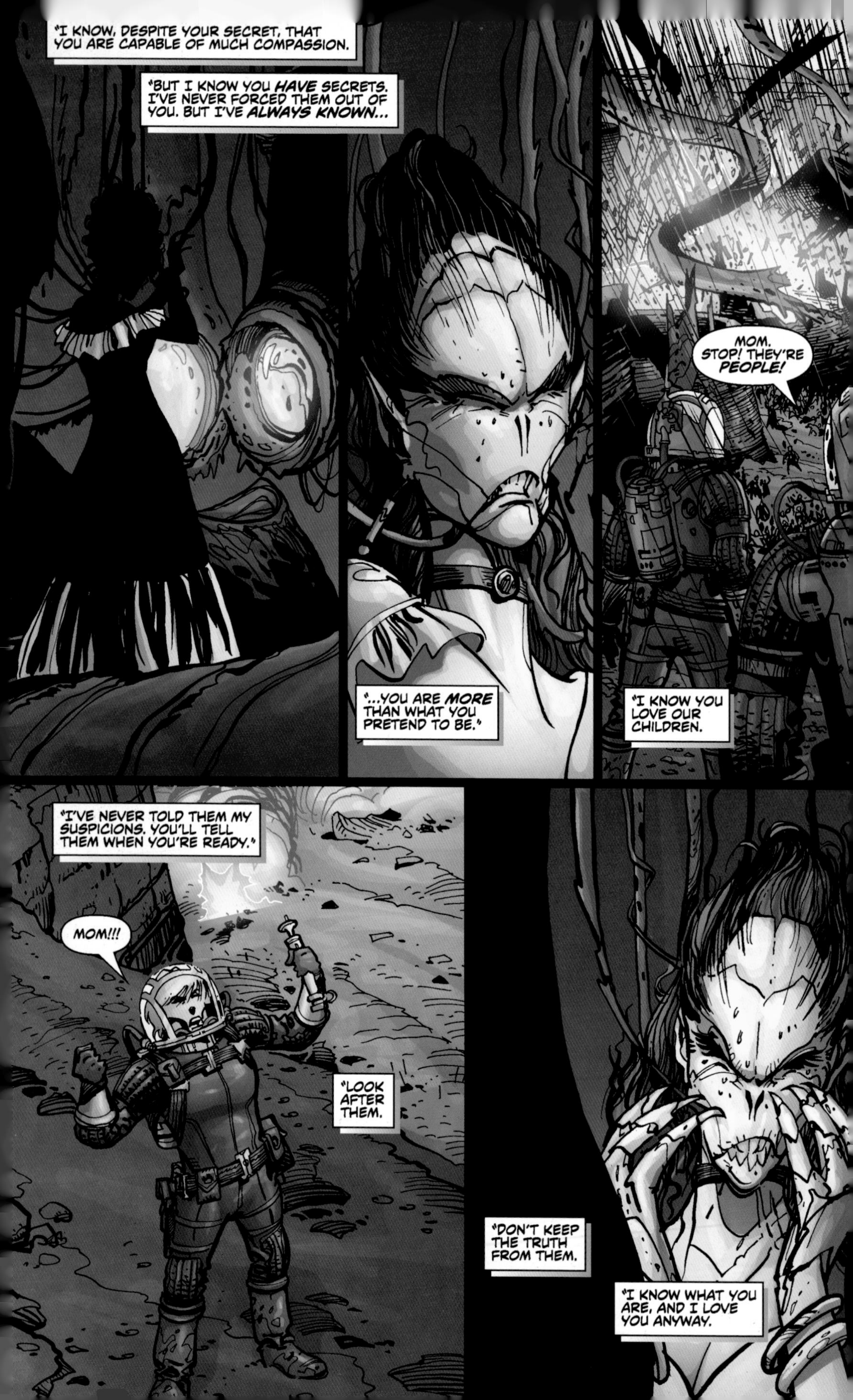

"I KNOW, DESPITE YOUR SECRET, THAT YOU ARE CAPABLE OF MUCH COMPASSION.
"BUT I KNOW YOU *HAVE* SECRETS. I'VE NEVER FORCED THEM OUT OF YOU. BUT I'VE *ALWAYS KNOWN...*
"...YOU ARE *MORE* THAN WHAT YOU PRETEND TO BE."
MOM. STOP! THEY'RE *PEOPLE!*
"I KNOW YOU LOVE OUR CHILDREN.
"I'VE NEVER TOLD THEM MY SUSPICIONS. YOU'LL TELL THEM WHEN YOU'RE READY."
MOM!!!
"LOOK AFTER THEM.
"DON'T KEEP THE TRUTH FROM THEM.
"I KNOW WHAT YOU ARE, AND I LOVE YOU ANYWAY.

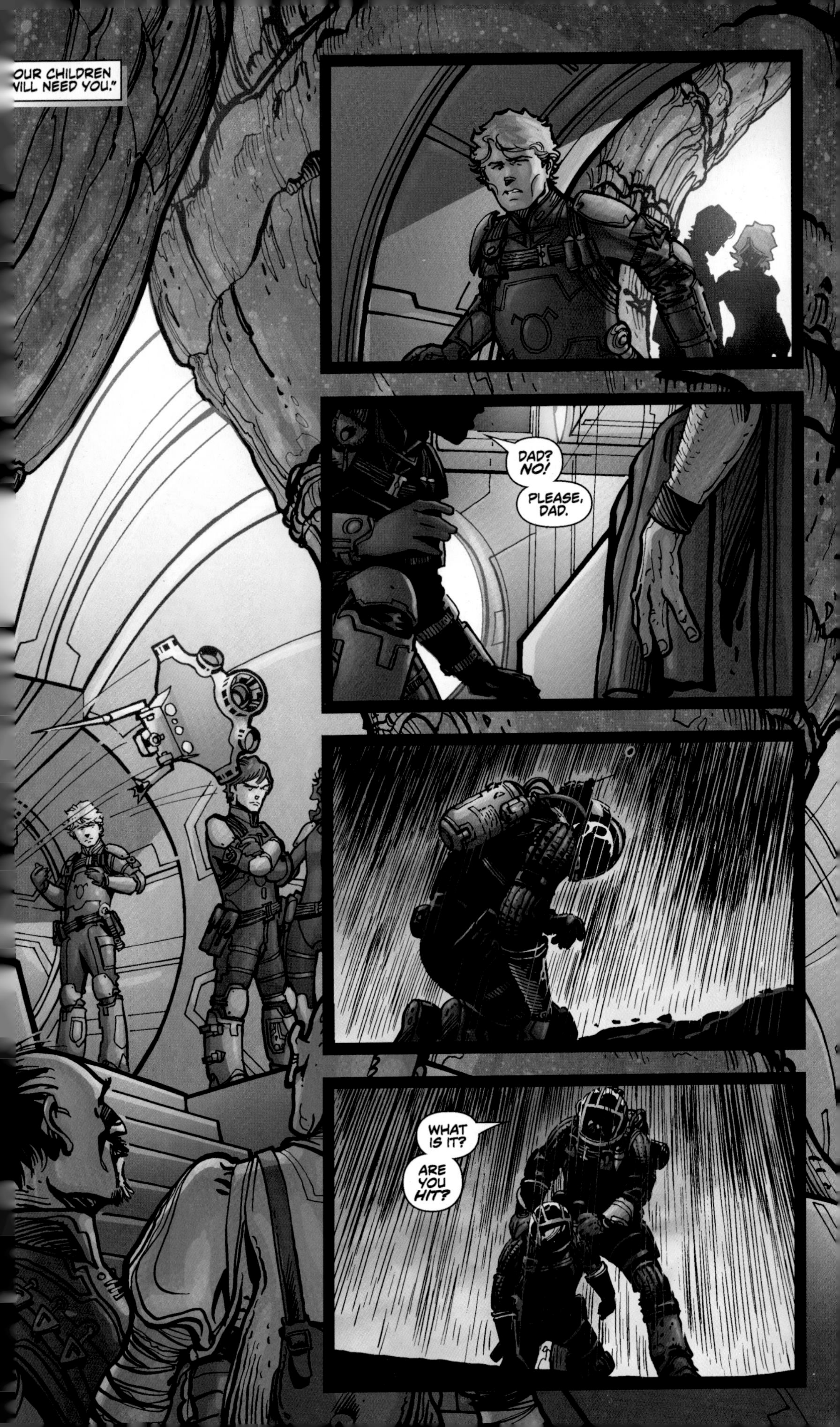
OUR CHILDREN WILL NEED YOU."
DAD? NO!
PLEASE, DAD.
WHAT IS IT?
ARE YOU HIT?

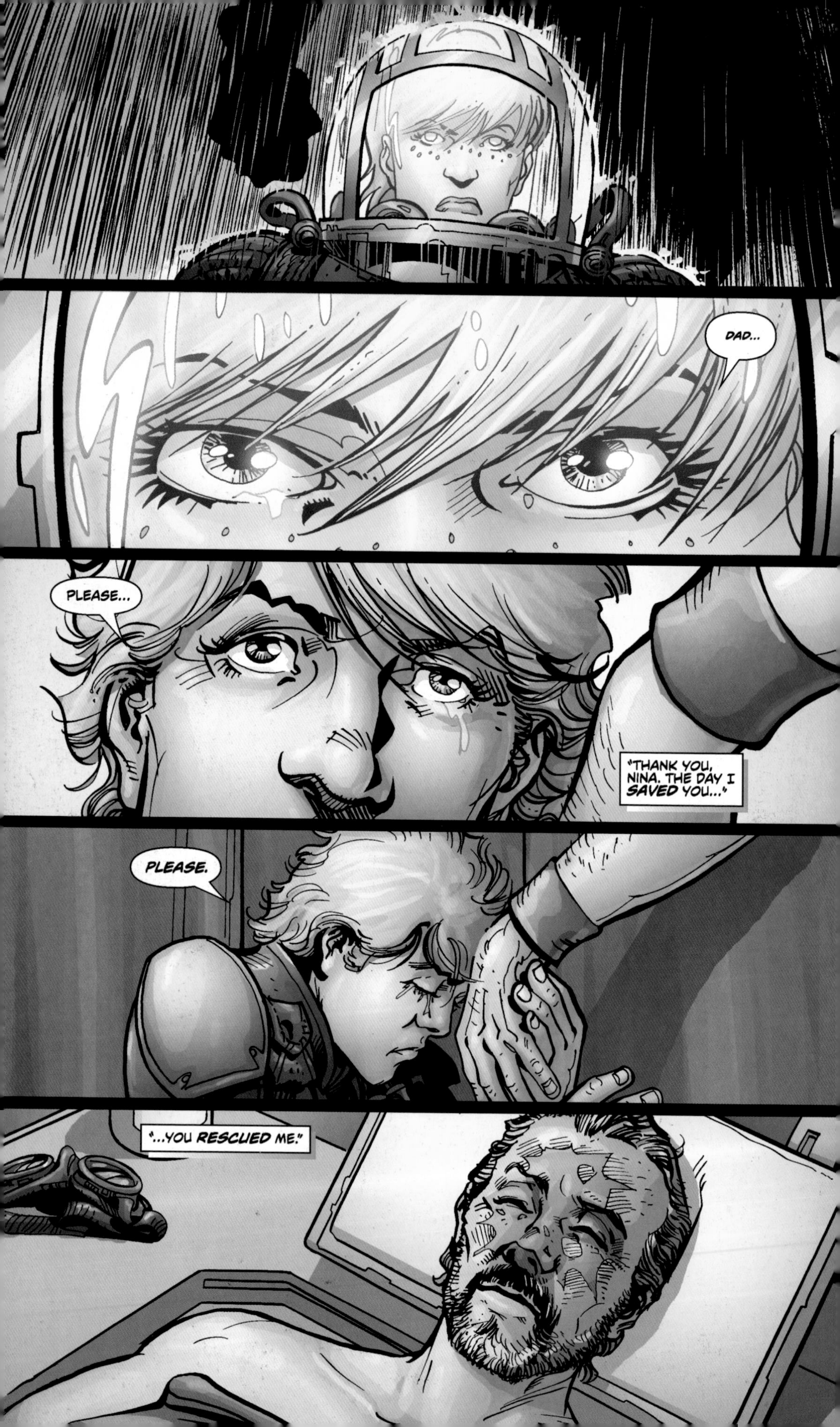
DAD...
PLEASE...
"THANK YOU, NINA. THE DAY I SAVED YOU..."
PLEASE.
"...YOU RESCUED ME."

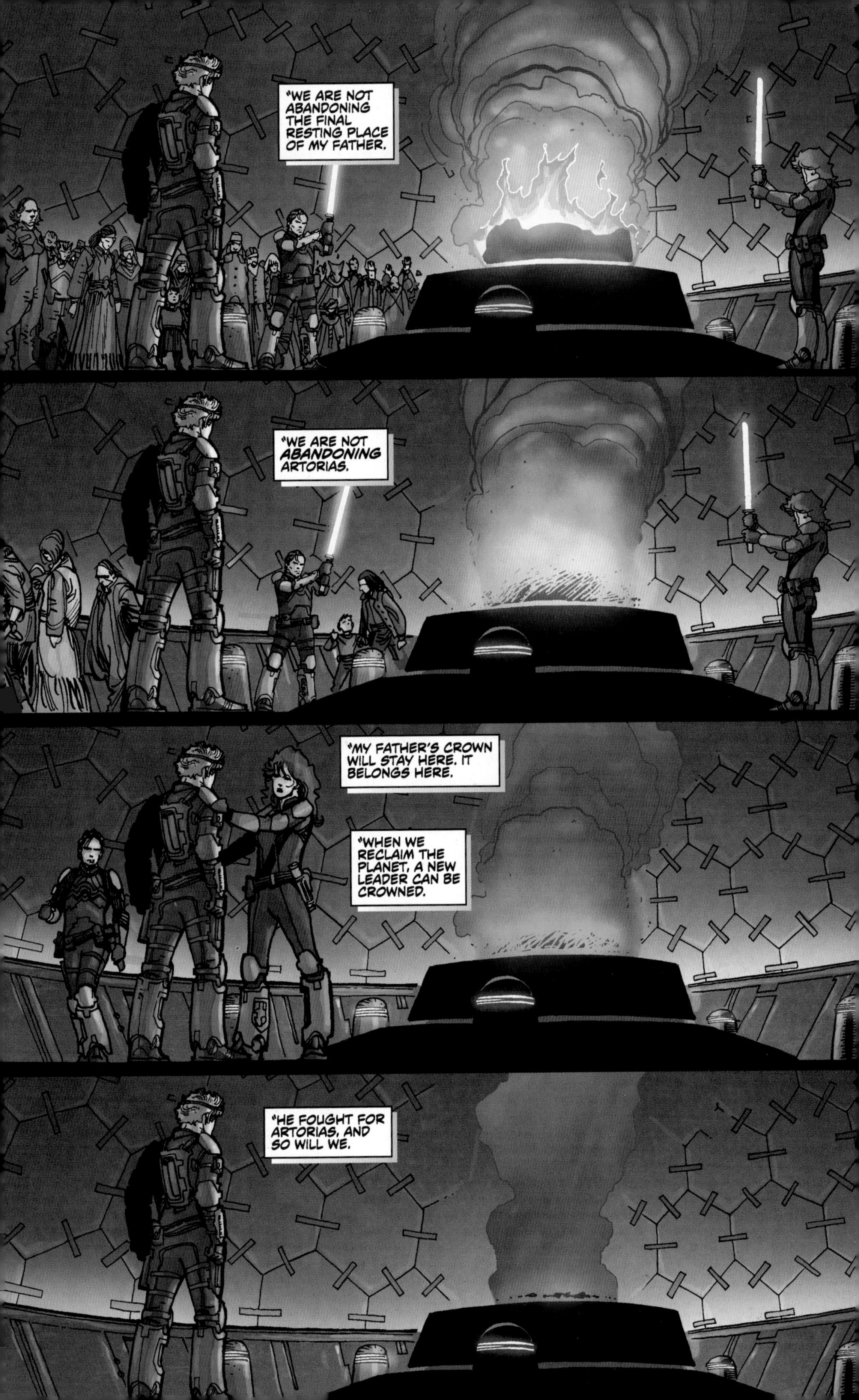
"WE ARE NOT ABANDONING THE FINAL RESTING PLACE OF MY FATHER.
"WE ARE NOT *ABANDONING* ARTORIAS.
"MY FATHER'S CROWN WILL STAY HERE. IT BELONGS HERE.
"WHEN WE RECLAIM THE PLANET, A NEW LEADER CAN BE CROWNED.
"HE FOUGHT FOR ARTORIAS, AND SO WILL WE.

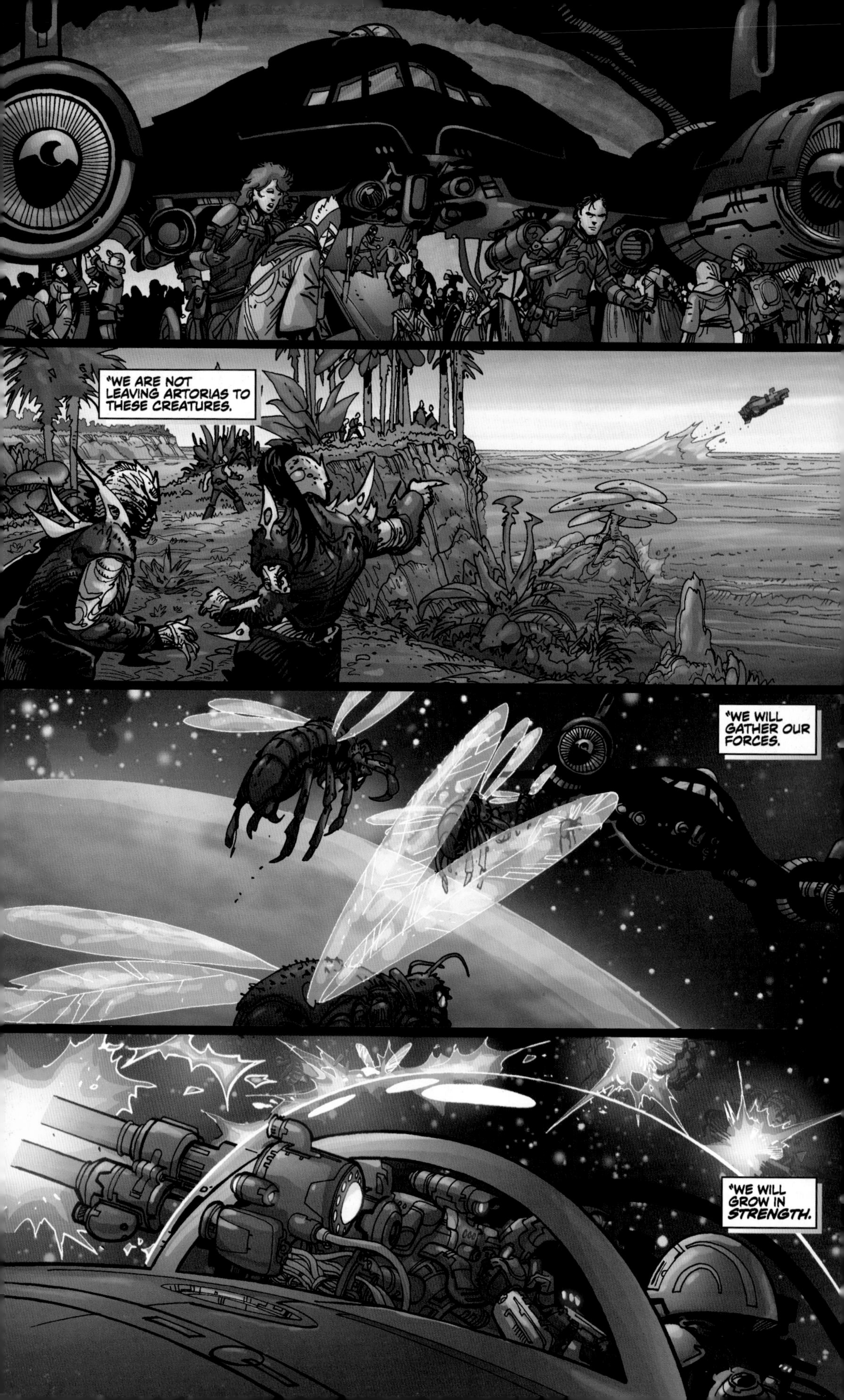
"WE ARE NOT LEAVING ARTORIAS TO THESE CREATURES.
"WE WILL GATHER OUR FORCES.
"WE WILL GROW IN *STRENGTH*.

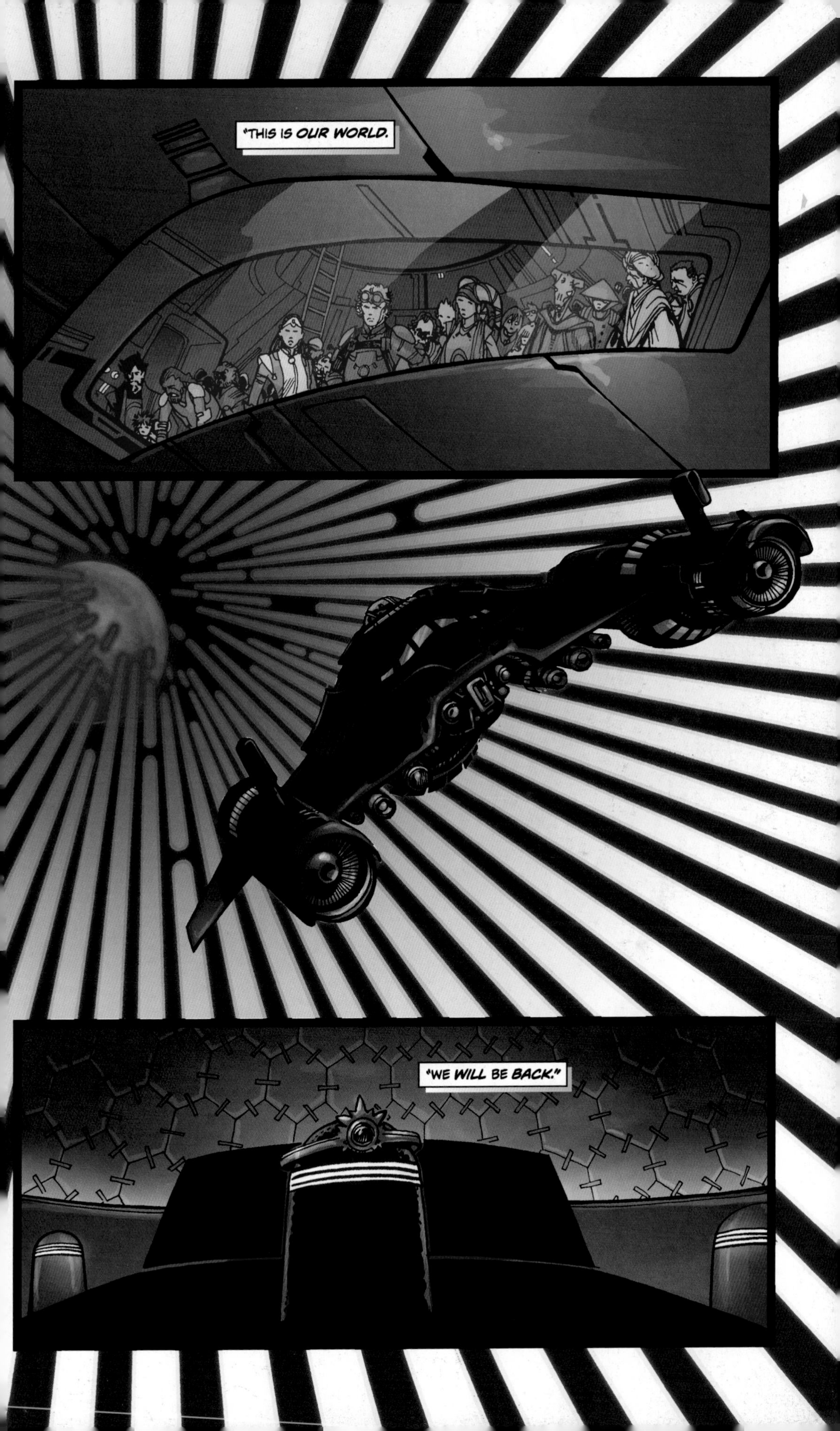
"THIS IS OUR WORLD.
"WE WILL BE BACK."

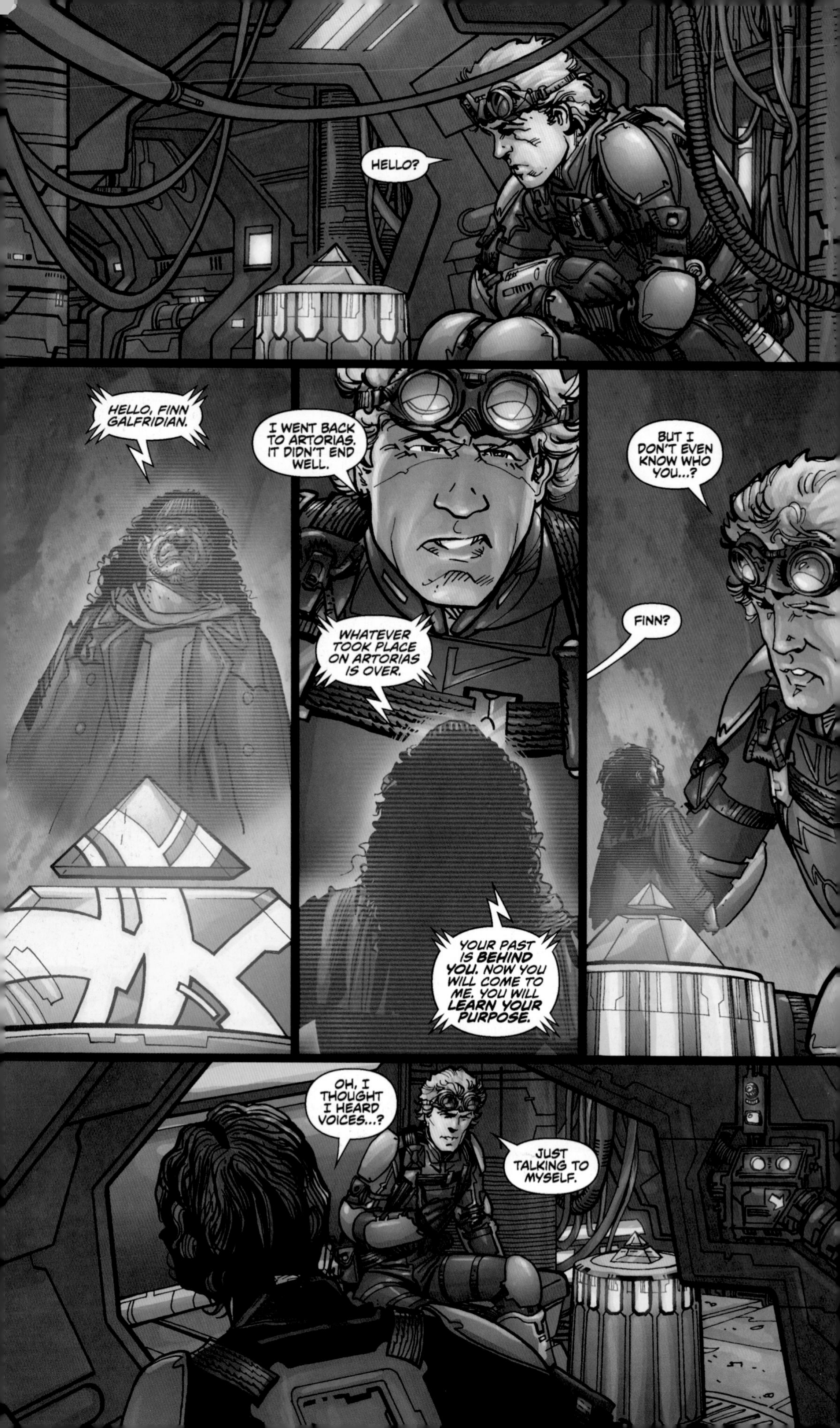
HELLO?
HELLO, FINN GALFRIDIAN.
I WENT BACK TO ARTORIAS. IT DIDN'T END WELL.
WHATEVER TOOK PLACE ON ARTORIAS IS OVER.
YOUR PAST IS BEHIND YOU. NOW YOU WILL COME TO ME. YOU WILL LEARN YOUR PURPOSE.
BUT I DON'T EVEN KNOW WHO YOU...?
FINN?
OH, I THOUGHT I HEARD VOICES...?
JUST TALKING TO MYSELF.

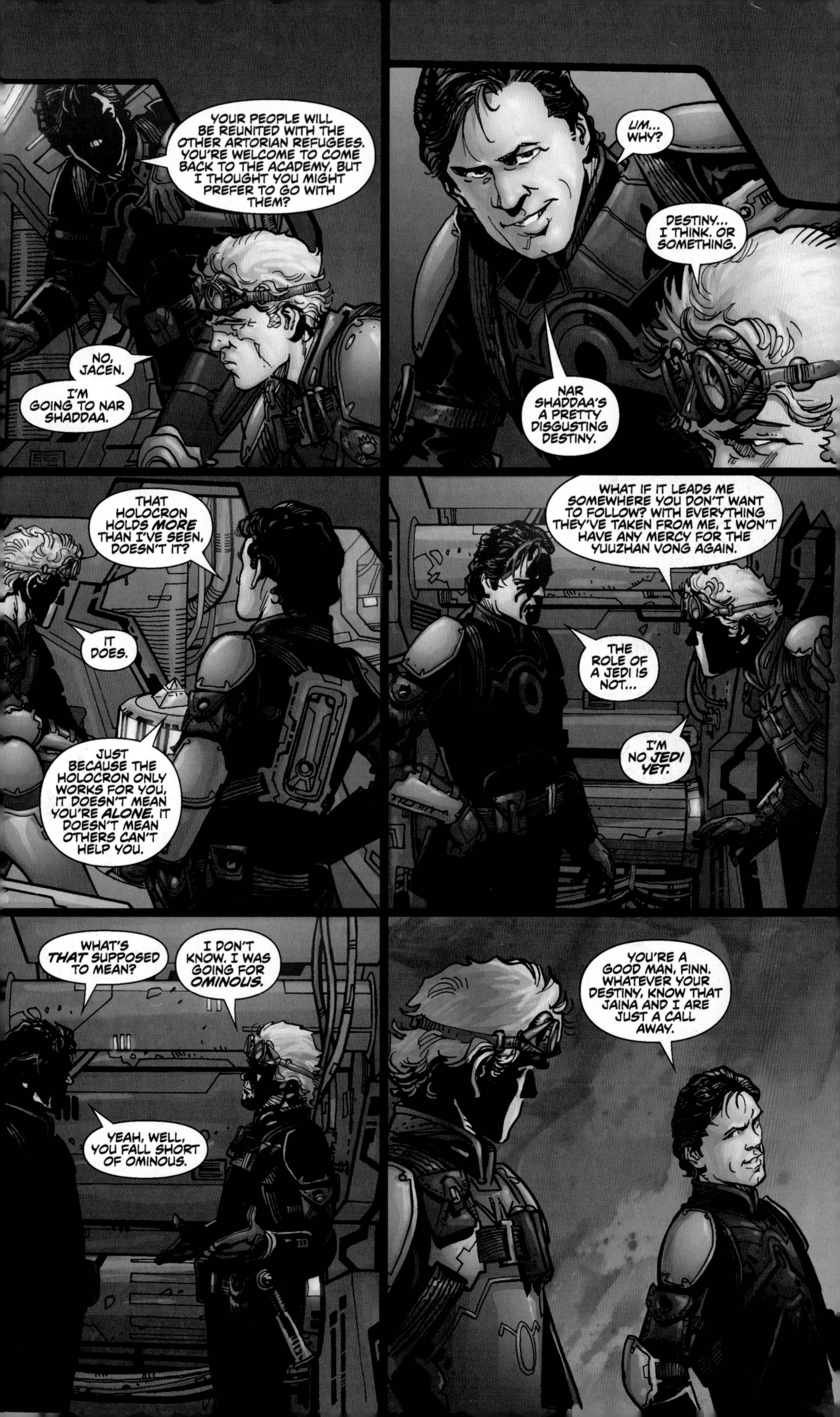
YOUR PEOPLE WILL BE REUNITED WITH THE OTHER ARTORIAN REFUGEES. YOU'RE WELCOME TO COME BACK TO THE ACADEMY, BUT I THOUGHT YOU MIGHT PREFER TO GO WITH THEM?
NO, JACEN.
I'M GOING TO NAR SHADDAA.
UM... WHY?
DESTINY... I THINK. OR SOMETHING.
NAR SHADDAA'S A PRETTY DISGUSTING DESTINY.
THAT HOLOCRON HOLDS MORE THAN I'VE SEEN, DOESN'T IT?
IT DOES.
JUST BECAUSE THE HOLOCRON ONLY WORKS FOR YOU, IT DOESN'T MEAN YOU'RE ALONE. IT DOESN'T MEAN OTHERS CAN'T HELP YOU.
WHAT IF IT LEADS ME SOMEWHERE YOU DON'T WANT TO FOLLOW? WITH EVERYTHING THEY'VE TAKEN FROM ME, I WON'T HAVE ANY MERCY FOR THE YUUZHAN VONG AGAIN.
THE ROLE OF A JEDI IS NOT...
I'M NO JEDI YET.
WHAT'S THAT SUPPOSED TO MEAN?
I DON'T KNOW. I WAS GOING FOR OMINOUS.
YEAH, WELL, YOU FALL SHORT OF OMINOUS.
YOU'RE A GOOD MAN, FINN. WHATEVER YOUR DESTINY, KNOW THAT JAINA AND I ARE JUST A CALL AWAY.

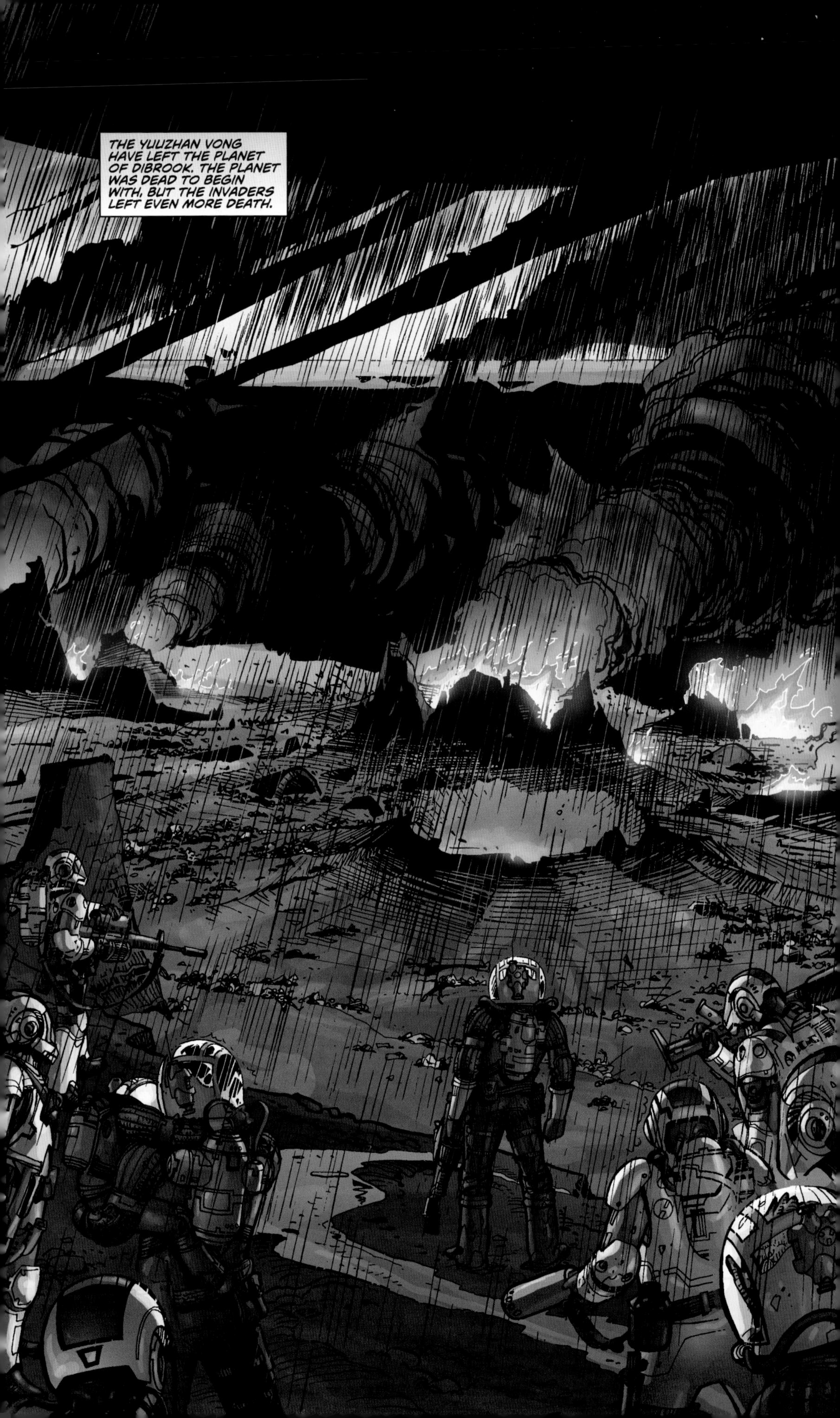
THE YUUZHAN VONG HAVE LEFT THE PLANET OF DIBROOK. THE PLANET WAS DEAD TO BEGIN WITH, BUT THE INVADERS LEFT EVEN MORE DEATH.

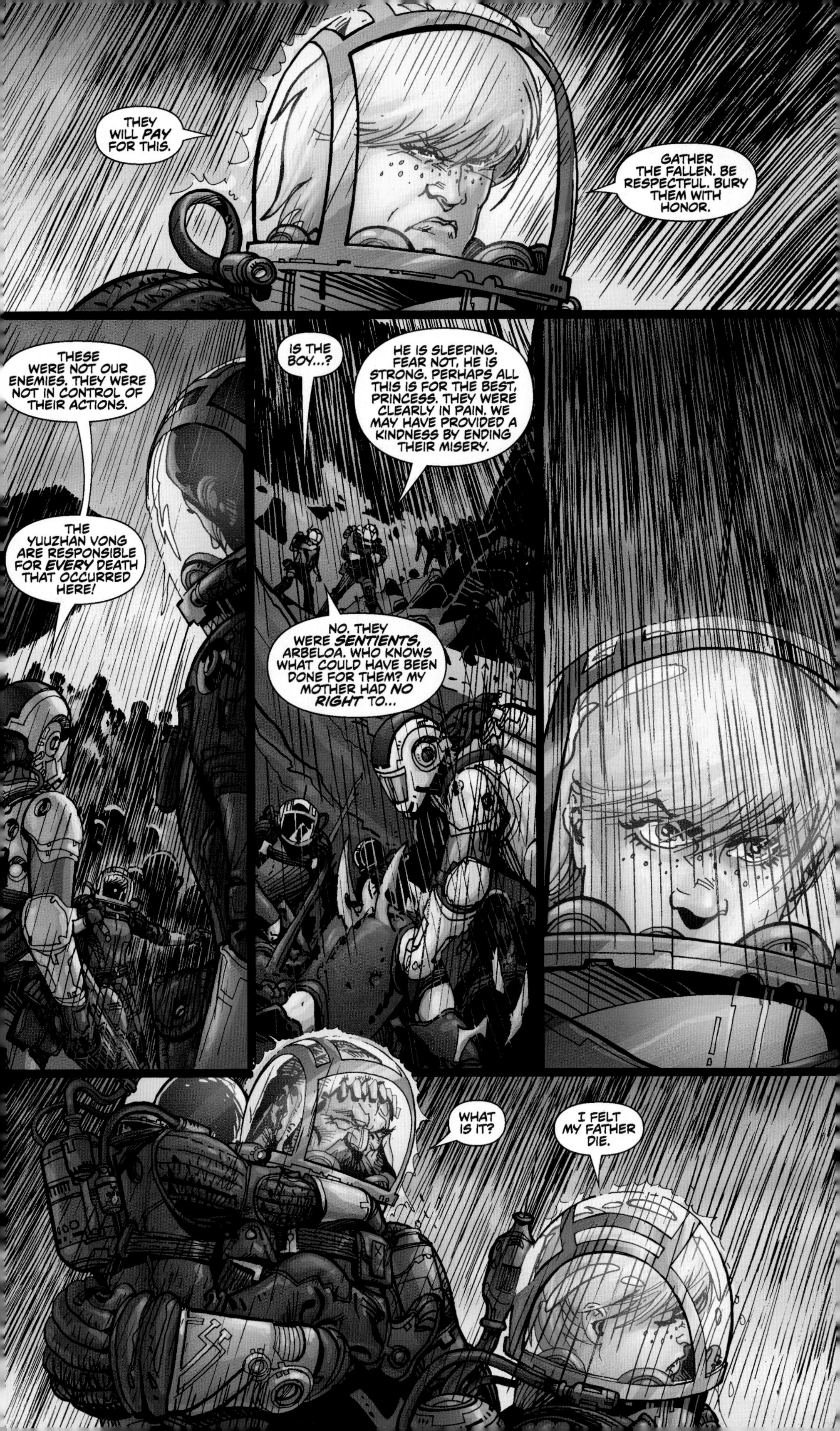
THEY WILL PAY FOR THIS.
GATHER THE FALLEN. BE RESPECTFUL. BURY THEM WITH HONOR.
THESE WERE NOT OUR ENEMIES. THEY WERE NOT IN CONTROL OF THEIR ACTIONS.
THE YUUZHAN VONG ARE RESPONSIBLE FOR EVERY DEATH THAT OCCURRED HERE!
IS THE BOY...?
HE IS SLEEPING. FEAR NOT, HE IS STRONG. PERHAPS ALL THIS IS FOR THE BEST, PRINCESS. THEY WERE CLEARLY IN PAIN. WE MAY HAVE PROVIDED A KINDNESS BY ENDING THEIR MISERY.
NO. THEY WERE SENTIENTS, ARBELOA. WHO KNOWS WHAT COULD HAVE BEEN DONE FOR THEM? MY MOTHER HAD NO RIGHT TO...
WHAT IS IT?
I FELT MY FATHER DIE.

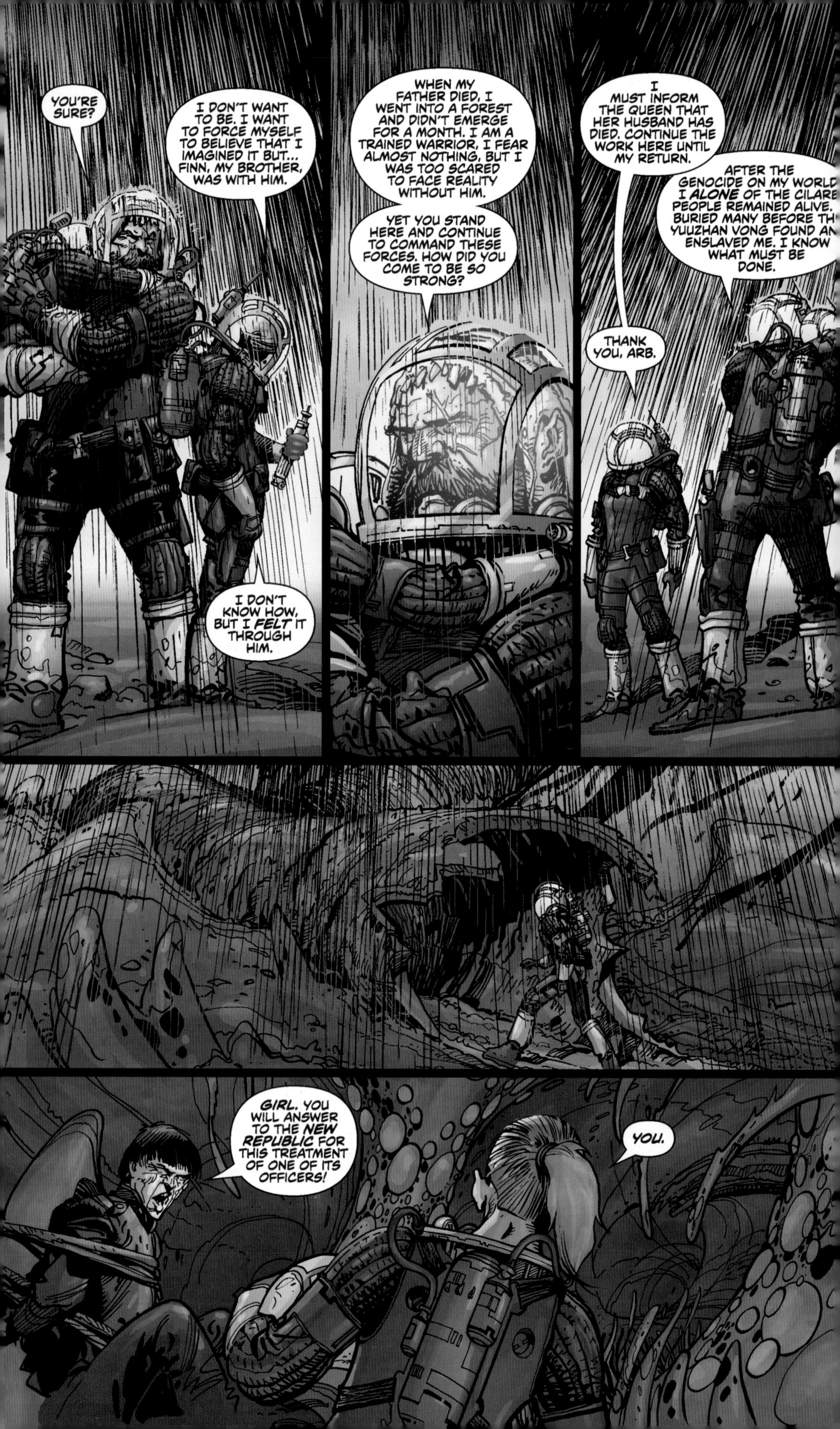
YOU'RE SURE?
I DON'T WANT TO BE. I WANT TO FORCE MYSELF TO BELIEVE THAT I IMAGINED IT BUT... FINN, MY BROTHER, WAS WITH HIM.
I DON'T KNOW HOW, BUT I *FELT* IT THROUGH HIM.
WHEN MY FATHER DIED, I WENT INTO A FOREST AND DIDN'T EMERGE FOR A MONTH. I AM A TRAINED WARRIOR, I FEAR ALMOST NOTHING, BUT I WAS TOO SCARED TO FACE REALITY WITHOUT HIM.
YET YOU STAND HERE AND CONTINUE TO COMMAND THESE FORCES. HOW DID YOU COME TO BE SO STRONG?
I MUST INFORM THE QUEEN THAT HER HUSBAND HAS DIED. CONTINUE THE WORK HERE UNTIL MY RETURN.
AFTER THE GENOCIDE ON MY WORLD I *ALONE* OF THE CILARE PEOPLE REMAINED ALIVE. BURIED MANY BEFORE TH YUUZHAN VONG FOUND AN ENSLAVED ME. I KNOW WHAT MUST BE DONE.
THANK YOU, ARB.
GIRL. YOU WILL ANSWER TO THE *NEW REPUBLIC* FOR THIS TREATMENT OF ONE OF ITS OFFICERS!
YOU.

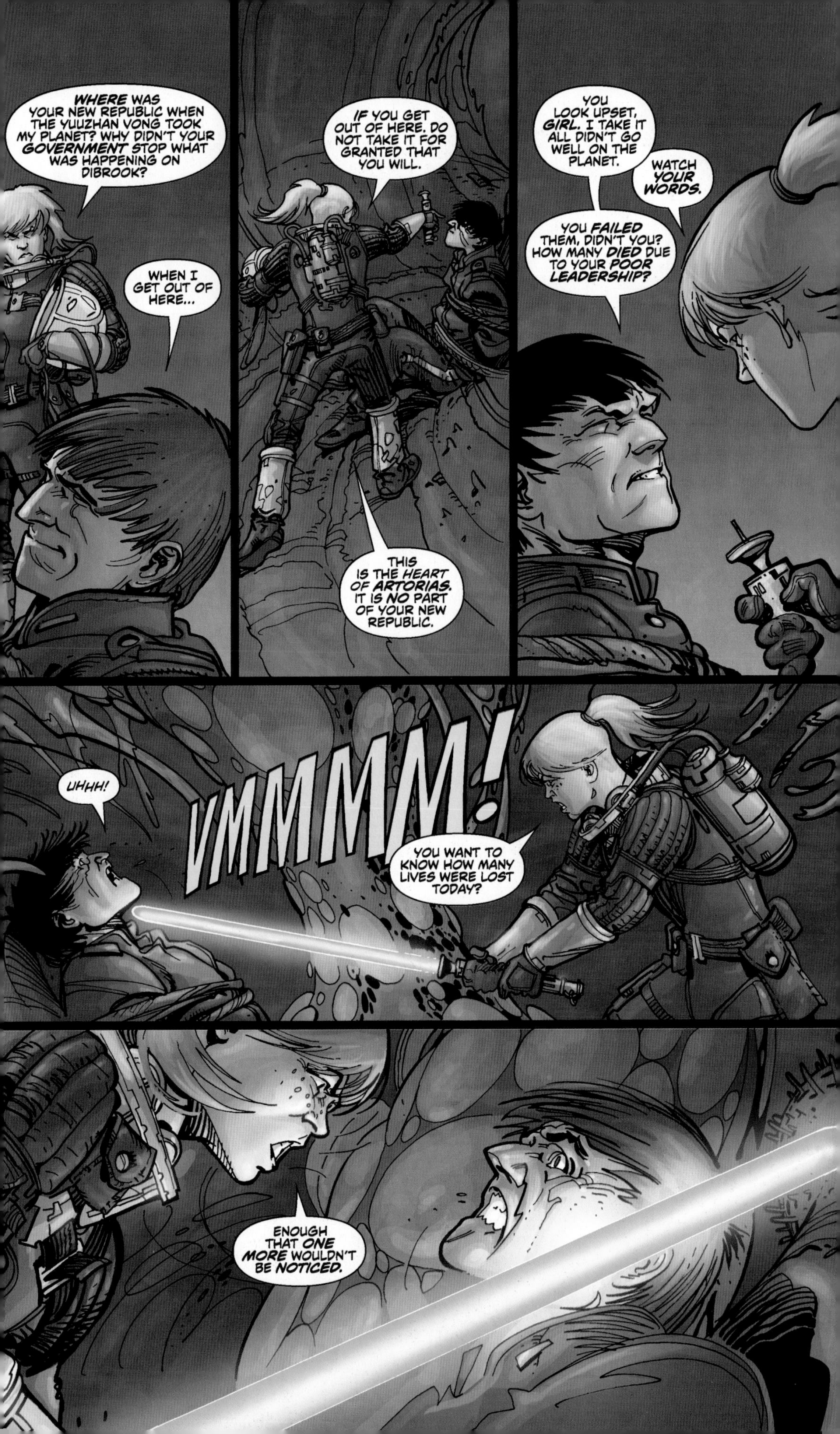
WHERE WAS YOUR NEW REPUBLIC WHEN THE YUUZHAN VONG TOOK MY PLANET? WHY DIDN'T YOUR GOVERNMENT STOP WHAT WAS HAPPENING ON DIBROOK?
WHEN I GET OUT OF HERE...
IF YOU GET OUT OF HERE. DO NOT TAKE IT FOR GRANTED THAT YOU WILL.
THIS IS THE HEART OF ARTORIAS. IT IS NO PART OF YOUR NEW REPUBLIC.
YOU LOOK UPSET, GIRL. I TAKE IT ALL DIDN'T GO WELL ON THE PLANET.
WATCH YOUR WORDS.
YOU FAILED THEM, DIDN'T YOU? HOW MANY DIED DUE TO YOUR POOR LEADERSHIP?
UHHH!
VMMMM!
YOU WANT TO KNOW HOW MANY LIVES WERE LOST TODAY?
ENOUGH THAT ONE MORE WOULDN'T BE NOTICED.

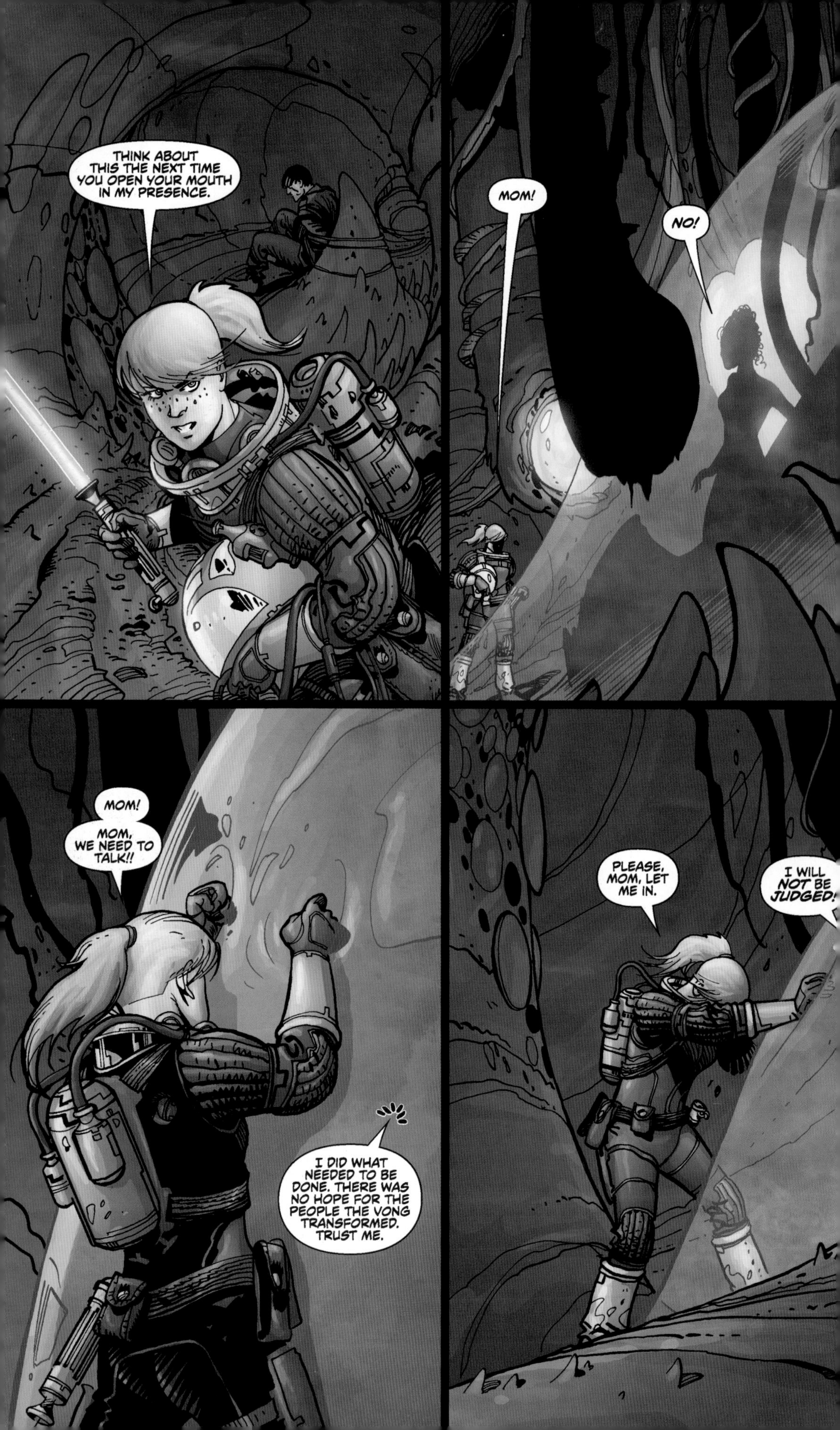
THINK ABOUT THIS THE NEXT TIME YOU OPEN YOUR MOUTH IN MY PRESENCE.
MOM!
NO!
MOM!
MOM, WE NEED TO TALK!!
I DID WHAT NEEDED TO BE DONE. THERE WAS NO HOPE FOR THE PEOPLE THE VONG TRANSFORMED. TRUST ME.
PLEASE, MOM, LET ME IN.
I WILL NOT BE JUDGED!

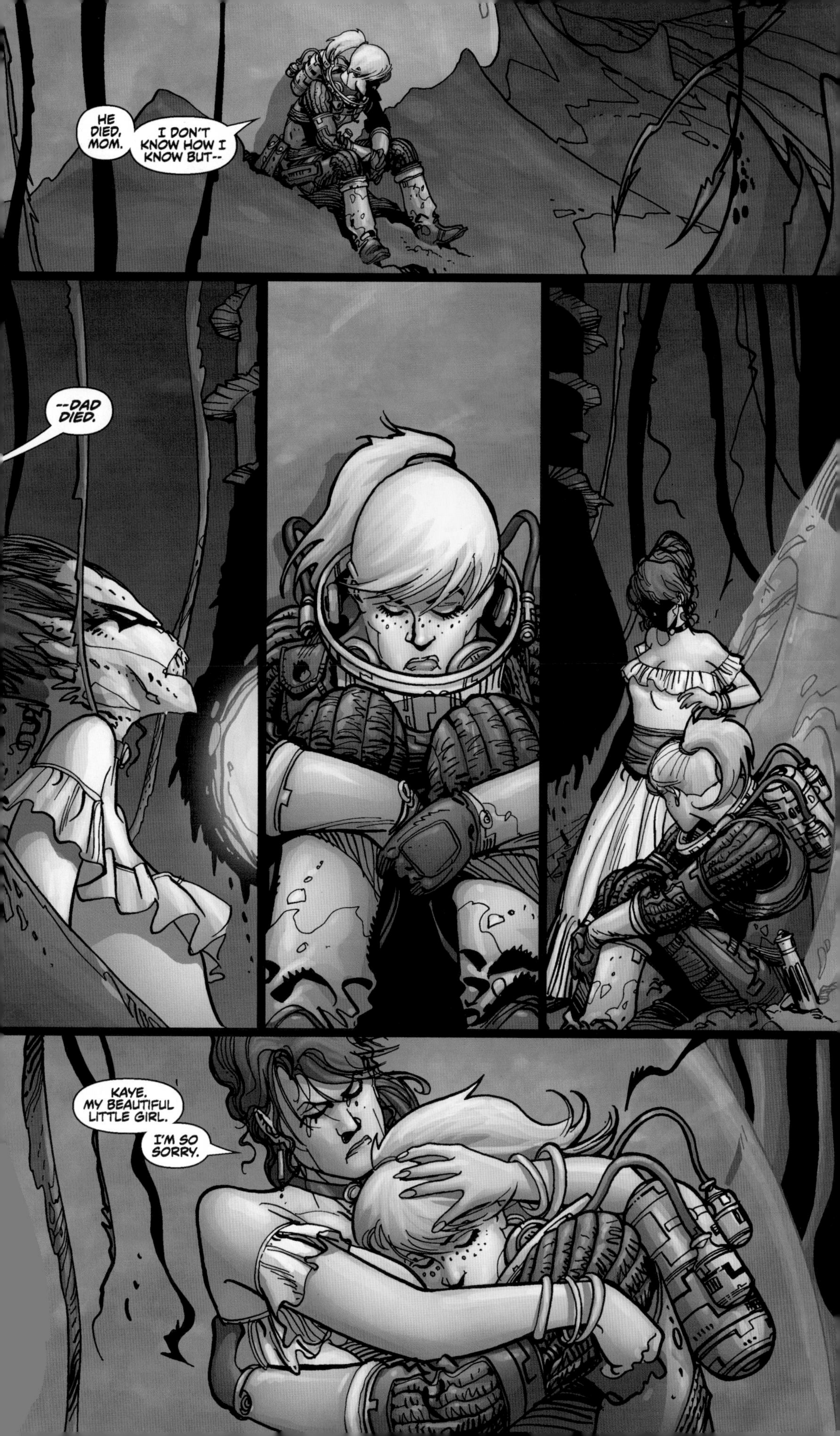
HE DIED, MOM.
I DON'T KNOW HOW I KNOW BUT--
--DAD DIED.
KAYE. MY BEAUTIFUL LITTLE GIRL.
I'M SO SORRY.

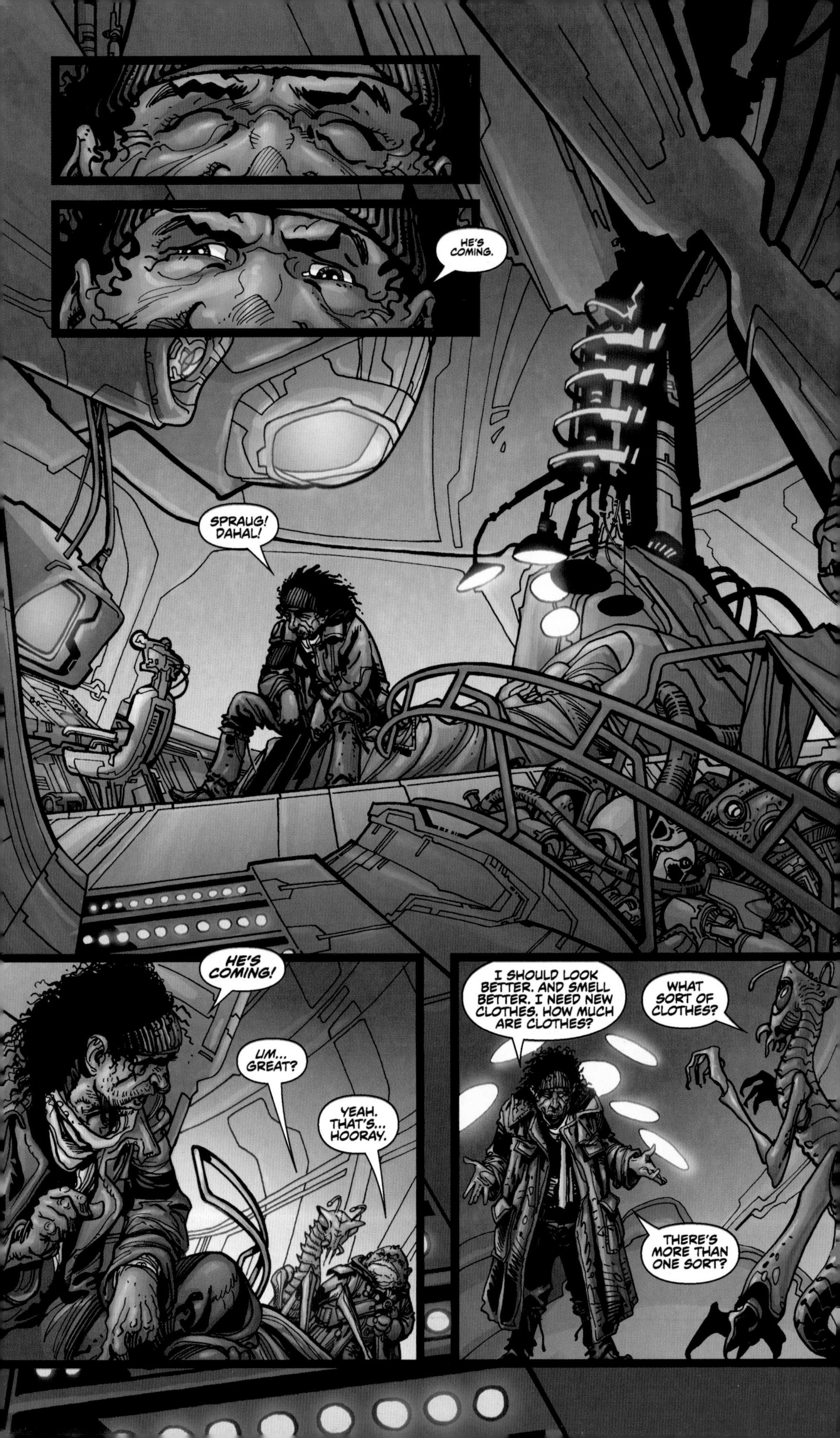
HE'S COMING.
SPRAUG! DAHAL!
HE'S COMING!
UM... GREAT?
YEAH. THAT'S... HOORAY.
I SHOULD LOOK BETTER. AND SMELL BETTER. I NEED NEW CLOTHES. HOW MUCH ARE CLOTHES?
WHAT SORT OF CLOTHES?
THERE'S MORE THAN ONE SORT?

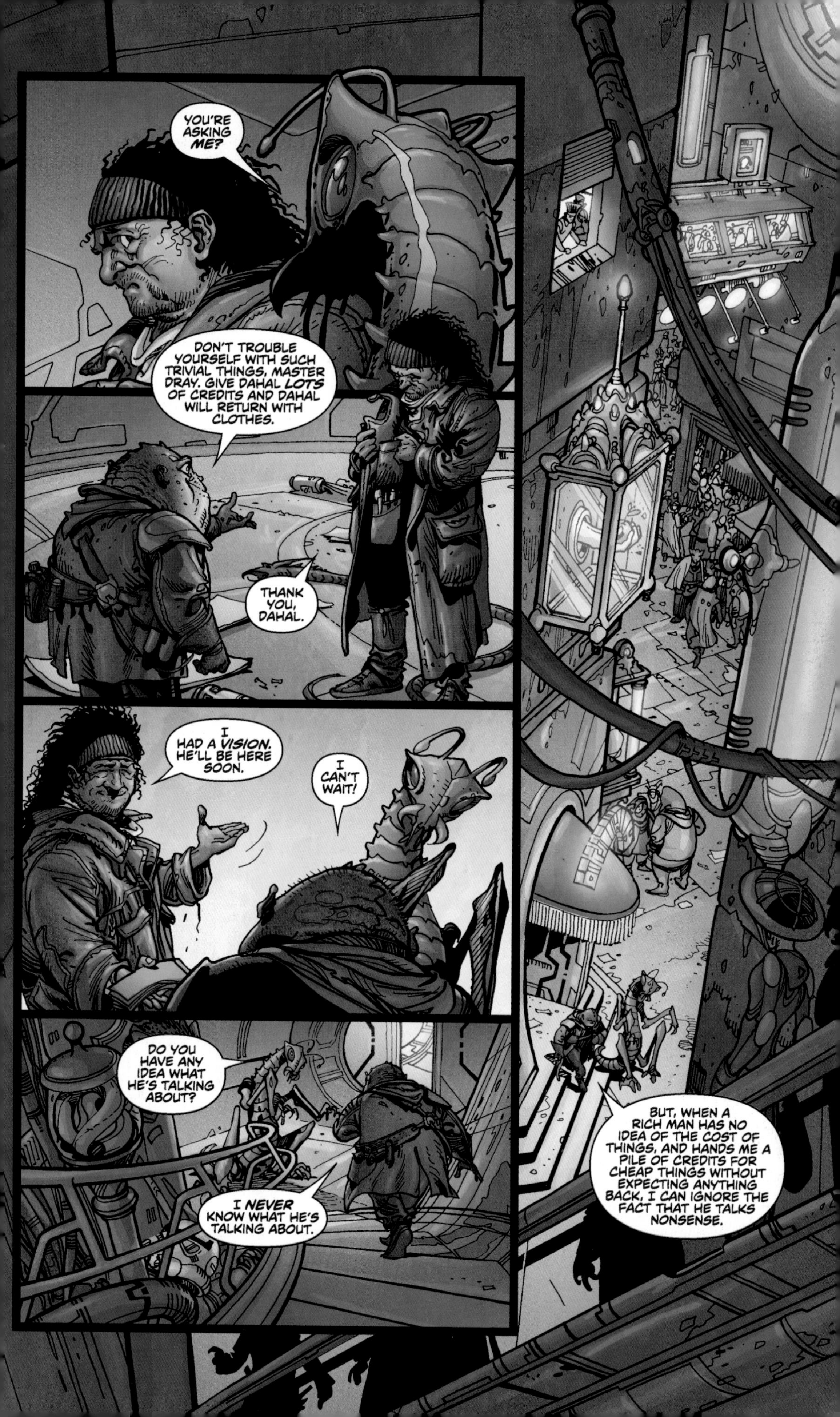
YOU'RE ASKING *ME?*
DON'T TROUBLE YOURSELF WITH SUCH TRIVIAL THINGS, MASTER DRAY. GIVE DAHAL *LOTS* OF CREDITS AND DAHAL WILL RETURN WITH CLOTHES.
THANK YOU, DAHAL.
I HAD A *VISION*. HE'LL BE HERE SOON.
I CAN'T WAIT!
DO YOU HAVE ANY IDEA WHAT HE'S TALKING ABOUT?
I *NEVER* KNOW WHAT HE'S TALKING ABOUT.
BUT, WHEN A RICH MAN HAS NO IDEA OF THE COST OF THINGS, AND HANDS ME A PILE OF CREDITS FOR CHEAP THINGS WITHOUT EXPECTING ANYTHING BACK, I CAN IGNORE THE FACT THAT HE TALKS NONSENSE.

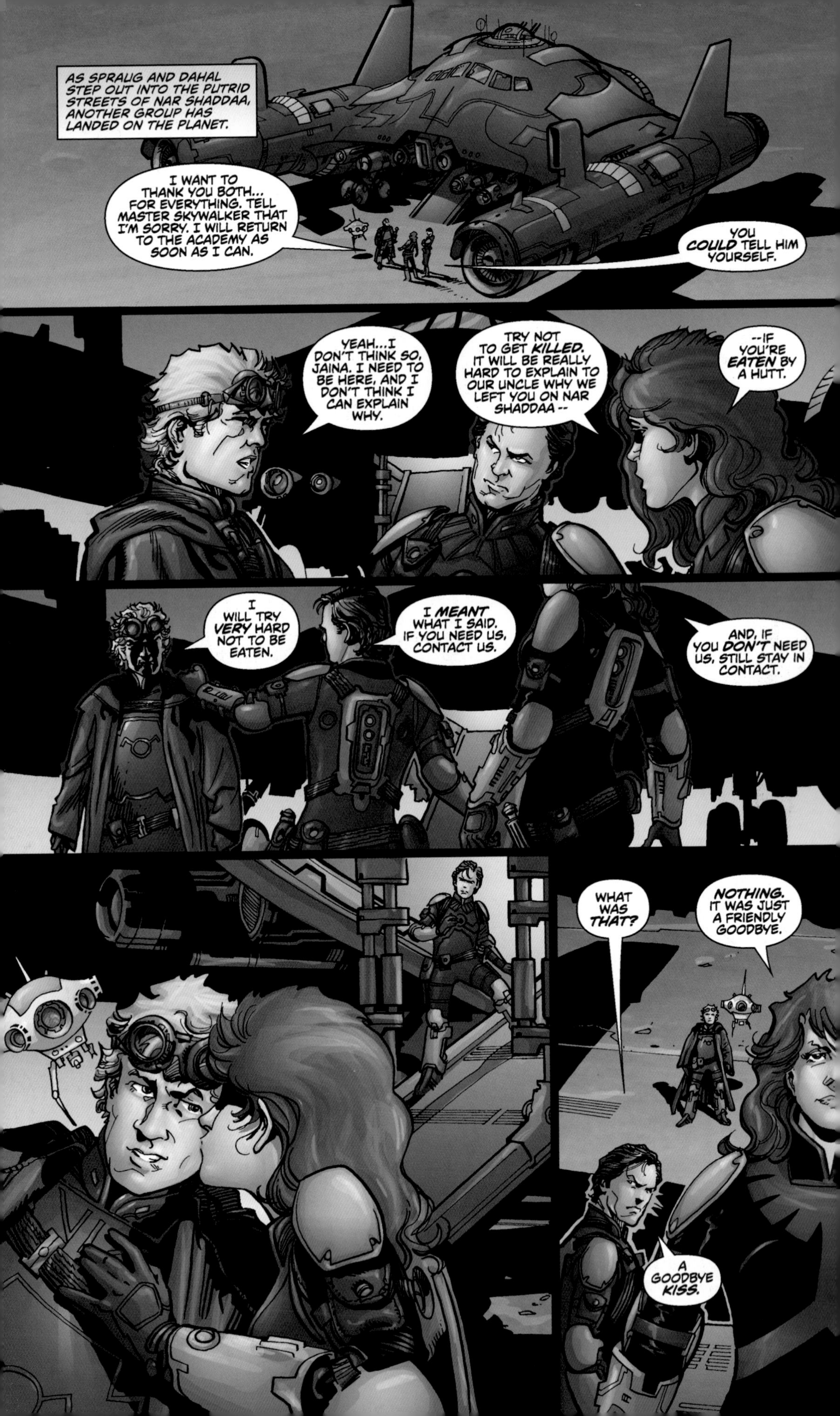
AS SPRAUG AND DAHAL STEP OUT INTO THE PUTRID STREETS OF NAR SHADDAA, ANOTHER GROUP HAS LANDED ON THE PLANET.
I WANT TO THANK YOU BOTH... FOR EVERYTHING. TELL MASTER SKYWALKER THAT I'M SORRY. I WILL RETURN TO THE ACADEMY AS SOON AS I CAN.
YOU COULD TELL HIM YOURSELF.
YEAH...I DON'T THINK SO, JAINA. I NEED TO BE HERE, AND I DON'T THINK I CAN EXPLAIN WHY.
TRY NOT TO GET KILLED. IT WILL BE REALLY HARD TO EXPLAIN TO OUR UNCLE WHY WE LEFT YOU ON NAR SHADDAA --
--IF YOU'RE EATEN BY A HUTT.
I WILL TRY VERY HARD NOT TO BE EATEN.
I MEANT WHAT I SAID. IF YOU NEED US, CONTACT US.
AND, IF YOU DON'T NEED US, STILL STAY IN CONTACT.
WHAT WAS THAT?
NOTHING. IT WAS JUST A FRIENDLY GOODBYE.
A GOODBYE KISS.

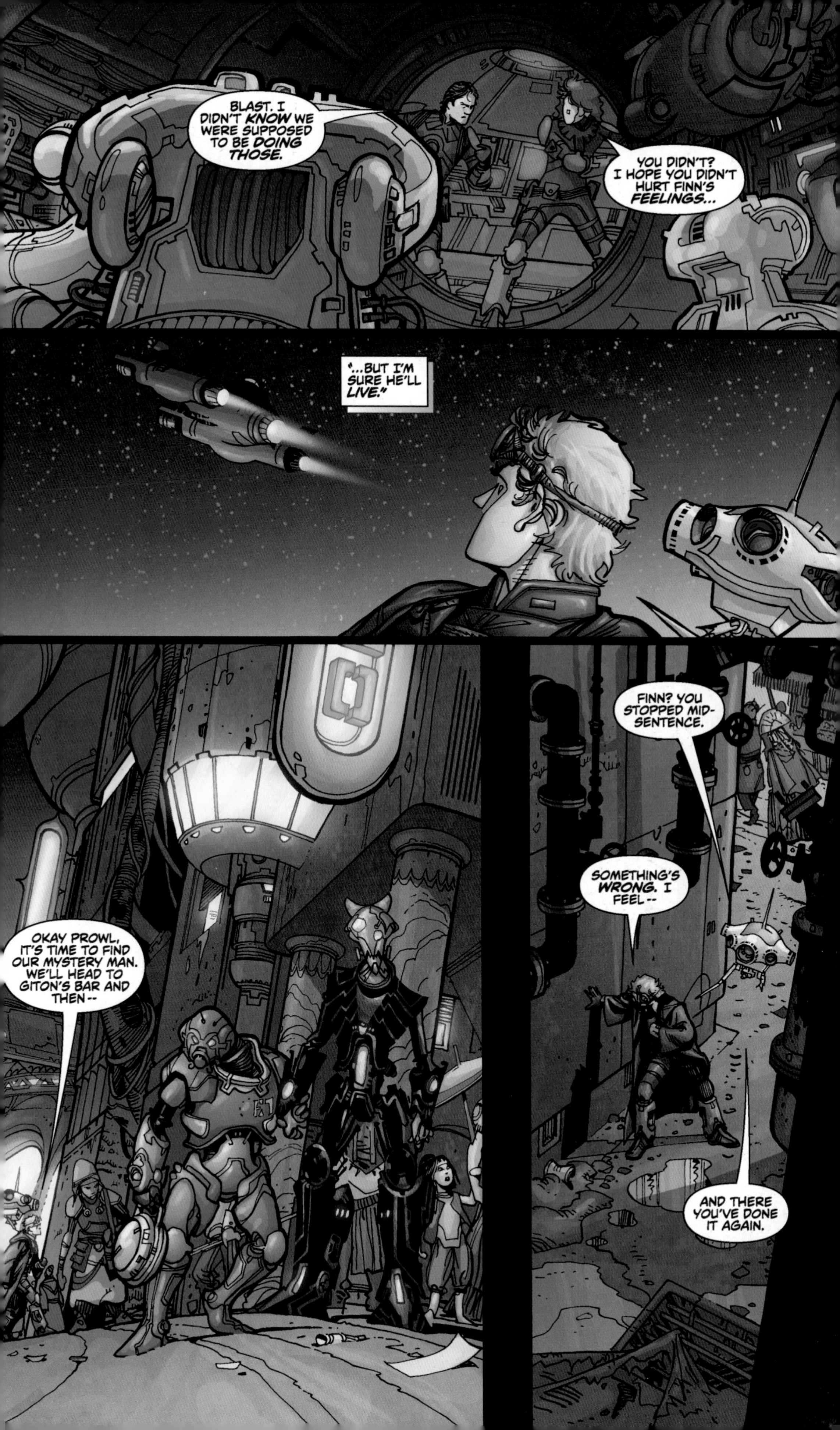

BLAST. I DIDN'T KNOW WE WERE SUPPOSED TO BE DOING THOSE.
YOU DIDN'T? I HOPE YOU DIDN'T HURT FINN'S FEELINGS...
"...BUT I'M SURE HE'LL LIVE."
OKAY PROWL, IT'S TIME TO FIND OUR MYSTERY MAN. WE'LL HEAD TO GITON'S BAR AND THEN --
FINN? YOU STOPPED MID-SENTENCE.
SOMETHING'S WRONG. I FEEL --
AND THERE YOU'VE DONE IT AGAIN.

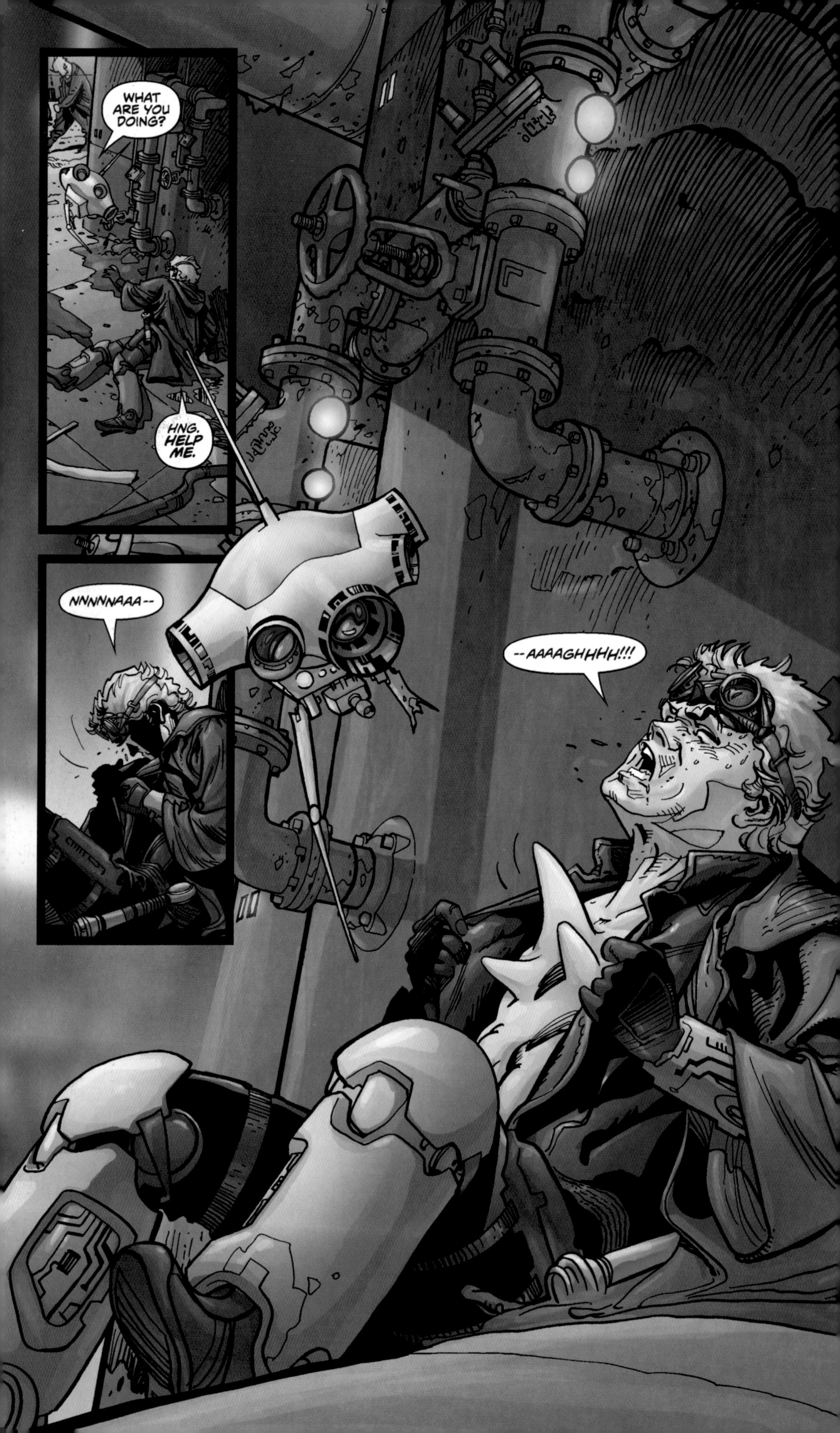
WHAT ARE YOU DOING?
HNG. HELP ME.
NNNNNAAA--
--AAAAGHHHH!!!

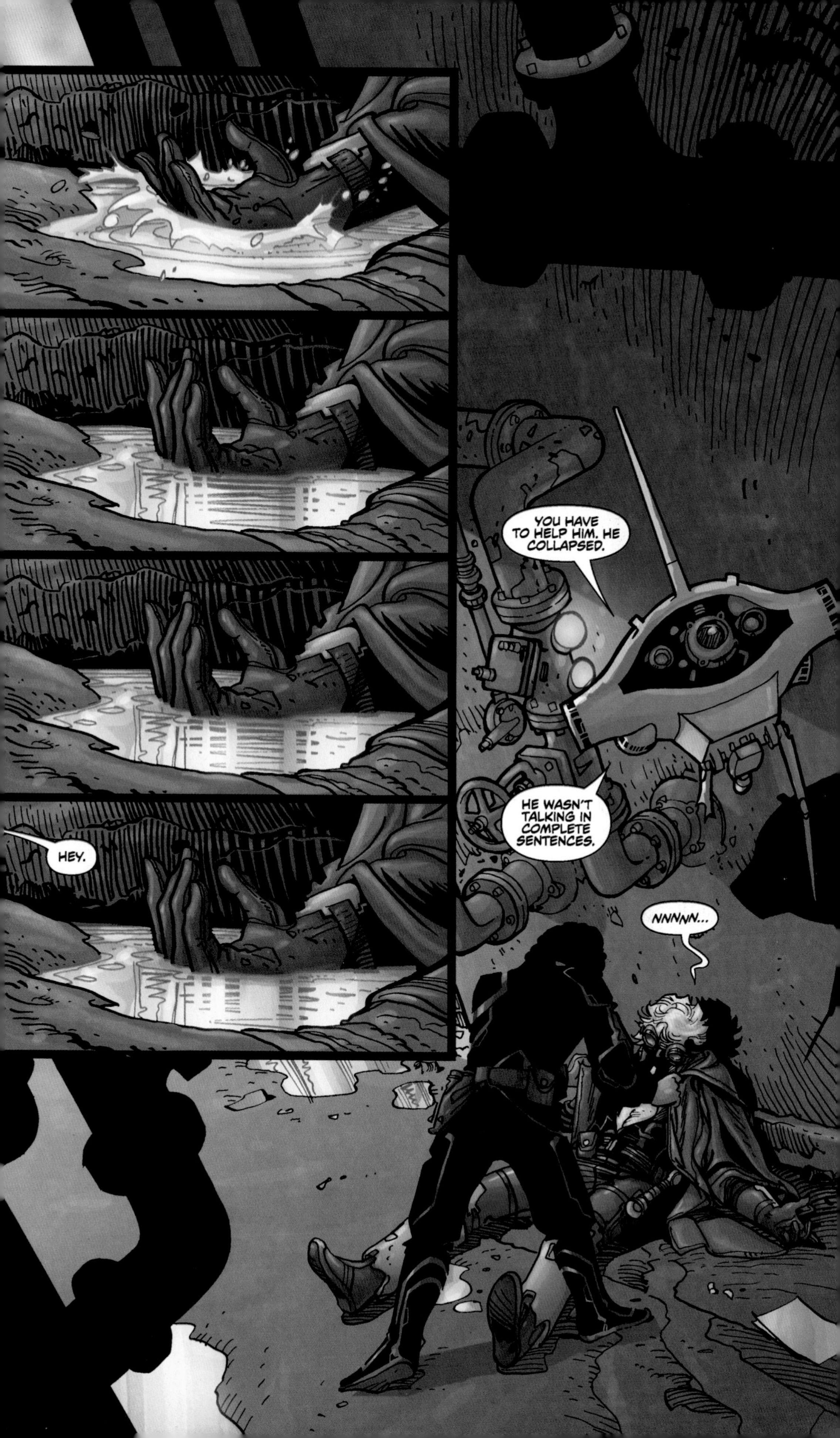
HEY.
YOU HAVE TO HELP HIM. HE COLLAPSED.
HE WASN'T TALKING IN COMPLETE SENTENCES.
NNNNN...

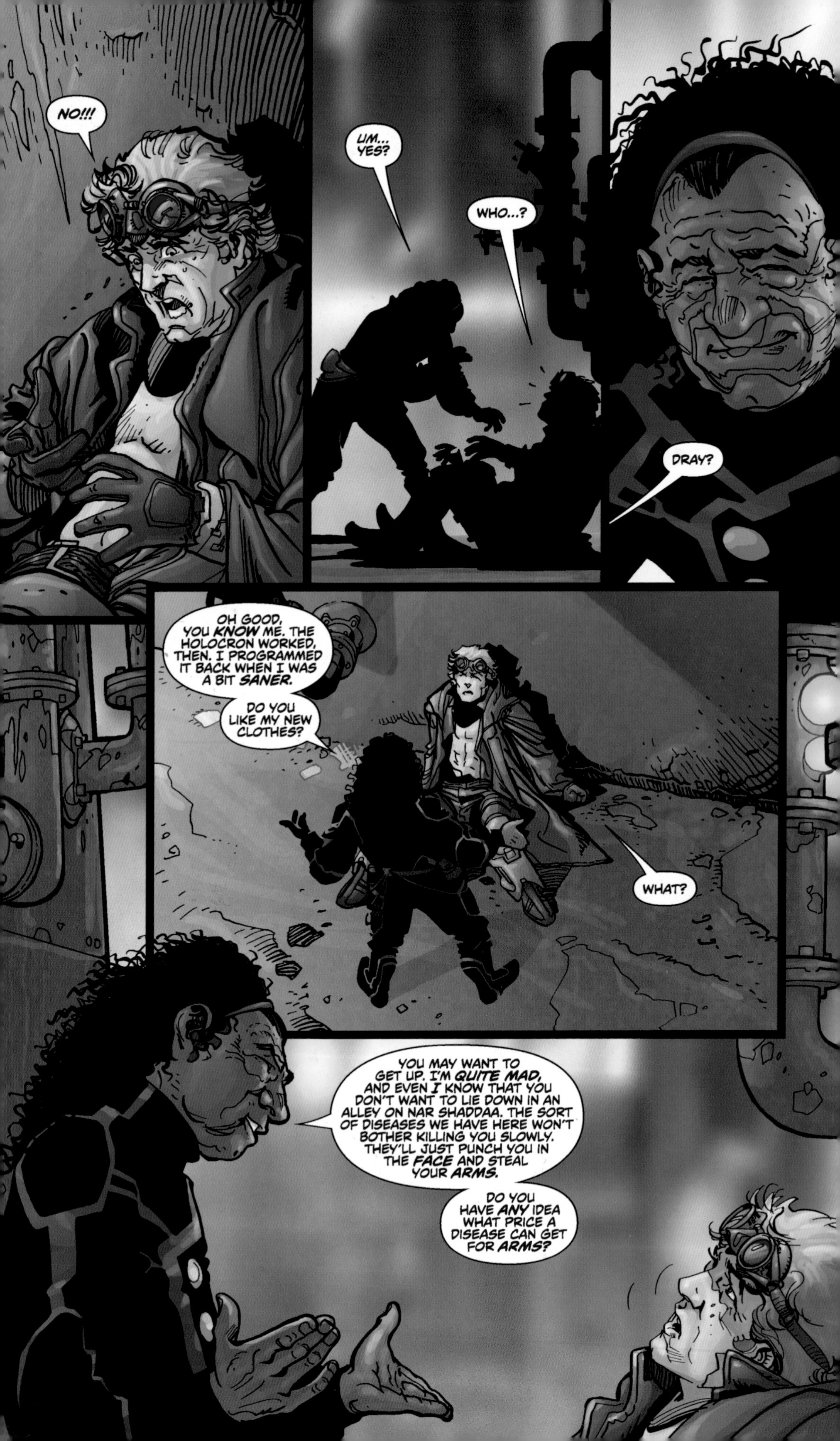
NO!!!
UM... YES?
WHO...?
DRAY?
OH GOOD, YOU KNOW ME. THE HOLOCRON WORKED, THEN. I PROGRAMMED IT BACK WHEN I WAS A BIT SANER.
DO YOU LIKE MY NEW CLOTHES?
WHAT?
YOU MAY WANT TO GET UP. I'M QUITE MAD, AND EVEN I KNOW THAT YOU DON'T WANT TO LIE DOWN IN AN ALLEY ON NAR SHADDAA. THE SORT OF DISEASES WE HAVE HERE WON'T BOTHER KILLING YOU SLOWLY. THEY'LL JUST PUNCH YOU IN THE FACE AND STEAL YOUR ARMS.
DO YOU HAVE ANY IDEA WHAT PRICE A DISEASE CAN GET FOR ARMS?

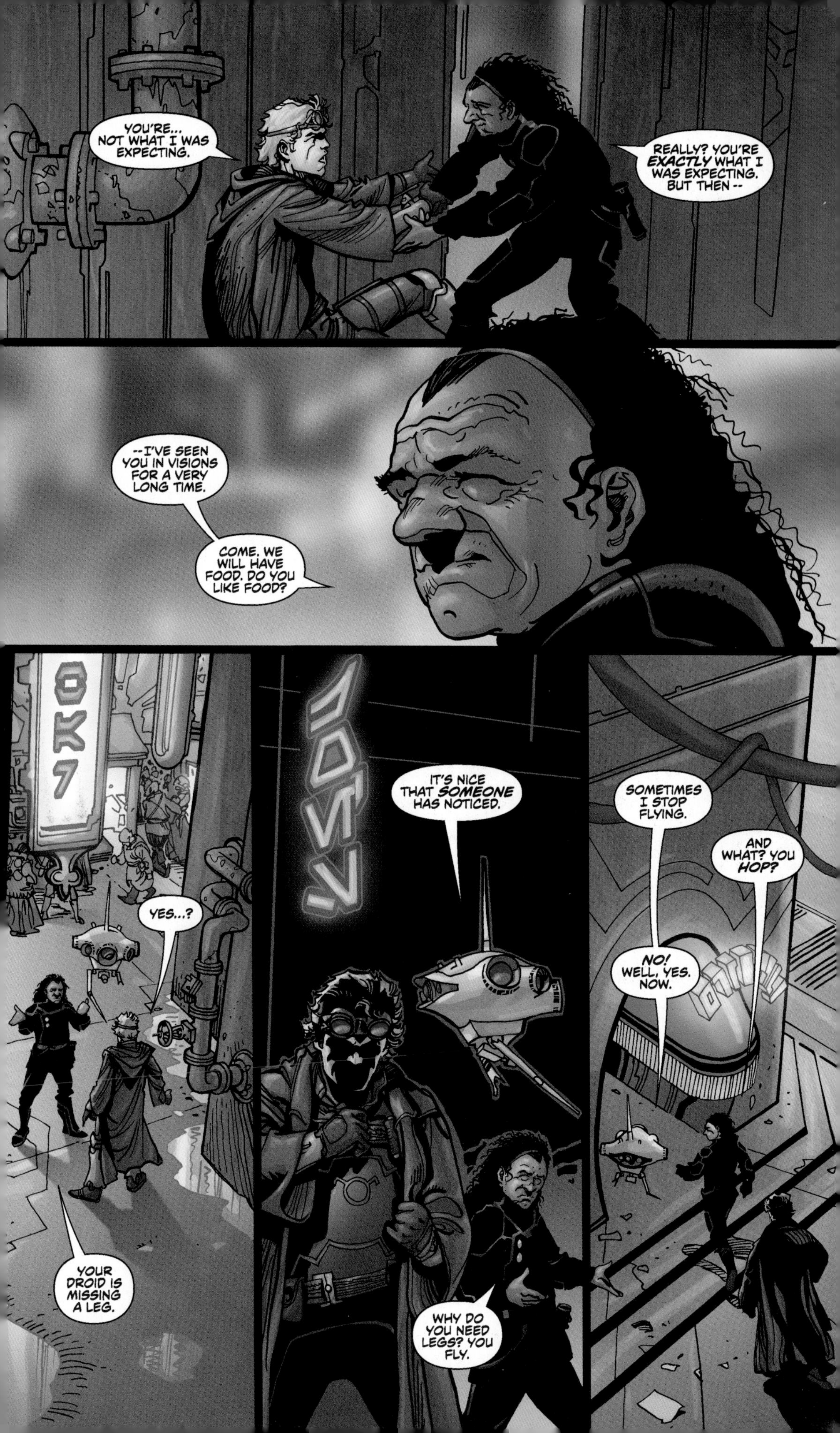
YOU'RE... NOT WHAT I WAS EXPECTING.
REALLY? YOU'RE *EXACTLY* WHAT I WAS EXPECTING. BUT THEN --
--I'VE SEEN YOU IN VISIONS FOR A VERY LONG TIME.
COME. WE WILL HAVE FOOD. DO YOU LIKE FOOD?
YES...?
YOUR DROID IS MISSING A LEG.
IT'S NICE THAT *SOMEONE* HAS NOTICED.
WHY DO YOU NEED LEGS? YOU FLY.
SOMETIMES I STOP FLYING.
AND WHAT? YOU *HOP?*
NO! WELL, YES. NOW.

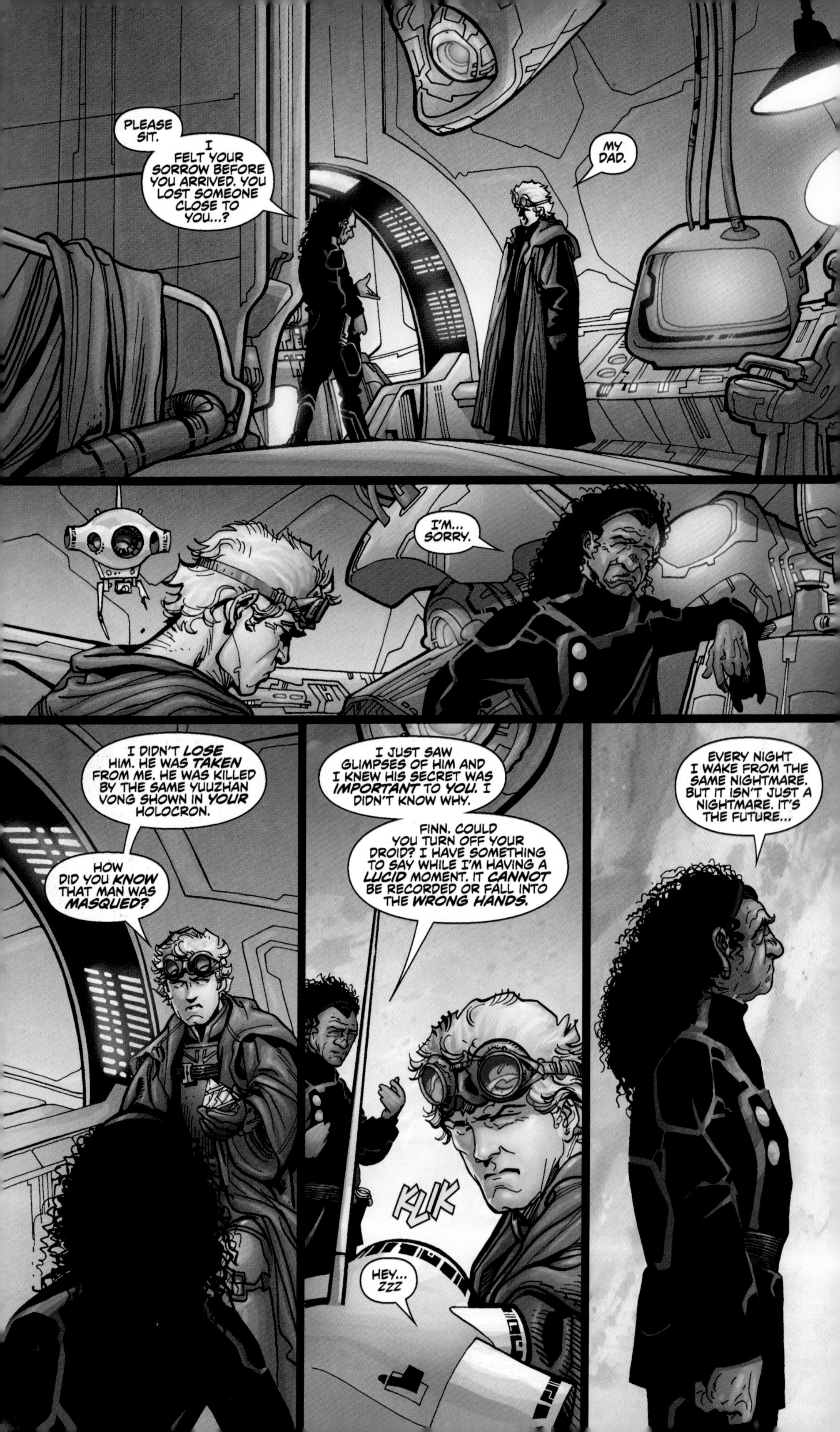

PLEASE SIT.
I FELT YOUR SORROW BEFORE YOU ARRIVED. YOU LOST SOMEONE CLOSE TO YOU...?
MY DAD.
I'M... SORRY.
I DIDN'T *LOSE* HIM. HE WAS *TAKEN* FROM ME. HE WAS KILLED BY THE SAME YUUZHAN VONG SHOWN IN *YOUR* HOLOCRON.
HOW DID YOU *KNOW* THAT MAN WAS *MASQUED?*
I JUST SAW GLIMPSES OF HIM AND I KNEW HIS SECRET WAS *IMPORTANT* TO *YOU.* I DIDN'T KNOW WHY.
FINN. COULD YOU TURN OFF YOUR DROID? I HAVE SOMETHING TO SAY WHILE I'M HAVING A *LUCID* MOMENT. IT *CANNOT* BE RECORDED OR FALL INTO THE *WRONG HANDS.*
KLIK
HEY... ZZZ
EVERY NIGHT I WAKE FROM THE SAME NIGHTMARE. BUT IT ISN'T JUST A NIGHTMARE. IT'S THE FUTURE...

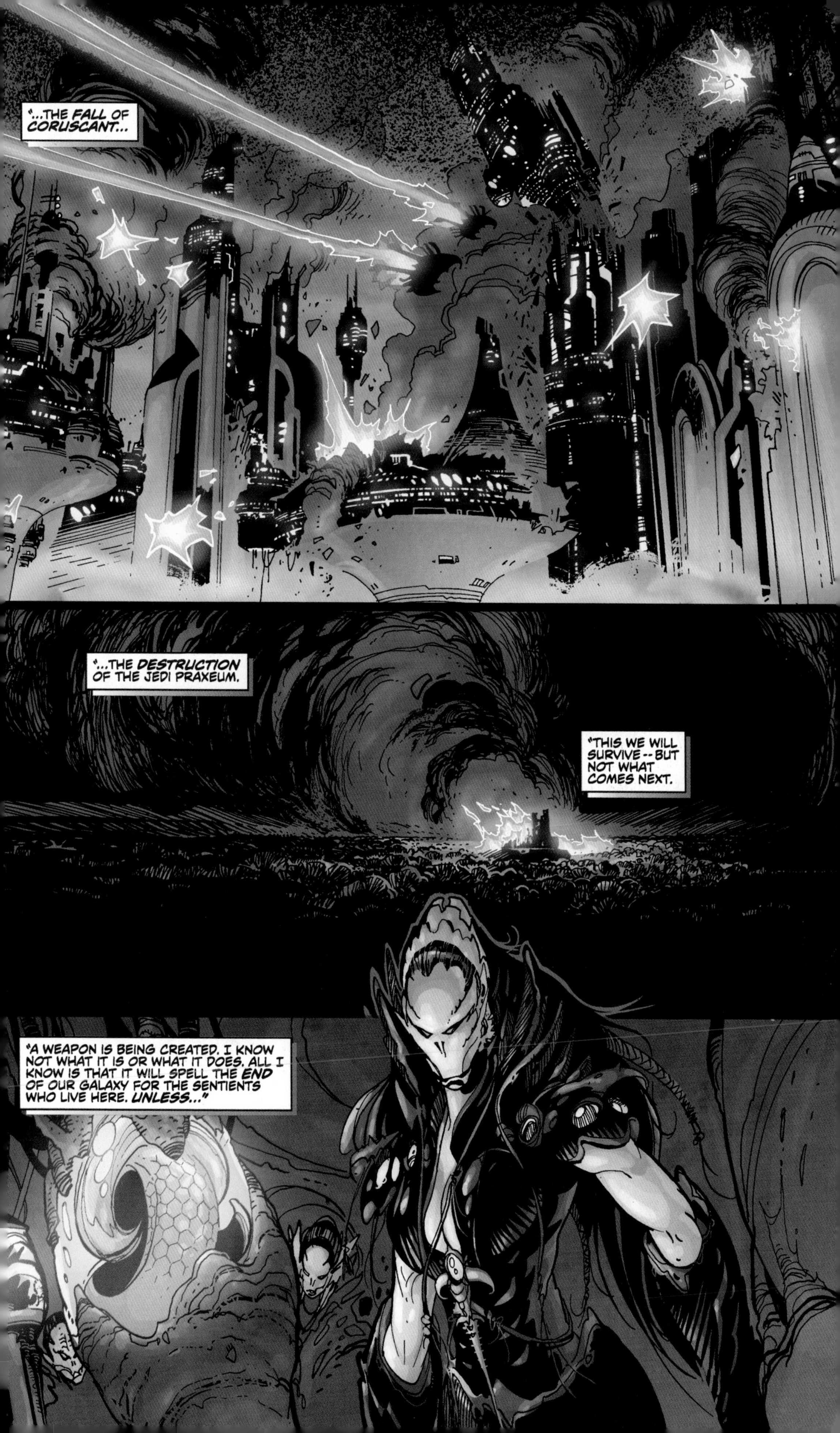
"...THE FALL OF CORUSCANT...
"...THE DESTRUCTION OF THE JEDI PRAXEUM.
"THIS WE WILL SURVIVE -- BUT NOT WHAT COMES NEXT.
"A WEAPON IS BEING CREATED. I KNOW NOT WHAT IT IS OR WHAT IT DOES. ALL I KNOW IS THAT IT WILL SPELL THE END OF OUR GALAXY FOR THE SENTIENTS WHO LIVE HERE. UNLESS..."

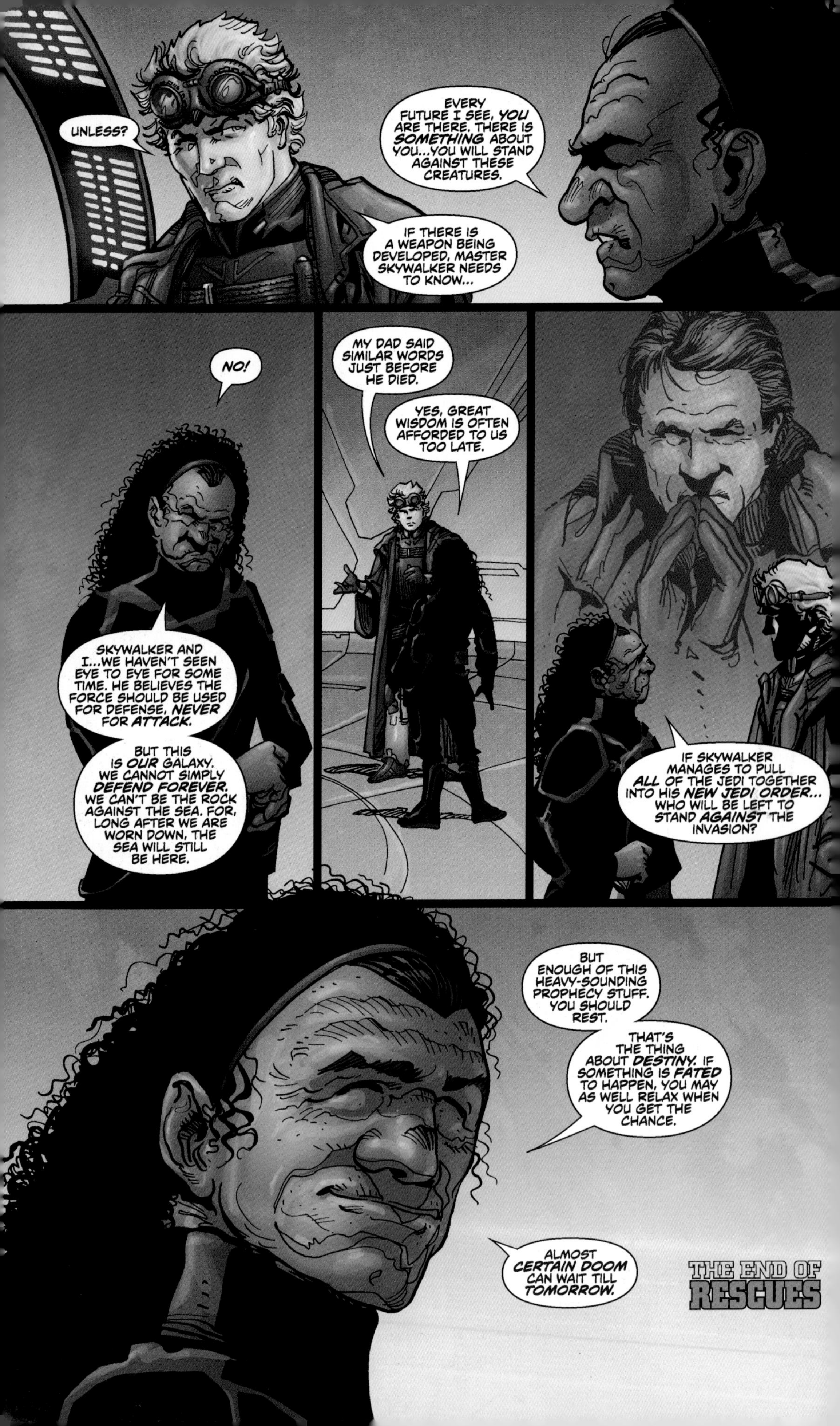
UNLESS?
EVERY FUTURE I SEE, YOU ARE THERE. THERE IS SOMETHING ABOUT YOU...YOU WILL STAND AGAINST THESE CREATURES.
IF THERE IS A WEAPON BEING DEVELOPED, MASTER SKYWALKER NEEDS TO KNOW...
NO!
SKYWALKER AND I...WE HAVEN'T SEEN EYE TO EYE FOR SOME TIME. HE BELIEVES THE FORCE SHOULD BE USED FOR DEFENSE, NEVER FOR ATTACK.
BUT THIS IS OUR GALAXY. WE CANNOT SIMPLY DEFEND FOREVER. WE CAN'T BE THE ROCK AGAINST THE SEA. FOR, LONG AFTER WE ARE WORN DOWN, THE SEA WILL STILL BE HERE.
MY DAD SAID SIMILAR WORDS JUST BEFORE HE DIED.
YES, GREAT WISDOM IS OFTEN AFFORDED TO US TOO LATE.
IF SKYWALKER MANAGES TO PULL ALL OF THE JEDI TOGETHER INTO HIS NEW JEDI ORDER... WHO WILL BE LEFT TO STAND AGAINST THE INVASION?
BUT ENOUGH OF THIS HEAVY-SOUNDING PROPHECY STUFF. YOU SHOULD REST.
THAT'S THE THING ABOUT DESTINY. IF SOMETHING IS FATED TO HAPPEN, YOU MAY AS WELL RELAX WHEN YOU GET THE CHANCE.
ALMOST CERTAIN DOOM CAN WAIT TILL TOMORROW.
THE END OF RESCUES

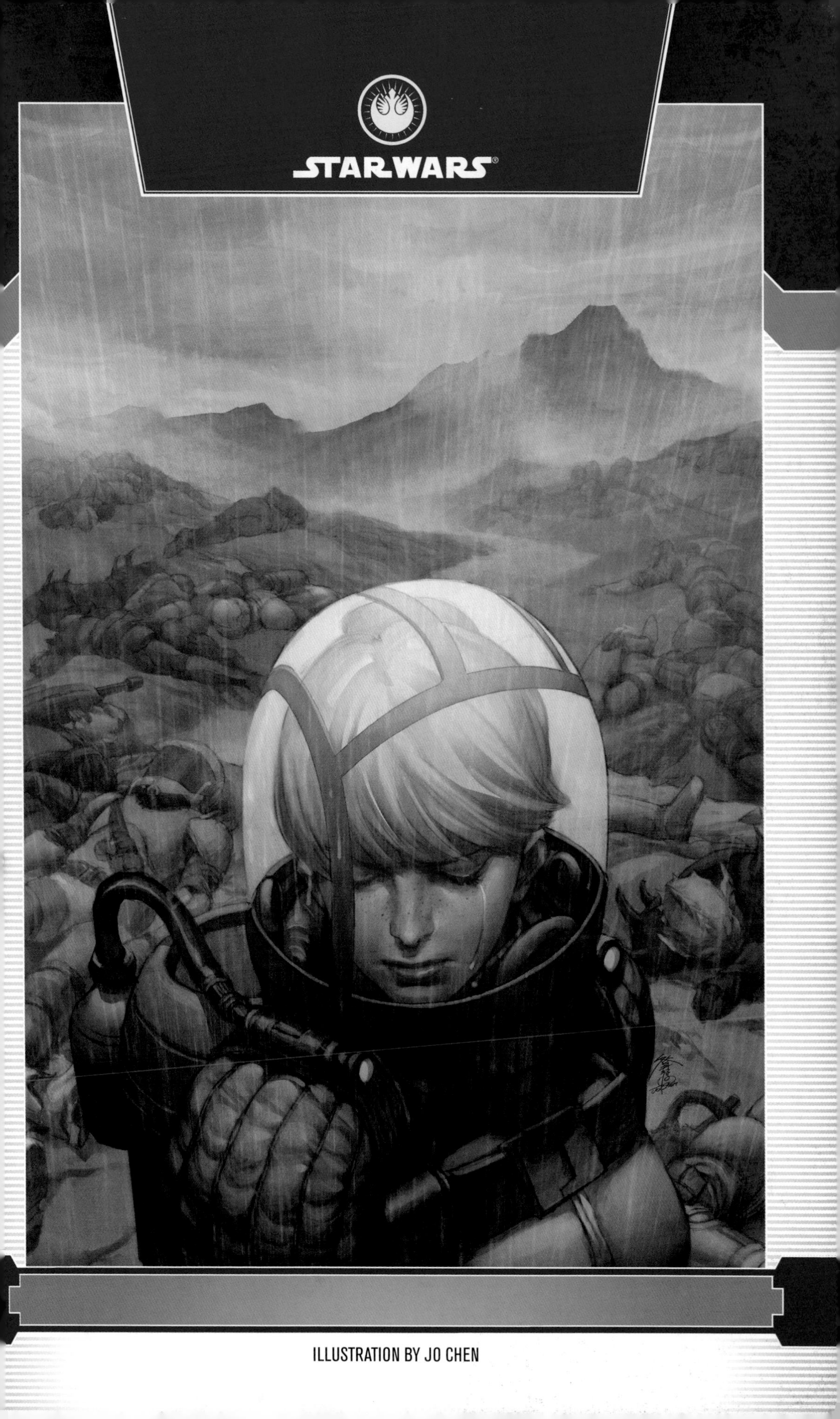
STAR WARS

ILLUSTRATION BY JO CHEN

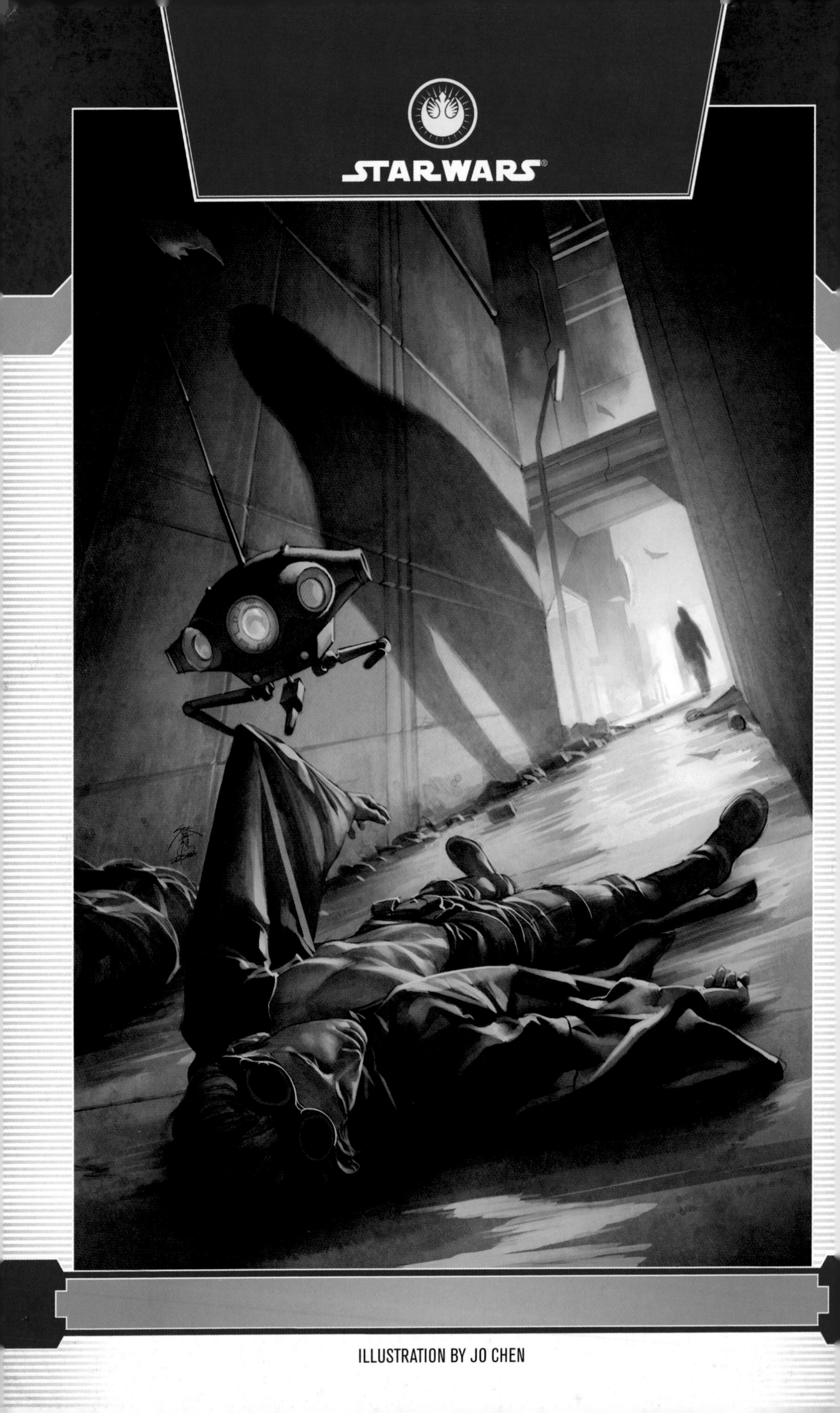

ILLUSTRATION BY JO CHEN

STAR WARS®
LEGACY

More than one hundred years have passed since the events in *Return of the Jedi* and the days of the New Jedi Order. There is new evil gripping the galaxy, shattering a resurgent Empire, and seeking to destroy the last of the Jedi. Even as their power is failing, the Jedi hold onto one final hope . . . the last remaining heir to the Skywalker legacy.

AVAILABLE AT YOUR LOCAL COMICS SHOP OR BOOKSTORE

DARK HORSE BOOKS
darkhorse.com

TO FIND A COMICS SHOP IN YOUR AREA, CALL 1-888-266-4226.
For more information or to order direct: *On the web: darkhorse.com *E-mail: mailorder@darkhorse.com
*Phone: 1-800-862-0052 Mon.-Fri. 9 A.M. to 5 P.M. Pacific Time.

STAR WARS © 2011 Lucasfilm Ltd. & ™ (BL 8015)

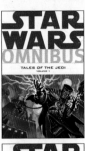

STAR WARS OMNIBUS COLLECTIONS

STAR WARS
OMNIBUS
TALES OF THE JEDI

STAR WARS: TALES OF THE JEDI

Including the *Tales of the Jedi* stories "The Golden Age of the Sith," "The Freedon Nadd Uprising," and "Knights of the Old Republic," these huge omnibus editions are the ultimate introduction to the ancient history of the *Star Wars* universe!

Volume 1 ISBN 978-1-59307-830-0 | $24.99 **Volume 2 ISBN 978-1-59307-911-6 | $24.99**

STAR WARS
OMNIBUS
X-WING ROGUE SQUADRON

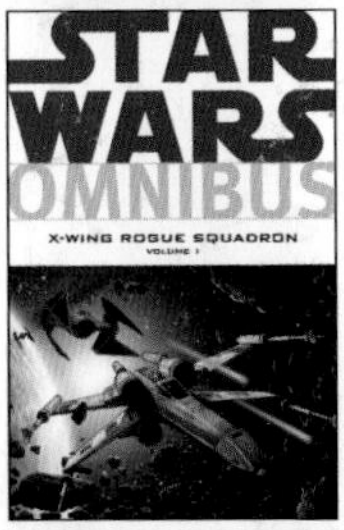

STAR WARS: X-WING ROGUE SQUADRON

The greatest starfighters of the Rebel Alliance become the defenders of a new Republic in this massive collection of stories featuring Wedge Antilles, hero of the Battle of Endor, and his team of ace pilots known throughout the galaxy as Rogue Squadron.

Volume 1 ISBN 978-1-59307-572-9 | $24.99 **Volume 2 ISBN 978-1-59307-619-1 | $24.99**

Volume 3 ISBN 978-1-59307-776-1 | $24.99

STAR WARS: BOBA FETT

Boba Fett, the most feared, most respected, and most loved bounty hunter in the galaxy, now has all of his comics stories collected into one massive volume!

ISBN 978-1-59582-418-9 | $24.99

STAR WARS
OMNIBUS
EARLY VICTORIES

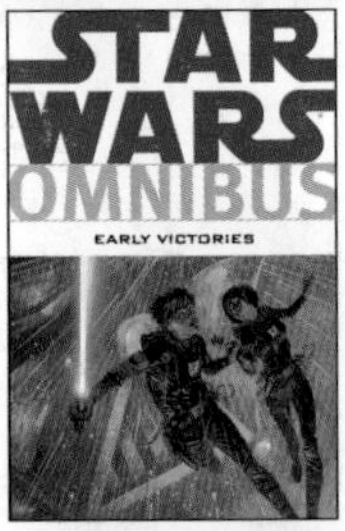

STAR WARS: EARLY VICTORIES

Following the destruction of the first Death Star, Luke Skywalker is the new, unexpected hero of the Rebellion. But the galaxy hasn't been saved yet–Luke and Princess Leia find there are many more battles to be fought against the Empire and Darth Vader!

ISBN 978-1-59582-172-0 | $24.99

STAR WARS
OMNIBUS
RISE OF THE SITH

STAR WARS: RISE OF THE SITH

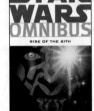

Before the name of Skywalker–or Vader–achieved fame across the galaxy, the Jedi Knights had long preserved peace and justice . . . as well as preventing the return of the Sith. These thrilling tales illustrate the events leading up to *The Phantom Menace*.

ISBN 978-1-59582-228-4 | $24.99

STAR WARS
OMNIBUS
EMISSARIES & ASSASSINS

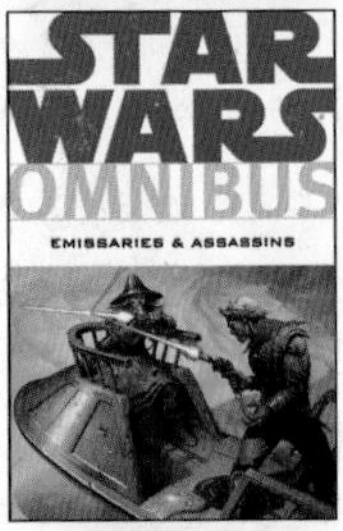

STAR WARS: EMISSARIES AND ASSASSINS

Discover more stories featuring Anakin Skywalker, Amidala, Obi-Wan, and Qui-Gon set during the time of Episode I: *The Phantom Menace* in this mega collection!

ISBN 978-1-59582-229-1 | $24.99

STAR WARS
OMNIBUS
MENACE REVEALED

STAR WARS: MENACE REVEALED

This is our largest omnibus of never-before-collected and out-of-print *Star Wars* stories. Included here are one-shot adventures, short story arcs, specialty issues, and early Dark Horse Extra comic strips! All of these tales take place after Episode I: *The Phantom Menace*, and lead up to Episode II: *Attack of the Clones*.

ISBN 978-1-59582-273-4 | $24.99

STAR WARS: SHADOWS OF THE EMPIRE

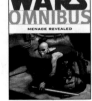

Featuring all your favorite characters from the *Star Wars* trilogy—Luke Skywalker, Princess Leia, and Han Solo—this volume includes stories written by acclaimed novelists Timothy Zahn and Steve Perry!

ISBN 978-1-59582-434-9 | $24.99

STAR WARS
OMNIBUS
A LONG TIME AGO . . .

STAR WARS: A LONG TIME AGO. . . .

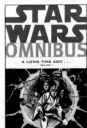

Star Wars: A Long Time Ago. . . . omnibus volumes feature classic *Star Wars* stories not seen in over twenty years! Originally printed by Marvel Comics, these stories have been recolored and are sure to please *Star Wars* fans both new and old.

Volume 1: ISBN 978-1-59582-486-8 | $24.99 **Volume 2: ISBN 978-1-59582-554-4 | $24.99**

Volume 3: ISBN 978-1-59582-639-8 | $24.99

AVAILABLE AT YOUR LOCAL COMICS SHOP OR BOOKSTORE!

To find a comics shop in your area, call 1-888-266-4226

For more information or to order direct: • On the web: darkhorse.com

• E-mail: mailorder@darkhorse.com • Phone: 1-800-862-0052 Mon.–Fri. 9 AM to 5 PM Pacific Time